P9-DHB-149

Also by Rushworth M. Kidder

Dylan Thomas: The Country of the Spirit

E. E. Cummings: An Introduction to the Poetry

An Agenda for the 21st Century

Reinventing the Future: Global Goals for the 21st Century

In the Backyards of Our Lives

Heartland Ethics: Voices from the American Midwest (editor)

Shared Values for a Troubled World:
Conversations with Men and Women of Conscience

HOW GOOD PEOPLE MAKE TOUGH CHOICES

Resolving the Dilemmas of Ethical Living

Rushworth M. Kidder

A FIRESIDE BOOK
Published by Simon & Schuster

To my parents,
Ruth and George Kidder,
who taught us ethics by their example

FIRESIDE
Rockefeller Center
1230 Avenue of the Americas
New York, NY 10020

First Fireside Edition 1996
Published by arrangement with William Morrow & Company, Inc.

FIRESIDE and colophon are registered trademarks
of Simon & Schuster Inc.

Designed by Arlene Schleifer Goldberg

Manufactured in the United States of America

20 19 18 17 16 15

Library of Congress Cataloging-in-Publication Data
Kidder, Rushworth M.
How good people make tough choices : resolving the dilemmas of ethical living / Rushworth M. Kidder.—1st Fireside ed.
p. cm.
"A Fireside book."
Include bibliographical references and index.
1. Business ethics. 2. Decision-making—Moral and ethical aspects. I. Title.
HF5387.K52 1996
658.4'03—dc20 96-4137 CIP

ISBN 0-684-81838-8

"Traveling Through Dark" is reprinted by permission of the Estate of William Stafford.

The lines from "Musée des Beaux Arts" are from *Collected Poems* by W. H. Auden © 1940 and renewed 1968 by W. H. Auden. Reprinted by permission of Random House, Inc.

Preface

The seeds of this book were sown when, one warm summer afternoon at her home in Cos Cob, Connecticut, in 1986, I had a quiet, long, and thoughtful conversation with Barbara Tuchman.

A historian of what she called "the small facts, not the big Explanation," she had twice won the Pulitzer Prize—and earned high praise for such books as *A Distant Mirror,* which used the fourteenth century and its Black Plague as a "mirror" for the twentieth century's confusions and violence. As a columnist and staff writer for *The Christian Science Monitor,* I was interviewing her for a series of articles based on the ideas of twenty-two leading thinkers around the world. Ultimately published as *An Agenda for the 21st Century* (MIT Press, 1987), this series sought to discover the major, first-intensity, high-leverage issues that humanity would have to address in order to negotiate the coming century successfully.

As we talked, I asked her how, if she were a twenty-first-century historian looking backward, she would characterize our century.

"I would call it an Age of Disruption," she said. She warned of the nuclear threat. She called attention to environmental problems. But her central concern, she said, lay in "the real disruption in public morality."

"There have always been times when people have acted immorally," she continued. But what was new, she felt, was "the extent of *public* immorality making itself so obvious to the average citizen."

The more I went forward with these interviews—with former president Jimmy Carter, industrialist David Packard, author and editor Norman Cousins, West German president Richard von Weizsäcker, former Nigerian head of state Olusegun Obasanjo, philosophers Mortimer Adler and Sissela Bok, Mexican novelist Carlos Fuentes, and the rest—the more I kept hearing about the centrality of morality for the twenty-first century. Finally, when the interviews had each appeared in the paper and it came time to write the concluding, what-does-it-all-mean piece, six issues stood out as central to our future agenda. Five were not surprising:

- The nuclear threat
- Environmental degradation
- The population explosion
- The North-South economic gap between the developed and the developing worlds
- The need for education reform

The sixth, surfacing in interview after interview, caught me by surprise: the breakdown of morality. It was as though these interviewees were saying, "Look, if we don't get a handle on the ethical collapses going on around us, we will be as surely doomed as we would be by a nuclear disaster or an environmental catastrophe." Ethics, they were saying, was no mere luxury: It was central to our survival.

That conclusion caused my colleagues and me at the *Monitor* to sit up and take notice. Like any top-ranked newspaper, we had writers who had specialized for years in the first five of these issues. But an "ethics beat"? What would that look like?

As a columnist, I had the freedom to choose my subjects each week. So I began writing frequently about ethical issues, working out as I went the language of public discourse that lets one talk about moral values without sounding preachy, naive, or old-fashioned. In the end, the subject proved too large and commanding for even a fine newspaper. So in 1990, in concert with the *Monitor*'s former editor, Katherine Fanning, and with support from the W. K. Kellogg Foundation, I founded the Institute for Global Ethics in Camden, Maine. As a think tank involved in publishing, education, and research, the Institute is designed to carry this work forward, extend it to a global reach, and provide time and resources to develop this language and these ideas still further.

This book is the result of these years of search and experimentation. It reflects, too, the Institute's recent work in providing executive ethics seminars for corporate, non-profit, academic, and governmental clients. Rather than using fictional, canned case studies in our seminars, I ask the participants to bring to the table examples of authentic dilemmas they have encountered. They may change names or local details if necessary to protect confidences. But they are urged to set out their tales in full complexity. As a result, our files are well supplied with examples of up-to-the-minute, tough dilemmas from some of the nation's most ethical organizations.

This book makes ample use of those dilemmas—stripped of all reference to identifiable individuals, of course, but rich with challenge. It sets them forth in the context of a number of ideas and constructs that we've found especially helpful, including the emphasis on "right versus right," the concept of the dilemma paradigms, and the "ethical fitness" analogy. Since busy people may have little time to read more than one book on ethics, this book brings together some of the best current thinking on this subject. In the end, it has one goal: to help change the way we think about the world and to provide, through that change, a practical set of mental tools by means of which good people can make tough choices.

Making moral choices, of course, is nothing new. Through the centuries, people facing ethical decisions have been aided by the twin traditions of religion and philosophy. This book owes a great deal to both traditions. Given the scope of the former and the exacting nature of the latter, however, it cannot hope to represent either with the depth that an audience of theologians or philosophers might expect. The audience for this book, by contrast, comprises the thoughtful nonspecialist, and while I have sought to bring the highest sense of scholarly and journalistic integrity to my use of sources, I have tried above all to be clear, direct, and relevant. There are some wonderful books to be written on the relations of religion and philosophy to the contemporary practice of ethics—topics on which this book only touches.

This book has benefited from the work of many hands. Those too numerous to name include the hundreds of seminar participants who reached into their own personal histories and supplied our sessions with real-life ethical dilemmas that were sometimes dazzling, often profound, and unfailingly engaging. Special thanks go to the staff of the Institute for Global Ethics for helping me think through the ramifications of this process: to Patricia Brousseau, who has been instrumental in transforming these ideas into highly effective workshops for secondary-school students; to Carol Shaw, who has done masterful work in research and manuscript preparation; to Betcie Byrd, who has organized our offices so well that I've had time to write; to Kaley Noonan, for patient footnoting; and to Karin Anderson, Kenneth Cardillo, Barton W. Emanuel, Carl Hausman, Beth Schuman, Melody Smith, and Jo Spiller for their interest and encouragement.

No non-profit executive could ask for a more supportive board—and no author for a more intelligent and penetrating set of advisors—than the directors of the Institute: James K. Baker, James D. Ewing, Katherine Fanning, Theodore J. Gordon, Willard Hanzlik, Michael K. Hooker, Elizabeth Kidder, Robert Pratt, and Randa Slim. Financial support for the project has come from many sources, including the Arvin Foundation, the Charles Stewart Harding Foundation, the W. K. Kellogg Foundation, the Florence & John Schumann Foundation, the Walker Group/Walker Family Foundation, Mr. and Mrs. Charles Rainwater, Mrs. William M. Correll, Mr. and Mrs. William F. Carl, and Mr. and Mrs. James K. Baker. Two corporate leaders who played a central role in this book, Timothy P. Smucker of The J. M. Smucker Company and Dr. Earl Hess of Lancaster Laboratories, were among the first to invite us to hold seminars for their executives and employees: They provided, as it were, the workbench upon which the model was tested and refined. Raphael Sagalyn provided invaluable editorial advice that helped define the tone and scope of this book in its early stages.

Finally, I owe boundless gratitude to the ethical exemplars who have helped shape my own life in ways that made this book possible. Chief among them I count my wife, Elizabeth, whose hand on the ethical tiller is the steadiest I've ever seen, and my parents, Ruth and George Kidder, who have proved that an abiding affection is at the very heart of the moral universe, and to whom this book is dedicated.

—RUSHWORTH M. KIDDER
Camden, Maine

Contents

Chapter One

Overview: The Ethics of Right Versus Right

All of us face tough choices.

Sometimes we duck them. Sometimes we address them. Even when we address them, however, we don't always decide to resolve them. Sometimes we simply brood endlessly over possible outcomes or agonize about paths to pursue.

And even if we *do* try to resolve them, we don't always do so by energetic self-reflection. Sometimes we simply bull our way through to a conclusion by sheer impatience and assertive self-will—as though getting it *resolved* were more important than getting it *right*.

This is a book for those who want to address and resolve tough choices through energetic self-reflection. Those are the people, after all, whom we often think of as "good" people. They are good, we say, because they seem to have some conscious sense of vision, some deep core of ethical values, that gives them the courage to stand up to the tough choices. That doesn't mean they face fewer choices than other people. Quite the opposite: Those who live in close proximity to their basic values are apt to agonize over choices that other people, drifting over the surface of their lives, might never even see as problems. Sound values raise tough choices; and tough choices are never easy.

That was the case with a librarian who, several years ago, was working the reference desk at the public library in her community.

The phone rang. The questioner, a male, wanted some information on state laws concerning rape. The librarian asked several questions to clarify the nature of his inquiry. Then, in keeping with long-established library policy designed to keep phone lines from being tied up, she explained that she would call him back in a few minutes after researching his question. She took down his first name and phone number, and hung up.

She was just getting up to do the research when a man who had been sitting in the reading area within earshot of the reference desk approached her. Flashing a police detective's badge, he asked for the name and number of the caller. The reason: The conversation he had overheard led him to suspect that the caller was the perpetrator of a rape that had happened the night before in the community.

What should she do? On one hand, she herself was a member of the community. She felt very strongly about the need to maintain law and order. As a woman, she was particularly concerned that a rapist might be at large in the community. And as a citizen, she wanted to do whatever she could to reduce the possibility that he might strike again. After all, what if she refused to tell—and another rape happened the following night?

On the other hand, she felt just as strongly that her professional code as a librarian required her to protect the confidentiality of *all* callers. She felt that free access to information was vital to the success of democracy, and that if people seeking information were being watched and categorized simply by the kinds of questions they asked, the police state was not far behind. The right of privacy, she felt, must extend to everyone. After all, what if this caller was simply a student writing a paper on rape for a civics class?

The choice she faced was clearly of the right-versus-right sort. It was right to support the community's quest for law and order. But it was also right to honor confidentiality, as her professional code required. What made the choice so tough for her? The fact that her values were so well defined. Had she been less concerned about the confidentiality of information—which, in its highest form, grows out of a desire to respect and honor everyone in her community—she might not have hesitated to turn over the name to the detective. She might have bowed so entirely to the authority of the officer—or sought so willingly to help him bring the criminal to justice—that she would never have noticed how quickly, in her mind, "the caller" became "the criminal" before he had even been questioned. On the other hand, had she been single-mindedly committed to her profession as a gatekeeper of society's information, she might never even have considered her obligations to the larger community. She might simply have stood on the principle of confidentiality, and seen no conflict with the urgency of a social need.

Tough choices don't always involve professional codes or criminal laws. Nor do they always involve big, headline-size issues. They often operate in areas that laws and regulations don't reach. That was the case for a corporate executive with a nationwide manufacturing firm, who faced such a choice shortly after becoming manager of one of his company's plants in California. Every year, he learned, the producer of one of Hollywood's best-known television adventure series shot a segment for one of its shows in the plant's parking lot. Every year, the upper management at his firm's corporate headquarters allowed the crew to do the filming free of charge—typically on a Saturday, when the lot was empty. And every year Mr. Gray, the former plant manager, had given up weekend time with his family in order to be on location and assist the television crew.

So this year the new plant manager did the same. The shoot went as planned. At the end of the day, the producer came up to him, thanked him for his help, and asked how the check for five hundred dollars should be made out. Surprised, the manager replied that it should be made out to the corporation. Surprised in turn, the producer said, "Oh, okay. In the past we've always made it out to Mr. Gray. Shouldn't we just make it out to you?"

Tough choice? In a sense, yes. The corporation, which incurred no expenses and sustained no losses because of the shoot, neither asked for nor expected any payment. The plant manager, on the other hand, had given up an entire weekend day with no additional compensation. Yet the asset that made the shoot possible belonged not to him but to the corporation. Whose money was this? Was this a payment to the corporation or a contribution for his personal services? If the latter, was it a bribe to ensure that the same site would be available next year, or a gesture of appreciation for his helpfulness? Furthermore, if he *did* turn over the check to the corporation, would that lead to questions about what happened to last year's money and cause trouble for Gray, who may have reasoned out the issue in a different way and felt comfortable accepting the payment? Or might such an investigation lead to the discovery that this incident was part of a deceptive pattern established by Gray, who might have been regularly using corporate assets to produce personal gain? The manager knew that many people in his position would have pocketed the check with a murmur of appreciation and a live-and-let-live shrug. For him, it was hardly that simple—because of his core values of honesty, integrity, and fairness, and his desire to avoid even the appearance of evil. All in all, he felt that there was some right on both sides—that it was right for him to be compensated, and yet right for the company to receive whatever payments were made.

Tough choices, typically, are those that pit one "right" value against another. That's true in every walk of life—corporate, professional, personal, civic, international, educational, religious, and the rest. Consider that:

• It is right to protect the endangered spotted owl in the old-growth forests of the American Northwest—and right to provide jobs for loggers.

• It is right to honor a woman's right to make decisions affecting her body—and right to protect the lives of the unborn.

• It is right to provide our children with the finest public schools available—and right to prevent the constant upward ratcheting of state and local taxes.

• It is right to extend equal social services to everyone regardless of race or ethnic origin—and right to pay special attention to those whose cultural backgrounds may have deprived them of past opportunities.

• It is right to refrain from meddling in the internal affairs of sovereign nations—and right to help protect the undefended in warring regions where they are subject to slaughter.

• It is right to bench the star college quarterback caught drinking the night before the championship game—and right to field the best possible team for tomorrow's game.

• It is right to resist the importation of products made in developing nations to the detriment of the environment—and right to provide jobs, even at low wages, for citizens of those nations.

• It is right to condemn the minister who has an affair with a parishioner—and right to extend mercy to him for the only real mistake he's ever made.

• It is right to find out all you can about your competitors' costs and price structures—and right to obtain information only through proper channels.

• It is right to take the family on a much-needed vacation—and right to save that money for your children's education.

• It is right to speak up in favor of a minority viewpoint in your club—and right to let the majority rule.

• It is right to support the principle of creative and aesthetic freedom for the curator of a photography exhibition at a local museum—and right to uphold the community's desire to avoid displaying pornographic or racially offensive works.

• It is right to "throw the book" at good employees who make dumb decisions that endanger the firm—and right to have enough compassion to mitigate the punishment and give them another chance.

Right versus right, then, is at the heart of our toughest choices. Does that mean that there are no right-versus-wrong choices? Is "wrong" only someone else's definition of what I think is "right"?

No. The world, unfortunately, faces plenty of right-versus-wrong questions. From cheating on taxes to lying under oath, from running red lights to inflating the expense account, from buying under-twelve movie tickets for your fourteen-year-old to overstating the damage done to your car for insurance purposes—the world abounds with instances that, however commonplace, are widely understood to be wrong. But right-versus-wrong choices are very different from right-versus-right ones. The latter reach inward to our most profound and central values, setting one against the other in ways that will never be resolved simply by pretending that one is "wrong." Right-versus-wrong choices, by contrast, offer no such depth: The closer you get to them, the more they begin to smell. Two shorthand terms capture the differences: If we can call right-versus-right choices "ethical dilemmas," we can reserve the phrase "moral temptations" for the right-versus-wrong ones.

When good people encounter tough choices, it is rarely because they're facing a moral temptation. Only those living in a moral vacuum will be able to say, "On the one hand is the good, the right, the true, and noble. On the other hand is the awful, the wicked, the false, and the base. And here I stand, equally attracted to each." If you've already defined one side as a flat-out, unmitigated "wrong," you don't usually consider it seriously. Faced with the alternatives of arguing it out with your boss or gunning him down in the parking lot, you don't see the latter as an option. To be sure, we may be tempted to do wrong—but only because the wrong appears, if only in some small way and perhaps momentarily, to be right. For most people, some sober reflection is all that's required to recognize a wolflike moral temptation masquerading in the lamb's clothing of a seeming ethical dilemma.

The *really* tough choices, then, don't center upon right versus wrong. They involve right versus right. They are genuine dilemmas precisely because each side is firmly rooted in one of our basic, core values. Four such dilemmas are so common to our experience that they stand as models, patterns, or paradigms. They are:

- Truth versus loyalty
- Individual versus community
- Short-term versus long-term
- Justice versus mercy

The names for these patterns are less important than the ideas they reflect: Whether you call it law versus love, or equity versus compassion, or fairness versus affection, you're talking about some form of justice versus mercy. So too with the others. But while the names may be flexible, the concepts are not: These four paradigms appear to be so fundamental to the right-versus-right choices all of us face that they can rightly be called *dilemma paradigms.* These paradigms are more fully explained in Chapters Five and Six. Here, however, is an example of each:

• **Truth versus loyalty.** As a professional working for a large defense electronics firm, Stan found himself riding a roller coaster of concern about layoffs. Every few years, it seemed, top management slashed jobs as work slacked off—only to hire again when things started looking up. So when Stan and his team members noticed that the executives were again meeting behind closed doors, they suspected the worst.

Stan's boss, however, was a good friend—and also a voluble talker. So Stan felt no qualms asking him about the future. His boss explained the contingency plan at length—mentioning that, if layoffs were needed, Stan's team member Jim would be slated to lose his job. He also made it plain that Stan was to keep that information confidential.

Not long after that conversation, Jim approached Stan and asked whether he could confirm what the rumor mill was saying: that he himself would be the target. That request landed Stan squarely in the truth-versus-loyalty dilemma. Because he knew the truth, honesty compelled him to answer accurately. But he had given his word to his boss not to break a confidence, and felt a strong loyalty to that relationship.

Whichever course he chose, then, would be "right." And he could not choose both.

• **Individual versus community.** In the mid-1980s, the administrator of a residential care facility in California received a letter from a nearby university hospital, where his elderly residents typically went for medical attention. The letter reminded him that five of his residents had recently had surgery at the hospital. It also informed him that the medical staff suspected that some of the blood used in their transfusions may have been tainted with the HIV virus. While making it clear that the probabilities of infection were low, the letter asked him to call the hospital immediately and arrange further testing for these five.

That letter, he recalled, presented him with a stark and direct question: What should he tell, and to whom should he tell it? Given the public and professional ignorance about AIDS—this was, remember, the mid-1980s, when the disease was little understood and legal regulations offered him no clear guidance—he felt certain that, if he told his staff, their fear would be so great that they would refuse to enter the rooms of those five, making it impossible to deliver even minimal care to them. But suppose he did not tell the staff and one of them contracted AIDS: Surely he would be culpable.

As it happened, none of the five ultimately tested positive. But that crucial fact was unknown at the time. What was he to do? He knew it was right to honor the individual rights of each of those five residents—the privacy of their medical histories, the expectation of high-quality care at his facility, their dignity as individuals. It was right, in other words, to say nothing.

On the other hand, he knew it was right to protect the community from disease. The staff had not signed on for hazardous duty. Most of them saw themselves as unskilled hourly workers, not members of a life-endangering profession to which they had been called by noble duty and prepared by intensive training. Never mind that they might all phone in sick the day after the announcement: They deserved protection so they could continue to deliver care, with full regard for safety, to the many other residents who were *not* among the five. So it was right to tell them.

Both sides were right, and he couldn't do both.

• **Short-term versus long-term.** When he graduated from college with a degree in science, Andy had found a solid job in his profession, married, and had two sons. Twelve years later, he moved to another company that promised steady advancement within its managerial ranks. A devoted family man, he admired his wife's dedication to raising the boys. But he also observed that his sons, approaching their teen years, benefited greatly from his fatherly friendship and counsel—especially as they approached what he and his wife realized could prove to be a difficult transitional period in their upbringing. So he made a commitment to spend plenty of time with them, playing baseball and helping with their schoolwork.

But he also loved his work, and did well at it. And it quickly became apparent that, to advance rapidly up the managerial ranks, he needed an MBA. A nearby university offered the degree in an attractive evening-and-weekend program that would allow him to continue full-time employment. But it would soak up the next several years of his life and throw most of the family activities into his wife's hands.

Andy's dilemma set the short-term against the long-term. It was right, he felt, to honor his family's short-term needs—to stick close to his sons at a time when a father's influence seemed so important. Yet it was right to build for the long-term needs of his family—to equip himself with an education that would make him a better provider in the coming years, when he would presumably need to pay college tuitions.

Both were right, and he couldn't do both.

• **Justice versus mercy.** As feature editor for a major daily newspaper, I found myself in charge of a broad array of different departments. Like most newspapers, ours ran features on education, books, science, and the arts—as well as on cars, chess, stars, gardening, and food. I quickly learned that what makes any of these departments sing is the skill of the writing—and that even in areas where I had no discernible interest, a well-crafted story could seize and hold my attention just as well as a breaking front-page sizzler. So we always sought to hire young staff members who, whatever other talents they might have, were good writers.

We had just such a young woman on the food page. She had come to us from one of the nation's finest colleges, and had progressed rapidly to the point where, as assistant editor, she wrote regularly. So one summer day, when I noticed that she had submitted a story on Maine blueberries, I was pleased to see it in the queue, awaiting publication in several more days.

The next day I looked up from my computer terminal to find the food editor herself—a woman with decades of experience, one of the best in the business—standing silently in front of my desk. In one hand she held a copy of her young assistant's story on blueberries. In the other hand she held a battered, tan cookbook some thirty years old. She laid each on my desk. And there, on the pages of that cookbook, was our young friend's story, printed word for word.

Among the few cardinal sins of journalism, one stands supreme: You don't plagiarize. Nothing should be drummed more insistently into the minds of young journalists; nothing destroys a career more rapidly; nothing defrauds your readers more egregiously; and nothing is more difficult to detect. This was no right-versus-right ethical dilemma. For our young friend, it was a pure and simple case of right-versus-wrong moral temptation—and she had chosen wrong.

For me, however, it *was* an ethical dilemma. I found myself torn by two conflicting desires. Half of me wanted to lunge from my desk, brush past the senior editor, and make a beeline for the assistant's desk—whereupon I would overturn it, scatter its contents across the newsroom floor, grab her by the scruff of her neck, heave her out into the street, and call out after her, "Never, *never* come back—and never let me hear that you are working in journalism anywhere else!" The other half of me wanted to walk over to her desk, quietly pull up a chair, and say, "What on earth has come over you? You know better than that! Is there something going wrong in your personal life that I haven't been aware of? Let's go have a cup of coffee—you and I have to talk!"

Half of me, in other words, wanted to see justice done in no uncertain terms—punishment swift and sure, the example emblazoned forever into the annals of American journalism—despite the fact that, were I to take such a course, half the newsroom might well line up on one side muttering, "Hard-hearted fascist, too rigid to care!" The other half yearned to be merciful, to extend the hand of compassion in a situation that seemed so desperately to need it—even though, were I to do so, I could foresee the rest of the newsroom lining up on the other side and muttering, "Bleeding-heart liberal, soft on crime!"

It was right to be merciful. It was right to enforce justice. And I could not do both at once.

This last situation offers two useful lessons. First, dilemmas have actors. Any analysis must begin with the question, Whose dilemma is this? For the young writer, it was a case of right versus wrong. For me, it was right versus right. For the senior food editor, I'm sure, it was a different sort of right versus right: Do I approach my young assistant directly, or do I take the case to a higher authority?

Second, the way this problem was eventually resolved illustrates an important point about solutions. Resolutions often arise when, in analyzing an apparently stark, rigidly bipolar ethical dilemma, we see a middle way open up between the two rights. In this case, we found that middle course. We learned that the young assistant was indeed having some serious personal problems. And since her blueberry piece had not yet been published, we had some latitude in our actions. So we moved her to an editing slot, with the understanding that she was to do no more writing. She remained in that position several years, eventually leaving to take a job outside journalism.

In listening to and analyzing hundreds of ethical dilemmas like these, I have found that they generally fit one (or more) of the four paradigms. But so what? How does this process of determining a paradigm help us make tough choices?

I think it does so in three ways:

• It helps us cut through mystery, complexity, and confusion—assuring us that, however elaborate and multifaceted, dilemmas can be reduced to common patterns. By doing so, it reminds us that *this* dilemma—the one that just landed on my desk in the middle of an otherwise ordinary Tuesday afternoon—is not some unique event created sui generis out of thin air and never before having happened to anyone in the universe. It is, instead, an ultimately manageable problem, bearing strong resemblance to lots of other problems and quite amenable to analysis.

• It helps us strip away extraneous detail and get to the heart of the matter. Under this sort of analysis, the fundamental fact that makes this an authentic dilemma—the clashing of core moral values—stands out in bold relief. Looking at this clash, we can easily see why we have a conflict: Each value is right, and each appears to exclude the other.

• It helps us separate right-versus-wrong from right-versus-right. The more we work with true ethical dilemmas, the more we realize that they fall rather naturally into these paradigms. So any situation that fits one or more of the paradigms must in fact be an issue of right versus right. But what about those situations that strike us as ethical conundrums but resist every effort to fit themselves into the paradigms? Usually there's a simple reason they don't fit: They turn out to be right-versus-*wrong* issues. Any attempt to make them square with one of these four patterns typically mires itself in frustration. While one side immediately appears right, the other side doesn't. Why? Because there's nothing right about it: It's wrong. In this way, the litmus of the paradigms helps us spot the difference between ethical dilemmas and moral temptations.

But merely to analyze a dilemma—even to fit it into the above paradigms—is not to resolve it. Resolution requires us to choose which side is the *nearest* right for the circumstances. And that requires some principles for decision-making.

The three principles outlined here are drawn from the traditions of moral philosophy. Of the many theories that have been propounded for ethical decision-making, these represent three that are particularly useful in helping us think through right-versus-right issues. Each gives us a way to test the twin rights of a dilemma. Each has a long and noble tradition behind it. Each, as we shall see in later chapters, has powerful arguments in its support—and significant refutations lodged against it. For clarity, we'll give them three shorthand labels: *ends-based, rule-based*, and *care-based.* These principles are more fully discussed in Chapter Seven. Here, in thumbnail detail, is the gist of each:

• **Ends-based thinking.** Known to philosophers as *utilitarianism*, this principle is best known by the maxim *Do whatever produces the greatest good for the greatest number.* It demands of us a kind of cost-benefit analysis, determining who will be hurt and who helped and measuring the intensity of that help. It is the staple of public policy debate: Most legislation, these days, is crafted with this utilitarian test in mind.

At the heart of this principle is an assessment of consequences, a forecasting of outcomes. Philosophers typically refer to utilitarianism, in fact, as a form of *consequentialism*—or, more precisely, as a *teleological* principle, from the Greek word *teleos*, meaning "end" or "issue." Why? Because you cannot determine the "greatest good" without speculating on probable futures. Hence the "ends-based" label: Utilitarianism examines possible results and picks the one that produces the most blessing over the greatest range.

• **Rule-based thinking.** Often associated with the name of the German philosopher Immanuel Kant, this principle is best known by what Kant somewhat obtusely called "the categorical imperative." Kant put it this way: "Act only on that maxim through which you can at the same time will that it should become a universal law." Simply put, that means, "Follow only the principle that you want everyone else to follow." In other words, act in such a way that your actions could become a universal standard that others ought to obey. Ask yourself, "If *everyone in the world* followed the rule of action I am following, would that create the greatest good or [in Kant's words] the greatest 'worth of character'?"

This mode of thinking stands directly opposed to utilitarianism. Arguing that consequentialism is hopelessly flawed—how, after all, can we *ever* imagine we know the entire consequences of our actions?—the rule-based thinker pleads for acting only in accord with fixed rules. Never mind outcomes: Stick to your principles and let the consequential chips fall where they may. Based firmly on duty—on what we ought to do, rather than what we think might work—it is known among philosophers as *deontological* thinking, from the Greek word *deon*, meaning "obligation" or "duty."

• **Care-based thinking.** Putting love for others first, this third principle comes into play most frequently in the Golden Rule: *Do to others what you would like them to do to you.* It partakes of a feature known to philosophers as *reversibility*: In other words, it asks you to test your actions by putting yourself in another's shoes and imagining how it would feel if you were the recipient, rather than the perpetrator, of your actions. Often associated with Christianity—Jesus, after all, said, "All things whatsoever ye would that men should do to you, do ye even so to them" (Matt. 7:12)—it is in fact so universal that it appears at the center of every one of the world's great religious teachings. While some philosophers (including Kant) have disputed its standing as a practical principle, it is for many people the only rule of ethics they know, deserving consideration for the moral glue it has provided over the centuries.

How do these three principles apply? First, some hypotheticals. You're walking through an outdoor shopping mall one day when the woman ahead of you opens her purse and pulls out a handkerchief. Unknown to her, a ten-dollar bill floats out of her purse onto the pavement. You pick it up and hand it back to her.

From the Kantian perspective, you have just invoked a rule or maxim—in this case, "Don't ever steal"—that you would wish to see universalized. It's not hard to see that, if everyone in the world did what you have just done in similar circumstances, the world would indeed be a better place.

But suppose it's later in the day and you're eating an ice-cream cone. You've nearly finished, except for the soggy, damp, and altogether unappealing butt-end of the cone. You're worried that, if you hold it much longer, the melted ice cream will begin running down your hand and along your arm. There's not a trash container to be seen. There is, however, a low hedge beside you, under which are lodged a few bits of trash. You consider chucking the cone into the hedge—but not until (being in an unusually philosophical mood) you ask yourself what the three resolution principles would counsel you to do.

Start with the utilitarian principle. A quick assessment of consequences suggests that (1) the mall probably employs sweepers to clean up trash, and (2) the hedge is probably visited regularly by squirrels, birds, and ants, and (3) there's no one else around eating a cone. Your little butt-end will make hardly any difference to the hedge or to the general neatness of the mall: It will, in other words, be a largely inconsequential act. So throw it away.

Not so fast, says the Kantian. Remember, you are setting the standard for the entire world. Throw it in the hedge, and you must be prepared to have *everyone,* from now until eternity, chuck away the butt-ends of their ice-cream cones under hedges, until shoppers all across the malls of the world are up to their eyeballs in soggy cone-tips. An extreme example? Certainly. But it helps remind us that the only reason we feel we can "get away" with the utilitarian principle is that there are only a few others who will do what we've just done, and that our tiny act will be of small consequence in a large universe. Yet is that, the Kantian would ask, any reason to break rules? Is that really the way you want others to behave?

Which, of course, is just what the Golden Rule would instruct: Don't do what you don't want others doing. How would you react if that woman ahead of you flipped *her* cone-end into the hedge? What about the rest of her hot dog? What about her cigarette butt? What about the entire contents of her sack of fast-food leftovers? Would you not be even slightly offended that she was degrading the orderliness of *your* experience? Then what about the woman behind you as you toss away your cone—and for that matter, what about the child she has with her? Do you want other adults to set good examples for your children, even in situations where an action that might be construed as a *bad* example is probably pardonable and might even be justified?

The point, here, is not to perform three tests and then vote to score a three-to-nothing or two-to-one victory. The point is to reason. The usefulness of these principles is not that they will deliver an airtight answer to your dilemma. They are not part of a magic answer kit that produces infallible solutions: If they were, ethics would be infinitely easier than it is, and the moral problems of the world would have been satisfactorily sorted out centuries ago. No, the principles are useful because they give us a way to exercise our moral rationality. They provide different lenses through which to see our dilemmas, different screens to use in assessing them. To see how the principles work, look at two of the dilemmas raised above: the case of the librarian facing the question about rape, and the case of the young journalist who plagiarized the blueberry story.

What should the librarian do? Analyzing her dilemma, it seems most readily to fit the paradigm of individual versus community: the lone caller's right to privacy versus the community's right to live in safety. The utilitarian, looking at consequences and numbers affected, may well urge the librarian to hand over the phone number to the detective. The good of the community, in this view, must prevail over the rights of the individual. What if he is innocent? What if the police, in their zeal to get a confession, make his life most unpleasant? That's unfortunate, but that's what is implied in utilitarianism: The fact that the greatest good goes to the greatest number suggests that every once in a while the not-as-good—even, at times, the very bad—will go to the few. Suppose (continues the utilitarian) the librarian refused to hand over the number—and that very night a second rape occurred. And suppose that happens night after night. Doesn't the community have the right to be protected?

The categorical imperative puts it in a different light. Arguing the hallowed regard for duty, the Kantian may well urge the librarian to elevate to first place her sense of obligation to her profession. The rule is simple and direct: You don't divulge the names of those who call for information. No matter what the circumstances, you simply don't do it—because, if you do, you are saying that every librarian in the world should do what you're about to do.

In explaining her reasoning to us, in fact, the librarian who originally related this dilemma backed it with another example. Suppose a small business entrepreneur in your community gets a flash of inspiration and decides to set up a miniature golf course. He calls the library to get information about how to build one. That information is immediately made public—and a big-bucks developer, who already has a piece of land and plenty of cash, decides he'll build it before this little guy even has a chance to explore the possibilities. Her point: Librarians have a sacred trust to protect the identity of information-seekers, in order to ensure the free use of libraries and promote the most inventive and productive society possible.

But would Mr. Big Bucks really do that, asks the utilitarian? Aren't the chances of that happening pretty slim? And isn't there a huge difference between rape and miniature golf? Surely the end result of a developer's financial coup pales in contrast to a criminal's conviction.

There you go again (replies the Kantian), speculating on consequences—as though you really could read the future. Since you can't, the only safe course is to stick to your duty: Don't tell. And remember: Whatever this librarian does in this case is going to set the standard for every librarian for all time. That's the imperative of the category of action she is creating. Go down this road, and you open yourself up to all sorts of consequences. Yes, every suspected rapist may be behind bars. But the libraries will all be bugged, and we'll all live free from crime and full of terror in a Soviet-style police state.

And the Golden Rule? Here the issue turns on whom we mean by *others*. If the other is the caller, he doesn't want to be turned in—particularly if he's just a student working on a paper. If the other is the detective, however, he really needs that number. If the others are women in the community, they too might well want the detective to know. How the librarian decides will depend in part on which one she thinks of as "the other." But only in part. It will also depend on her concept of what it means to *care for* others. Can she express the highest sense of caring by defending the long-term interests of a free society, where no one is put at risk merely by asking for information? Or does her highest sense of caring lie in protecting the community from what might be an immediate threat?

Three principles, three ways to think—and no clear vote. Whether you put the individual above the community, or the community above the individual, depends on the weight each of the lines of reasoning carries for you.

That's true as well for the blueberry story and its justice-versus-mercy paradigm. There, the utilitarian will urge an examination of consequences. Sure, throw the book at her: But what will you do if, the next day, you read that she committed suicide? That her private life was so entangled that she was driven to desperation—and you pushed her over the brink without even bothering to find out what was wrong? Or what if she sues you for sexual harassment because of your vigorous actions? What if, and what if? All things considered, the utilitarian might argue for bending the principle that plagiarism is a cardinal evil—leaning toward mercy, even if just this once.

The Kantian will want to ask not about the *what ifs* but about the rules. Remembering that whatever you do will be done by every editor in similar circumstances from now on, the Kantian wants to lay down a firm standard. If you must always obey one or the other side, which will it be? Here the logic may lean toward justice—an enforcement of the rules, with no concern for the consequences of your action in this particular case, but with a clear eye on the larger duty of eradicating plagiarism. After all, to lean in the other direction—to make mercy the infallible rule—would in essence make justice void. If every editor always acted as though justice could be set aside "just this once," what good is justice?

The Golden Rule, focusing on reversibility, asks, What would I want to have my superior do to me in such circumstances? What, I might ask, would have driven me to do such a thing? Am I struggling with overwhelming personal problems? Then maybe I want counsel. Am I frightened by the possibility of failure? Then maybe I want to be encouraged. Am I driven by a need to succeed at all costs? Then maybe I need to be brought to my senses by the tough, swift response of my boss. Maybe, in fact, this is an unconscious plea for help—a situation so blatant that it cries out to be caught, punished, and reformed.

The decisions examined here are all tough. And they are all tough in the same way. They all pit one powerful right against another. In the following chapters, we'll look at the concept of right versus wrong (Chapter Two). We'll examine what it means to be ethically fit (Chapter Three). We'll consider where we get our sense of what's right and how we develop our core of values (Chapter Four). We'll examine in much more detail the dilemma paradigms (Chapters Five and Six) and the resolution principles (Chapter Seven). In Chapter Eight, we'll apply these paradigms and principles to a rich array of examples drawn from the private and public realms. Finally, in Chapter Nine, we'll consider the nature of ethics in the twenty-first century and our individual relation to it.

First, however, we need to explore some twentieth-century answers to some age-old questions.

What about right and *wrong*?

Doesn't it matter that people do bad things?

As we move through the final years of this millennium, what's the reading on our moral barometer—and how important is that reading?

Does ethics really *matter*?

Chapter Two

Right Versus Wrong: Why Ethics Matters

There is something faintly surreal about the road to Chernobyl. It twists through the streets of Kiev, climbs the muscular steel bridge over the Dnieper River, and snakes beside gritty factories and railroad sidings overhung with power lines. Then it leaves the city, crawling across the flat Ukrainian farmland on a levee flanked with rows of poplars. Now and then it bisects a village where squat white houses, trimmed with bright blue and roofed in dark red, proclaim the persistence of a human spirit that longs to coax color out of a gray and sullen landscape. Here and there it carries old men in worn black suit jackets bicycling along the shoulders, or uniformed children carrying satchels to school. From time to time it passes women with round, impassive faces scarved in babushkas, leaning on rakes beside smoky leaf-fires. But for the most part it carries jeeps, motorcycles with sidecars, army buses, dump trucks, construction cranes, and cement mixers—a dusty entourage of equipment that, because this road now goes nowhere else, is destined to dead-end at the nuclear power station at Chernobyl, ninety miles from Kiev.

As I crossed this stretch of land in a mustard-yellow government van one Monday morning at the end of an oddly snowless March in 1989—as one of the first Western journalists ever taken to get such a close look at the ill-fated Reactor Number Four at Chernobyl—I remember noticing that the fields were already green with a carpet of winter wheat. That March, of course, was odd in other ways as well. Poised between the launch of Mikhail Gorbachev's perestroika and a political conclusion that was soon to bring the wholesale dissolution of the Soviet Union, the spring of 1989 hung unsteadily in a curious mix of heady freedom and palpable anxiety. You could feel it in the air. A people numbed by the seventy-year hammerlock of authoritarianism were wriggling loose—especially in this part of Ukraine, where they were rediscovering the voice of their long-suppressed nationalism in the musical language and brightly embroidered costumes of their heritage. Yet even now, as they peeped over the edge of their mental parapets to survey a world that should have promised freedom, what they saw along this stretch of road was a landscape still under the moral shadow of the worst industrial accident in the history of humankind: the meltdown and explosion at Chernobyl three years earlier.

The story I heard that March Monday—from some of the Soviet engineers who had been called in just after the explosion to help clean it up—was not only a tale of physical catastrophe. It was, in the end, the story of a moral meltdown. It was the tale of a lapse in conscience so profound as to compel us to rethink the role of ethics in contemporary society. It was the story of two electrical engineers working into the early morning hours of April 26, 1986, at the control panel of Reactor Number Four. Without any real authority—or so the Soviet authorities later reported to the International Atomic Energy Agency in Vienna—they decided to see how long the turbine would freewheel when the power was removed. So they began shutting down the reactor. To do so, they had to override six separate computer-driven alarm systems. The alarms kept flashing signals up on the screen—the Russian equivalents of *Stop! Go no farther! Reverse course!* Refusing to shut down their experiment, they switched off the alarms. When the cleanup crews got into the facility sometime after the explosion, they found valves padlocked in the open position to prevent them from automatically shutting down in a fail-safe mechanism that might have prevented the disaster.

It must have been sometime after midnight that these two men closed down the last alarm. By then, the reactor—an RBMK graphite-based, water-cooled device of a design notoriously unstable at low power—had dropped to a fraction of its normal output. Suddenly, within seconds, the power began rising rapidly. Sensing the danger, the engineers cut loose the cooling rods hanging above the reactor core. The rods should have fallen by gravity into holes in the core and moderated the reaction. But the intense heat from the reaction, well on its way to a temperature that would finally exceed 2,250 degrees Celsius, had already warped the rods. Jammed in their tracks, they would not fall into place. At 1:24 A.M. that Saturday morning there was a loud explosion, followed almost immediately by another. In blasts that blew the roof off the huge machinery hall, chunks of radioactive graphite spewed high into the air—and a plume of radioactive cesium 137 and iodine 131 began climbing three miles upward into the atmosphere.

The damage from that blast is still being measured. The explosion itself killed thirty-one Soviet workers—officially. Unofficially, hundreds more have since died from radioactive effects. The plume rained measurable doses of fallout on every nation in the Northern Hemisphere, poisoning reindeer in Sweden and lambs in Britain and driving tens of thousands into exile from their farmlands in Ukraine and Belarus. A circle around Chernobyl, eighteen miles in radius, is still too "hot" for human habitation: Even fish caught in its streams and mushrooms gathered under its towering pines cannot be eaten. The cost of the cleanup, still rising, has been pegged at $14 billion—as much, say some experts, as the entire Soviet investment in its nuclear power industry since its beginnings in 1954. What remains behind is the ominous cement sarcophagus, built up around Reactor Number Four like an immense gambrel-roofed barn. It contains an estimated ton of plutonium. To be safe, it must remain intact for centuries—as long, some say, as the Egyptian pyramids have already been standing.

Who were these two engineers, known to us only in an almost fictional middle distance, like characters in a movie one has heard about but never seen? One thing is sure: They were not dumb. In those days, a job at Chernobyl was a real plum. Those men were among the brightest their country had to offer. Nor were they lacking in scientific or technical skill: Clearly they knew enough not only to operate the control panels but to override and disable the warning systems. What was missing, clearly, was something that goes far beyond the requirements of intelligence. What was missing—not only within those two individuals, but in the entire structure of command and control that either encouraged or permitted such an unconscionable experiment to go forward that night—was a framework for discerning right from wrong. What was absent was what most people around the world would describe, quite simply, as conscience, morality, or ethics.

This is no small point. Indeed, it gets to the heart of the matter. It seems obvious that what broke down at Chernobyl, long before the reactor exploded, was not simply some scientific understanding, some aspect of the knowledge base. What failed was a system of inner restraints. Before a single computer alarm could have been overridden, there must have been a moral override. The age-old values of responsible authority, integrity, respect for the community and the environment and the future—where were they? Had the finely tuned scientific education of these men left no space for such considerations? Had the complexities of present-day technology demanded so much time and attention from its students that the grand humanistic issues, the richly nuanced landscape of Russian and Ukrainian culture, could find no niche in their curriculum? Was there no room for a moral philosophy equal to the sophistication of their scientific and technical understanding? Or did the system simply drive it out of them, compelling them to swallow their scruples for the sake of loyalty to their superiors?

We'll never know: Those two did not survive. The reporting from the Soviet authorities—who stonewalled for several days after the accident, until the radioactive plume reached Sweden and the secret could no longer be contained—leaves much to be desired. Still, these questions need asking. Never mind that, in some quarters, such queries about morality are thought to be mere metaphysical luxuries, quaint throwbacks to a more leisured, less confidently scientific nineteenth century. Never mind that, in our coolly technical age, we feel we've outgrown the need for an education rooted in philosophical wrestlings—that the ethics of technology, if pursued at all, can safely be relegated to the margins of elective courses, avocational interests, and "soft" conversations among experts in "hard" areas.

Chernobyl proves otherwise.

Yet was the moral meltdown at Chernobyl really such a new phenomenon? Hasn't every age had its egregious and unconscionable actors, its endemic amorality, its towering selfishnesses? Are we any worse than our ancestors? Does not every generation envision some apparently ethical golden age of the past and contrast with it the moral corruption of the present? Were those engineers, or even that Soviet system, any lower on the moral barometer than their predecessors?

Perhaps they weren't. Here is how William Wordsworth put it when, in 1802, he looked longingly back to the "virtue" embodied by John Milton, whose epic poem *Paradise Lost* had appeared 135 years earlier:

> Milton! thou shouldst be living at this hour:
> England hath need of thee: she is a fen
> Of stagnant waters: altar, sword, and pen,
> Fireside, the heroic wealth of hall and bower,
> Have forfeited their ancient English dower
> Of inward happiness. We are selfish men; . . .
>
> (Sonnet VIII, "London, 1802")

The impulse to condemn the ethical present—"We are selfish men"!—has always been there, as has the longing for the return of whatever will give us goodness. That perpetual impulse, however, should not blind us to the quantitative and qualitative differences between our past and present technologies. Was there a system in Wordsworth's age that, if you could have turned it over to two engineers like those at Reactor Number Four and said, "Do the most unconscionable thing you can imagine," would have produced a Chernobyl? Where in the nineteenth century (to change the example) could you have found a ship large enough to load with some toxic substance, put a drunken captain in charge, and run it aground in Prince William Sound in Alaska to have done the damage caused by the *Exxon Valdez* oil spill on March 24, 1989? Or where in the past could you have found a massive, nongovernmental financial system, handed it over to the moral equivalent of U.S. financier Charles Keating, and said, "Do whatever you like," that would have caused anything like the economic chaos wrought by the collapse of the American savings and loan institutions in the 1980s?

What's new, then, is not simply our knowledge. It's the sheer scale and power of our systems—scientific, technological, financial, governmental, educational, and so forth. Widespread, designed for great speed, often decentralized, such systems are increasingly susceptible to misuse or manipulation by a single individual making a single wrong decision. Why is that fact so important? Simply because such systems leverage our ethics so highly. Like megaphones, they amplify small whispers of wrongdoing into vast bellows of amorality. In that megaphone effect, a single moral lapse—a single ethical Chernobyl—can now affect millions for centuries.

But hasn't that always been so? Isn't it the case that, from Attila the Hun to Adolf Hitler, moral perversion has slaughtered millions? True enough. But these days the danger lies not only in the hands of madmen, tyrants, or obvious exponents of evil. Nowadays it also lies in the hands of more-or-less well-meaning experts—whose only failings, perhaps, are a fuzziness at the moral core and a consequent limiting of the vision. The danger increasingly lies in the hands of otherwise ordinary people—people you and I know and like. They are not willfully setting out to create the next Chernobyl. Yet they may be operating in a systemic and personal ethical vacuum that, in the end, leaves them unable to tell right from wrong. The great danger, it seems, is that at the critical moment of decision they may simply not understand the one most crucial fact—that they are walking straight into a world-class moral temptation.

Fifteen Minutes at Bath Iron Works

All temptations, fortunately, are not of a global scale. Some are personal and internal. But wherever they lie along the scale stretching from private guilt to public calamity, they call out for ethical clarity. And they are never, in the end, small. Even the more-or-less personal ones can lead to what an acquaintance of mine has called "the CEM." When I asked him what he meant, he reminded me of a situation that arose with a defense contractor on the coast of Maine—the sad tale of a navy contract, a much-respected corporate leader, and a fifteen-minute ethical lapse.

The story begins on May 16, 1991, when a group of executives at Bath Iron Works in Bath, Maine, sit down in their conference center for their quarterly meeting with the navy. Joining them is a consultant from PRC, Inc., a Virginia-based firm hired by the navy to help with financial analysis. On the table for discussion: a review of BIW's progress in building the destroyer *Arleigh Burke*. And just over the horizon: the navy's announced intention of letting contracts later that year for five more Aegis destroyers, each worth about $250 million to the shipbuilder.

Those contracts, naturally, are to be given to U.S. shipbuilders. But since World War II, the number of domestic shipbuilders capable of building surface combatants has decreased from fourteen to two. One is Bath Iron Works, a century-old company that, with a peacetime record of 11,300 employees in 1989, is Maine's largest private employer. The other is Ingalls Shipbuilding in Mississippi, which like BIW is that state's largest private employer. Again and again these two shipyards have vied for navy contracts. Again and again they have done their best to second-guess each other's cost structure and schedules in order to craft the winning bid. That's not surprising: The stakes are tremendously high, the pressures intense. With the end of the Cold War, defense jobs are already declining. If BIW is to continue as a viable shipbuilder in the near term, it must continue to win at least two destroyers a year.

This time, the bidding process might have been no different, were it not for a sixty-seven-page navy document. Marked "Business Sensitive," it is left behind by the consultant and found on a chair by a maintenance worker cleaning up the meeting room at five o'clock the next morning. Launched up through the corporation's executive channels, it lands at nine o'clock on the desk of the chief executive officer of BIW, William Haggett. The Colby- and Harvard-educated son of a BIW pipefitter, Haggett has spent twenty-eight years working his way up the BIW ladder from buyer to CEO. Now, highly regarded in the community as an outstanding citizen and supporter of volunteer causes, he is respected in Washington as a weighty voice on shipbuilding issues and often mentioned as a potential 1994 candidate for governor of the Pine Tree State.

That morning, however, Haggett has to leave right away for a meeting in Portland, a half-hour's drive away. One glance tells him that the document is replete with analyses of Ingalls's and BIW's cost structures. He scans it for fifteen minutes. He discusses its contents with his vice presidents for finance and for contracts, who have already examined it. He is now apprised of its contents: page after page of numbers, detailing his competitor's financial estimates for building Aegis destroyers. It is invaluable information for BIW. But as Haggett also knows, it is forbidden information. Its circulation is severely restricted under the Procurement Integrity Act, a federal law that requires defense contractors bidding on government contracts to certify that they are not—and have never been—in possession of proprietary information. Pressed for time, Haggett leaves for Portland. First, however, he asks that the document be photocopied—and the original returned to the conference center where it was found.

During his absence in the next four hours, the document is analyzed carefully. Portions of it are entered into spreadsheets on the company computers. At 2:15 that afternoon, however, one of the executives decides he had better tell his boss, BIW president Duane D. "Buzz" Fitzgerald. Like Haggett, Fitzgerald also has ties with BIW that run deep: His father worked for forty years in the company's shipfitting department. A lawyer by training, he is sometimes described as "the conscience of the shipyard" because of his reputation for ethical probity. Now, feeling a deep uneasiness at the course of events, Fitzgerald moves to correct its cause. At about three o'clock, he orders the copy shredded and the computer data deleted. Haggett, returning from Portland, agrees with Fitzgerald's order and admits that he made what he later called "a bad decision." By 4:30 Haggett has delivered the original document to the local navy official, Captain Paul M. Robinson.

Yet even then the problems persist. The shipyard's own report of the incident, submitted on May 31 by BIW's Washington lawyer, Robert H. Koehler, contains a succinct and sobering description of Haggett's delivery of the document. Haggett, it reports, "determined that he would not volunteer the information to Capt. Robinson that BIW had photocopied the study . . . but that he would only state that 'no copies existed.' " Since by 4:30 that afternoon all copies had already been shredded or deleted, Haggett's statement is technically correct.

The navy, naturally, is concerned. Worried that the bidding process might have been compromised, they launch their own investigation. In July their report comes back: No material damage has been done to Ingalls in this case. BIW and Haggett are cleared of serious wrongdoing. Once BIW sequesters those who had access to the document, the bidding process can continue essentially as planned.

Yet on September 16, Haggett is standing in front of the microphones at a press conference in Bath, resigning his position as CEO. He is doing so not at the insistence of the navy but at the suggestion of his own colleagues, who are so concerned about BIW's reputation for integrity that they have asked him to step down. The reason, Haggett explains somewhat ruefully to an astonished public, is clear.

Fifteen minutes of ethical uncertainty, he says, has cost him his career. "With the benefit of hindsight, I think it was a bad decision on my part," he notes, adding, "I know it was." Replacing him as CEO: Buzz Fitzgerald.

That is what my friend meant by the term CEM: a "career-ending move."

There is, of course, a world of difference between Bath and Chernobyl—in scale, damage, cost, and effect on others' lives. No one would equate the almost technical blunder of a Bill Haggett—where a fast-moving schedule conspired with a desire to benefit his firm to produce a personal tragedy—with the global disaster arising from the deliberate and premeditated efforts of the Chernobyl engineers to circumvent safety procedures. Yet at bottom these cases have a notable similarity. Each happened rapidly. And each happened because three essential elements came together to set the conditions for the blunder: intelligence, size, and an ethical lapse. Had any of the three been missing, the problem might well have been averted. Had the Chernobyl engineers been bright and amoral—but working only in a small-scale system—the damage would have been minimal. Had they been *dumb* but unethical, they would not have known how to shut down the alarms. And, of course, had they been bright people *with strong moral characters* working in a large system, they probably would have avoided so disastrous a course of action.

So, too, with Haggett. No one doubts that his intelligence got him to the top of his company. And there is no question that, as CEO of a major defense contractor, he was part of a large-scale system. Had either of these conditions been lacking—had he not been smart enough to be at the top, or had he headed a small organization—the damage might have been forgivable and the career left intact, however deep the ethical lapse. Put all three together, however, and the conditions were prime for a CEM.

Three Ways to Be Wrong

Still another factor unites these two tales. Each involves a right-versus-wrong decision. In the blur of events, it may seem for a moment that testing your turbine at Chernobyl or bagging a bid in Bath may be "right" at any cost. But only for a moment. A bit of reflection about long-term consequences, individual motives, or moral rules makes it clear that neither of these cases involved a genuine ethical dilemma that pitted right against right. Instead, they exhibited moral temptations that set right against wrong.

In that sense, these are telltale examples. The world, after all, is full of wrongdoing. A significant chunk of every government's budget is devoted to discovering, policing, judging, incarcerating, and rehabilitating wrongdoers. A great deal of private charity is given over to rectifying such wrongs as drug abuse, street crime, and family violence. Private corporations annually spend millions to keep from losing more millions in employee theft and fraud. Each of these problems comprises a collection of individual acts of wrong. And each individual wrong begins with someone's decision to do something other than right. Right versus wrong, then, constitutes a formidable part of any consideration of today's ethics.

But what is the nature of wrong? How do we know it when we see it? Typically, we think of *wrong* in three ways:

• **Violation of law.** It is wrong, we say, to pass a stopped school bus, take a candy bar without paying the shopkeeper, cut trees on your neighbor's property, or fail to curb your dog. More significant, it is wrong to bribe public officials, refuse to pay the rent, pass bad checks, or beat your spouse. These kinds of wrongdoing involve failures of compliance with clearly specified laws. Lack of compliance can arise ignorantly or intentionally—either because we don't know the law and its applications, or because we willfully choose to violate the law.

Increasing numbers of corporations now designate "compliance officers," whose task it is to inform managers about the law and urge respect for it. As sources of information, they help warn managers away from preventable legal and regulatory problems; as promoters of respect for law, they tend to become the corporate ethics officers. While these two functions often fit neatly together in the organizational chart, blending them into a single office sometimes promotes a blurring of law and ethics that is detrimental to each—a problem examined in more detail in Chapter Three.

• **Departure from truth.** We also use *wrong* to describe that which does not accord with the facts as generally known. Claiming *five* as the product of *two times three,* observing that it's raining when in fact it's only the lawn sprinkler spraying the window, and asserting that Bach wrote the "1812 Overture" are all wrong. So is calling in sick when you are not, asserting that the gunk in the river is not from *your* factory when it is, or claiming that, as president, you didn't know about Watergate when you did.

Character Education

What should a society do about a world of wrongdoing? Many would say, "Teach ethics." The standard term for such activity these days is "character education." As James Leming has demonstrated, however, there are many different birds nesting in these branches—some of them better than others.

The current character education movement in America had several antecedents, most notably in the 1920s and the 1960s. In the 1920s it consisted largely of establishing and promoting codes of conduct and integrating them into school life. In 1928, however, a major review of the research by Hugh Hartshorne and Mark May found that "the mere urging of honest behavior by the teacher or the discussion of standards and ideals of honesty . . . has no necessary relation to conduct." By World War II, character education had all but disappeared from the schools.

In the 1960s the effort came to life again as Lawrence Kohlberg and Sidney Simon (see boxes, pp. 50 and 219) pioneered, respectively, the "moral dilemma" discussion approach and the "values clarification" approach. The former asked students to develop their moral reasoning, in hopes of raising them to a higher stage in Kohlberg's scale. The latter asked the teacher simply to serve as a neutral facilitator, rigorously excluding his or her own values from the classroom and respecting any and all values the students formulated. The latter approach, in particular, produced significant public concern about "values neutral" education devoid of any moral direction. Extensive research has also proved it to have been ineffective. Moral dilemma discussion, however, has generally been found successful.

Today, a growing character education movement is coming together under such umbrellas as that of the Character Education Partnership in Washington, D.C., and with the intellectual firepower of such books as Thomas Lickona's *Educating for Character: How Our Schools Can Teach Respect and Responsibility.* Today's movement seeks to steer a middle course between a values-neutral approach and a highly structured enforcement of quasi-religious codes. Research indicates that what most seems to raise the moral barometer among students are:

- Moral dilemma discussion programs;
- Cooperative-learning environments, where students take responsibility for their own and others' learning and behavior;
- School climates based on clear standards, mutual respect among students and educators, and shared governance; and
- Clear communication of a peer- and community-based consensus concerning appropriate behaviors.

If the current movement is to succeed where its predecessors failed, writes Professor Leming, "character education must become an activity with clear community support" that goes well beyond the schools and provides "clear rewards for teachers that take its goals seriously and develop the necessary competencies."

These sorts of "wrongs" lie at the core of the legal process, where a great deal of energy is spent trying to determine the relation between what the parties *say* happened and what *actually* happened. But such departures from truth go well beyond law into areas untouched by legislation. At their simplest, they concern honest misreadings of the data: If I bounce a check because the bank incorrectly calculated the balance on my statement, I have been "wrong" about my ability to pay, although in an entirely blameless manner. At their most complex, such departures shade into complicated issues of interpretation: The assertions that Christopher Marlowe wrote much of the *Henry IV* that we now attribute to Shakespeare, or that Lee Harvey Oswald acted alone in killing John F. Kennedy, may in fact be "wrong" in that these statements do not depict what actually happened—although, not being able to determine "what actually happened" in these cases, we may never know.

• **Deviation from moral rectitude.** Suppose I see someone shoplifting, but I say nothing to the supermarket manager. Suppose I don't get around to feeding my dog today. Suppose I promise to meet you at noon, but decide to lunch with someone else and don't bother to call you. If we have even the most rudimentary concept of duty, we will probably see these as lapses of ethics. And we would not hesitate to describe as "wrong" the situation in which a journalist passes off as his or her own a few words from an uncopyrighted source, or in which a doctor urges upon a patient an expensive procedure when a less expensive treatment would do, or in which a politician presents opposed and conflicting promises to different groups. These things are wrong not because they violate law or fail to comport with fact, but because they go against the moral grain. They don't square, in other words, with the code of fundamental, inner values that is so widely shared and broadly understood that it defines—at least for our place and time—the difference between right and wrong.

That reservation—"for our place and time"—is important. Values *can* change, as the history of Western civilization easily demonstrates. When it was still right to own slaves, it was already wrong to eat people. When it had become wrong to own slaves, it was still right to possess women as property. When that became wrong, it was still right to blow cigarette smoke in your neighbor's face. Now, with smoking in disgrace, it is still right to use and dispose of polystyrene foam cups, regardless of their long-term effects on the environment. More changes, clearly, are in the works.

Such changes arise not only from faddish cultural movements or passing social frights. They sometimes come from deep-seated shifts in the moral tectonics of the age. Yet however much individual values change, one fact is clear: There remains a kind of inner core, a fixed measure within us all, that helps us separate right from wrong. It may be almost out of sight. It may be shaped in large part by those around us. It may be based on clearly reasoned views or deep religious convictions—or, conversely, on hazy notions and unexamined intuitions. But it's there. Usually, in assessing whether an individual is doing right or wrong, we seek answers to two questions: How well developed is this core? and, How congruent are this person's actions with that core?

When the answer to either question is "Not very!" we can be reasonably sure that some kind of action we would call "wrong" is in the offing. If the inner moral compass is lacking—if there is a void at the center where the core values ought to be—the individual may never even recognize that his or her actions are wrong. We typically define that condition as *amoral.* At its extreme, the vacuum of amorality produces a moral idiocy that kills, rapes, pillages, cheats, and lies with impunity, doing abundant wrong in all three of our above categories (but especially the last) and feeling no qualm at all.

More often, however, this kind of vacuum produces a low-grade amorality, an ethical denseness that sees no real reason not to lie, that treats others as means rather than ends, and that elevates self so far above the community that it fails to connect to the values of the society around it. Such thinking may produce behavior that is both legally acceptable and scientifically accurate. But it has no comprehension of the demands of moral rectitude—nor even that such a thing exists.

Most people, fortunately, are not inherently amoral. Most wrongdoing arises instead from *immorality*—a violation of the precepts of morality. It arises, it seems, because actions are out of sync with values—either with the individual's inner values or with values we can reasonably take for granted in the community at large. Why this incongruity? Usually because those values have remained more or less undefined. If I have only a vague sense of what "truth" means, for example, I don't immediately see that my action fails to square with the underlying value of truthfulness. I may see it when I'm told; in fact, I may be horrified that I acted as I did, because I like to think that truth matters. But until I see it, my action is out of balance.

Hence the need for individuals to identify, systematically and deliberately, the values they and their communities hold. That process of identification (which is the focus of Chapter Four) occupies a good deal of attention in contemporary ethics training programs. Many of these programs confront individuals with issues requiring a decision, ask them to decide, and then urge them to articulate the reasons for their decision. Result: The individual recognizes that his or her deeply held values often do not support the action taken—and feels a certain pressure to change either the action or the values.

In a world of drowsy morality, this sort of confrontation-and-decision approach is sometimes helpful in awakening an ethical response. And the sharpest confrontations can often be elicited by presenting cases that embody a serious potential for wrongdoing. Not surprisingly, then, a great many case studies used to teach and discuss ethics these days focus not on right-versus-right but on right-versus-wrong issues. The following two cases, prepared by Douglas Wallace for *Career World* magazine, are typical:

> *Pam, a Minnesota college student, works part-time as a receptionist in an apartment building for elderly persons. Last winter, many of the building's tenants, who had become Pam's friends, complained to her that their apartments were cold. When she relayed these comments to her boss, Pam was told to tell the senior citizens that the furnace was out of order. But she knew that her boss had simply turned down the central thermostat to save money on heating bills.*
>
> *Pam hates lying to the tenants, but is certain she will lose her much-needed job if she refuses.*

> *You manufacture keys, and you are accused of providing master keys for automobiles to mail-order customers, even though it was obvious that some of the purchasers might be automobile thieves. Your defense is plain and straightforward. If there is nothing in the law to prevent you from selling your keys to anyone who wants them, it is not up to you to ask your customers' motives. Is it any worse for you to sell your keys by mail, you ask, than for mail-order houses to sell guns that might be used for murder?*
>
> *Are you responsible for the consequences of selling master keys?*

A third case comes from an ethics questionnaire prepared by Walker Research, Inc., of Indianapolis:

> *You are an interviewing supervisor [for a survey research firm] and are trying to get an assignment completed in a tough part of the inner city. Of the last three interviewers who went in there, two quit after one day, and the third was mugged and is now recovering at home. A new interviewer is recruited and comes in for the assignment. What do you tell him/her about past experience in this location?*

Notice what these cases have in common: the temptation to do wrong. Stepping back from each case, it's easy to see that a world in which tenants freeze and are lied to, auto thieves easily buy car keys, and employees are kept in the dark about on-the-job dangers is far from an ideal world. That doesn't mean these are badly constructed cases: far from it. They are realistic, in that these kinds of situations do indeed arise in the world. They also open a window onto the distinction between the legal and the ethical: Each is presented as though no laws were broken. They may even provide useful examples to present to individuals whose ethical barometer you would like to read: Asking potential employees how they would respond if they were Pam, the key-maker, or the supervisor will shed light on their moral stance.

At bottom, however, the world presented in these cases is not one of great moral complexity. It fairly quickly reduces itself to a black-and-white, right-versus-wrong world. Ask the question a different way—"What sort of world would *you* most like to live in?"—and it becomes pretty clear that Pam ought not lie, master keys ought not to be sold, and new employees should be told the whole truth. Why? Because to do otherwise is "wrong." There may be ways to weasel around that wrongness. And there will surely be temptations to overlook it. But the issue clearly does not involve two rights. One side is wrong.

Scanning the Moral Barometer

If you have come this far in this book, you probably have little trouble seeing the "wrong" in the above cases. But the world is largely composed of people who have not read this far. What is their world like these days? What's the reading on its moral barometer? If the need for ethics is as serious as I've suggested—and as serious as the protagonists of Chernobyl and Bath Iron Works should have understood it to be—how are we doing? How well are we equipped for an age in which our survival will depend just as much on telling right from wrong as on being smart and competent?

There are a few hopeful signs. One is that we're talking more about ethics, it seems, than ever before. The word has become an integral part of the language of public discourse: No week goes by without *ethics* figuring in the blare of our headlines and on the lips of our commentators. So pervasive is the idea that, as University of Montana ethics expert Deni Elliott has noted, *The New York Times* index from 1969 to 1989 reveals that the number of news stories indexed under *ethics* grew in that twenty-year period by 400 percent. Few readers of the *Times,* perhaps, would attribute that change to an idealistic editorial staff bent on preaching purity to an unregenerate world. The reason is much simpler: This is a group of savvy newspaper executives who prosper by giving the public the stories they want to read. Today, we want to read about ethics.

What we read under that heading, of course, is not uniformly encouraging. It is typically a rich broth of scandal, corruption, and vice. Sometimes the stories on ethics have to do with personal tragedies—which, to cite a classical definition of tragedy, involve the fall of great individuals from high places. Financiers Ivan Boesky and Michael Milken, politicians Jim Wright and Gary Hart, evangelists Jim Bakker and Jimmy Swaggart, athlete Pete Rose, hotelier Leona Helmsley, clergyman Bruce Ritter—the list goes on and on. Sometimes those stories have to do with entire nations, as in the corruption scandals that wracked Italy in 1993, the ongoing issues of political intrigue and million-dollar kickbacks in Japan, and the revelations of a knowing use of AIDS-tainted blood for transfusions in France in the 1980s. Sometimes, too, ethics reaches the headlines as we frame the debate over the agonizing international issues of our time: how Western nations should respond to "ethnic cleansing" in the former Yugoslavia, what guidelines to erect concerning the use of "heroic" medical technologies to keep alive the seriously ill, how to think about euthanasia and abortion, how to balance the pressures against violence in the media and the concern for freedom of expression, whether to distribute condoms in the schools.

Yet today's ethics stories are not all generated from some sad human failing, or from agonizing choices between two wrongs. Some of the headlines applaud the moral compass of single individuals who, like community college student Roger Wardell, found a satchel containing $6,100 in cash in a Tempe, Arizona, parking lot and gave it back—because, he said, "It's just a matter of principle. . . . My parents brought me up to be honest." Other stories focus on the willingness of teenagers to behave unselfishly: A 1991 survey by Independent Sector, for example, found that 61 percent of American twelve-to-seventeen-year-olds regularly do volunteer work, contributing an average of 3.2 hours of time each week to a charitable activity of their choice. Still other stories highlight the dawning recognition of the importance of ethics for our future: When Korn/Ferry International and the Columbia University School of Business polled 1,500 executives in twenty nations in 1989, they found that "personal ethics" came at the very top of a list of characteristics said to be required in the ideal corporate chief executive officer in the year 2000.

Still other stories center on the attitudes of entire sectors of society, who when asked whether ethics matters answer, "Yes, indeed":

- In annual polls by the Gallup Organization, the number of people insisting that a "strict moral code" is "very important" has risen steadily from 47 percent in 1981 to 60 percent in 1989.
- In 1991–92, when the Josephson Institute surveyed U.S. students, 78 percent of the high-schoolers said that cheating on exams is wrong, and 90 percent of the high school and college crowd said that "being kind and caring" is very important.
- When the Center for Business Ethics at Bentley College in Massachusetts surveyed *Fortune 1000* corporations in 1992, one third of the respondents said they had set up a formal "ethics officer" position in their corporation—of which nearly half had been established since 1989.
- When the Chicago-based management consulting firm of McFeely Wackerle Jett asked four thousand upper-level executives in 1987 whether "good ethics is good business in the long run," 90 percent strongly agreed.

And there's plenty of anecdotal evidence. A colleague of mine tells of taking his grandson to watch a liftoff of the space shuttle at Cape Canaveral. With the countdown in progress, the boy noticed a watch on the ground beneath the bleachers. Slipping through the seats, he retrieved it—a genuine Rolex, set about with diamonds. With the liftoff finished and people rushing to the parking lot to beat the crowd, he apologized to his grandfather for slowing them down, but insisted they take the watch to Lost and Found. On their way, the owner of the watch and her husband caught up with them, identified the watch, and, greatly relieved, offered the boy a reward. He refused. They insisted, explaining that he had done a rare and highly moral thing. He still refused. Why? Because, he explained, "I'm a Boy Scout." Ethics, to him, was not a rare and unusual exception. It was a proper and customary duty.

Unfortunately, however, any serious reading of the moral barometer also reveals a number of sobering signs. Among the most telling are the views that Americans take toward that very barometer—the kind of "How are we doing?" assessments that register the nation's attitudes toward itself. "By a margin of 63 percent to 33 percent," says a September 1992 report in the Knight-Ridder Newspapers based on a Gallup survey, "Americans believe the United States is in decline as a nation. The decline is not military—we are still the only superpower—but economic, moral, and spiritual." That last category—a moral and spiritual decline—received a "yes" vote from nearly two thirds of those responding. Similar comments surface in other places as well. Asked about the ethical standards of people today, 59 percent of the upper-level executives polled by McFeely in 1987 indicated dissatisfaction. And 80 percent of the respondents to a 1992 "Life in America" survey by Shearson Lehman Brothers felt that the United States was "pretty seriously on the wrong track."

As for who's doing things wrong, the figures over time seem to turn up the same parade of good guys and bad guys. Asked in a Harris Poll in 1992 to name the groups with good moral and ethical standards, American adults said:

- small business owners (64 percent)
- journalists (39 percent)
- business executives (31 percent)
- lawyers (25 percent)
- members of Congress (19 percent)

If Congress fares poorly here, look at how it came out in a survey by J. Walter Thompson researchers James Patterson and Peter Kim. There, in a ranking of the ten sleaziest ways to make a living, members of Congress and local politicians were surpassed only by street peddlers, prostitutes, TV evangelists, organized crime bosses, and drug dealers.

But perhaps the most serious evidence of a barometric decline comes from the numerous surveys that ask individuals to assess their own response to certain ethical situations. The challenge is especially acute among the rising generations, who are destined to provide the ethical leadership for the nation in the twenty-first century. How are *they* doing?

• In a Louis Harris survey conducted in 1989 for the Girl Scouts of America, 65 percent of the high-schoolers said that, faced with an important test for which they weren't sufficiently prepared, they would either try to copy answers from a good student nearby or glance at that student's paper for ideas.

• That figure is roughly equivalent to the one reported in a 1991–92 survey by the Josephson Institute, which found that three in five high-schoolers "admitted to having cheated on an exam at least once while in high school."

• Josephson also found that 83 percent of high-schoolers had lied to their parents at least once in the prior year.

• A 1989 survey by the Pinnacle Group, an international public relations firm, found that, when they got out into the world of business, "a total of 66 percent of students [in the United States] said they would consider lying to achieve a business objective." About the same number said they would "inflate their business expense report."

When these same students finish college and head for graduate school, their ethics apparently goes with them. Rutgers professor Donald McCabe, surveying more than six thousand students in thirty one colleges and universities around the nation during the 1990–91 academic year, found that over two thirds "indicated that they had cheated on a test or major assignment at least once while an undergraduate." The primary reason: tough competition to gain admission to graduate school. The breakout of undergraduate cheaters by their intended profession is especially interesting. The lowest percentage of admitted cheaters were heading for the nation's schools of education. That fact ought to comfort today's parents and educators—until they realize that the "low" number is 57 percent. Confessed cheaters in some other intended specialties:

- Law schools: 63 percent
- Arts programs: 64 percent
- Public service and government programs: 66 percent
- Medical schools: 68 percent

- Engineering programs: 71 percent
- Graduate schools of business: 76 percent

The presence of an honor code, apparently, had little deterrent effect: Of the thirty-one colleges and universities surveyed, fourteen have long-standing honor-code traditions. Asking why they cheated, Professor McCabe was led to conclude that "many students felt that some forms of cheating were victimless crimes, particularly on assignments that accounted for a small percentage of the total course grade."

Why Do Children Do Right?

As children mature, do they develop through stages of morality? The question has fascinated such notable educational theorists as Jean Piaget, who published *The Moral Judgment of the Child* in 1932. But it was developmental psychologist Lawrence Kohlberg who, in studies of boys between ten and sixteen undertaken in the 1950s, first found that children's responses to hypothetical moral dilemmas could be categorized into his now-famous "six stages of moral judgment" related to their age and based on their level of reasoning.

In Stage One, Kohlberg finds no higher reason for doing right than fear of punishment or respect for authority. Stage Two is characterized by increasing individualism and a sense of equal exchange and fairness. It is based, however, on a conviction that right is relative—and that rules should be followed only when someone's immediate interest (yours or another's) is served. These two stages Kohlberg labels "Pre-conventional."

In the two following "Conventional" stages, children increasingly take account of others. In Stage Three, they pay special heed to the expectations of those around them and the stereotypes of "good" behavior. They also develop a sense of caring based on the Golden Rule and on values such as trust, loyalty, respect, and gratitude. By Stage Four, recognizing for the first time that a generalized moral system defines the rules and roles, they strive to fulfill agreed-upon duties. To keep institutions from breaking down, they adhere to a form of Kant's categorical imperative, avoiding actions that if done by everyone would undermine the collective.

The final "Post-conventional" or "Principled" stages rise toward universal moral precepts. In Stage Five, while still believing that values are largely relative to one's own group, children nevertheless uphold these values out of regard for a social contract that requires obedience to shared laws. Asked what is right, they turn to utilitarianism, striving to make rational calculations of the greatest good for the greatest number. Stage Six, moving beyond such calculations, sees the development of personal commitment to universal moral principles such as justice, equal human rights, and individual dignity. In this stage, the rational individual must recognize that persons are not means but ends, and must treat them as such.

As theory, Kohlberg's work has been applauded for the order it brings to a baffling topic. In practice, however, it has given rise to controversial research and speculation attempting to explain how children develop from one stage to the next and why some go further than others. Even Kohlberg, who spent much of his later life in the alternative education movement developing teaching methods for moral reasoning, acknowledged that higher stages of moral reasoning do not necessarily signal changes in ethical behavior. Yet his work remains the touchstone for explaining how children think about morality.

You have only to ask who engineered the bridge you are about to cross, or where your doctor got his or her training, to begin questioning whether a widespread propensity for cheating among professionals—and the consequent danger of unleashing into the world a cadre of individuals who don't know what they are doing—is in fact a "victimless crime." And you have only to sit in the corporate hiring chair, watching the parade of bright young MBAs coming for interviews, to contemplate the statistical probability that three out of four of them cheated to get through your door in the first place.

More anecdotal is a recent "poll" by futurist Marvin Cetron, who asked ten deans of the nation's business schools to pose to one hundred of their students the following question: If you could do an illegal deal, get caught and tried and convicted, serve a three-year prison sentence, and emerge with $500 million from the deal, would you do it? Three in five of the business students, Cetron reports, said "Absolutely!"

When these people finally enter the workforce, do attitudes

change? Not according to a Roper survey done for Shearson Lehman Brothers in 1992. When eighteen-to-twenty-nine-year-olds were asked to identify the most important factors in getting ahead in the world, 89 percent said "who you know" and 69 percent "playing politics." Those responses could be innocent enough, if translated into less provocative terminology such as "networking" and "being politically astute." Unfortunately, there are no mitigating translations for two other "get ahead" factors—corruption and deceit—cited as important, respectively, by 37 and 39 percent of the young adults.

Are the not-so-young adults any better? There is some comfort in a 1991 Roper Survey reporting that only 23 percent of Americans find nothing wrong with telling their insurance company that "their car is kept in a location with lower insurance rates than where they actually live"—which means that, presumably, 77 percent would *not* do so. Other surveys are not so flattering: The J. Walter Thompson researchers found that nine in ten citizens regularly lie. When asked, "What are you honestly willing to do for $10 million?"—a curious question at best, given the multiple meanings of "honestly" in that context—respondents to the same survey said they would abandon their family (25 percent), become a prostitute for a week (23 percent), or kill a stranger (7 percent).

From the profusion of such data examining the moral barometer, two trends are discernible. Both are troubling, and both are significant. The first, comparing the young and the not-so-young, points to *an ebbing of moral attitudes as children get older:*

• A 1992 write-in survey by *USA Weekend*—admittedly unscientific, since the 126,000 teens estimated to have responded were not randomly selected—found that while 70 percent of the thirteen-year-olds said they would return an extra dollar mistakenly given to them in change, only 55 percent of seventeen-year-olds said they would do the same.

• Much more scientific are the results of the Girl Scouts survey, showing a similar pattern of ethics declining as age increases. In that survey, 65 percent of high-schoolers reported that they would cheat to pass an important exam—while only 21 percent of elementary school children and 53 percent of junior high students said the same. The inference is clear: For every year that our students stay in school, the willingness to cheat (or, to put it more accurately, the willingness to contemplate cheating as an acceptable behavior) increases.

• A similar and perhaps more discouraging figure comes from studies of college athletes. Assessing scores on moral reasoning tests given to incoming freshmen, various researchers note that the athletes generally score lower (indicating less proficiency in ethical awareness and analysis) than the nonathletes. More disturbing, however, is the fact that when these same tests are given later in the students' careers, the nonathletes' scores improve—while athletes involved in intercollegiate sports actually *decline* in their moral-reasoning abilities. If ever there was an old chestnut about a well-rounded education, it is the notion that sports makes the whole person, builds character, inculcates strong values, and generally creates ethical individuals. Yet intercollegiate sports, as currently played on the competitive, televised, and money-sodden fields of many of today's campuses, apparently does just the reverse. It takes whatever capacity for moral reasoning the athletes bring in with them and corrodes it slowly away as the seasons pass.

A second trend worth noting is *the comparison of past and present ethical ages:*

• When the Josephson Institute asked the out-of-school set (dominated by the over-thirty crowd) about their own past, they found that only 25 percent of them said they had cheated in their senior year in high school. That figure, of course, might simply reflect a rosy haze of misremembered nostalgia, or a less-than-candid willingness to speak the truth even in an anonymous survey. It could also, however, point to a significant increase in cheating: The figure for today's high school students in the same survey stands at over 60 percent.

• Less open to question is another of Josephson's findings, which is that while some 75 percent of college students agree that "most people will cheat or lie when it is necessary to get what they want," only half as many in the over-thirty group agree.

• Watching trends over the past several decades, University of Georgia professor Fred Schab found that in 1969 more than 80 percent of high-schoolers agreed that "honesty is the best policy"—a figure that had dropped to 60 percent by 1989. Asked whether they had ever signed their parents' name to an excuse, nearly half the students in 1989 said they had—up from 26 percent who said "Yes" in 1969.

• When upper-level executives were asked by McFeely Wackerle Jett whether "during the past twenty years people have become more ethical, less ethical, or stayed about the same," 56 percent said "less ethical" and 36 percent said "about the same."

There are, of course, innumerable explanations for these twin trends of declining ethics as students age and as history unfolds. Many observers point to the breakup of the family, where most people still feel values are best taught. Others point to a decline in religious commitment, the fracturing of the community, the influence of television, a more sexually permissive age "liberated" by birth control and abortion, an upsurge of cynicism, a decline in unselfishness, a glut of greed, a dearth of compassion, and so forth. A curious fact unearthed among the college students surveyed by Professor McCabe, however, suggests yet one more candidate: growing affluence. "Those from families with incomes over $150,000," he reports, "are 50 percent more likely to be regular cheaters than those whose parents earn less than $25,000." His finding, sadly enough, gives new relevance to that old descriptor *poor-but-honest.*

What, then, is the moral barometer telling us? Its current reading suggests a complex pattern, with tendencies toward moral decline married to evidence of rising concern. Reading the barometer to discern trends—inquiring into the state of the nation's youth, for example, as a predictor of the future—suggests a more poignant picture. America's young people are deeply confused about issues of right versus wrong. To their credit, they seem to know it: Cheating is wrong, they say, even while they go on cheating. As for what to do about it, they have none of the resistance to learning sound values that adults sometimes attribute to them: Asked whether the public schools should "teach basic values such as honesty, fairness and responsibility," 80 percent of the respondents to the 1992 *USA Weekend* survey said "Yes." But then, even the nation's business executives feel that way: By a margin of 84 percent, they either "strongly" or "somewhat" agree with the proposition that "Companies should provide employees at all levels with some type of education or training in ethics."

"There can be little debate that the character of youth is an increasingly serious problem for the United States," writes Professor James S. Leming, a specialist in ethics education at Southern Illinois University at Carbondale. The experience of schooling, he says, is

> *one of the few constants for all children in an increasingly fragmented and unstable environment. We as a nation cannot afford to continue the ser-*

endipitous character education of youth. The schools must begin to address this issue, for if we as a people fail to effectively pass on to our youth the character traits that have made the United States a great nation, then the future of both our youth and the society are in danger.

Yet the confusion about right and wrong remains, and it runs deep. Over dinner with a group of well-educated and highly intelligent students at one of California's finest liberal arts colleges not long ago, I repeated to them a story—said to be true—about a ten-year-old in one of Brooklyn's roughest sections. On his way to school one day, he found a wallet full of money and credit cards—and so full of identification that its owner could easily have been found. He took it with him to school, and could find no one there—no teacher or administrator—willing to tell him what was the "right thing to do" with that wallet.

"We can't tell you to keep it or to return it," they said in essence, "because that would be imposing our values on you. Besides, you're poor and he's pretty well off: What would your mom say if we suggested you return the wallet? She might be real upset. No, you'll have to figure that one out for yourself. We can't help you."

When I asked the students around that campus table what they thought should have happened, they all agreed: The school officials, they said, were absolutely right. There is no way you can impose your values on others, no way even to help instruct them into a clearer sense of right and wrong. That child would simply have to learn his values for himself.

It's almost halfway around the world from California to Chernobyl, where two engineers had apparently learned *their* values—such as they were—for themselves. We sat down to lunch that day in the town of Pripyat. Built to house thirty thousand people beside Chernobyl, it now stands deserted, an interlock of straight streets lined with five-story and twelve-story cement buildings. Their crumbling porches are painted in varying pastels; sunlight shines through empty rooms from windows on the far side. We pass streetlamps no longer working, their hinged glass covers hanging open like tongues. Near a crosswalk we pass a familiar triangular sign silhouetting two tots: CHILDREN PLAYING, it says without needing words. But nothing moves except our mustard-yellow van and, in the air overhead, a couple of crows.

At lunch in a made-over apartment block now serving as the nerve center for the research team, I sit across from Grigory, a lanky young radiochemist. As we talk about the malformed plants and animals growing up in the woods nearby, and about the effects of radiation on human populations and psyches, it is clear that for him this corner of the Ukrainian forest has ceased to be a human community. It has become instead a vast laboratory, a huge experiment upon nature whose hypotheses are still only dimly formulated.

Over a dessert of delicate fruit-filled meringues, I ask him a typical journalist's question: From what you know of the Soviet nuclear industry and the mental and moral makeup of those running it, will there be another Chernobyl-scale disaster in the future?

With a slight shrug—not of indifference, but of resignation in the face of what he takes to be a matter not of opinion but of statistics—he answers simply. "The probability," he says, "is one every ten years."

Chapter Three

Ethical Fitness

What if Grigory is right? What if every decade brings another Chernobyl? And what if the ethical barometer forecasts a society so adrift from its moral anchors that it cannot weather the world-class Chernobyls of the twenty-first century? How do we survive?

What's needed is a capacity to recognize the nature of moral challenges and respond with a well-tuned conscience, a lively perception of the difference between right and wrong, and an ability to choose the right and live by it. What's needed is *ethical fitness.*

One of the most compelling examples of ethical fitness to arise in our seminars came from a dilemma shared with us by a participant from Ohio. He told us that his father, an auto mechanic, was called early one morning to the scene of a wreck on a state highway. Arriving at the isolated, wooded spot, he could see immediately what had happened: A large flatbed truck had gone off the highway and hit a tree head-on. On impact, its load of steel had torn loose and slid forward through the back of the cab, pinning the driver helplessly inside. The cab was on fire, in danger of exploding at any minute.

As he arrived, so did a state police car. And as the trooper ran to the open cab window, the mechanic could hear the driver inside screaming, "Shoot me! Shoot me!" It was obvious that the trooper could not lift off that load of steel and free the driver. So, with the flames growing in intensity, the trooper slowly removed his service revolver from his holster. Then he paused, reconsidered, and slid the revolver back into his holster. And then, amid the driver's screams, he removed it a second time, paused, and put it back once again.

It was at that point in this agonized struggle that the mechanic saw the officer do a remarkable thing. Running back to his cruiser, he grabbed a small carbon tetrachloride fire extinguisher. It was hardly enough to quell the fire. But it was large enough to spray in the driver's face and put him to sleep, which is what he did.

Shortly afterward, the cab exploded.

What was going on in that trooper's mind? From this distance, we don't know. But in those few seconds he must have been wrestling with a conflict between two of humanity's mightiest moral principles:

- You must not kill.
- You must do all in your power to relieve suffering.

How could he kill a fellow human being? Yet how could he not accede to desperate pleas for merciful action?

In the heat of the moment, however, there was no time for reasoning. There was no opportunity to resort to the police manual, to tally up arguments on either side, or even to pull out of a wallet a small plastic reminder card listing the elements of an ethical decision-making process. Just as a lifeguard, seeing a child drowning in the undertow, has no time to go lift weights for a few weeks and get in physical shape for the swim she knows she must undertake, so the trooper had no time to get himself into ethical shape for the decision he knew he had to make. He had to choose instantly, according to his best understanding at the time. And he had to choose right.

To put it simply, he had to be ethically fit.

Notice how much ethical fitness is like physical fitness. You're not born into physical fitness. You reach it by giving a little effort each day. Sometimes that effort is unconscious, natural, almost accidental: You spend a summer as a child playing baseball, climbing trees, or mowing lawns, and without even noticing it you're in shape. At other times, getting in shape requires a conscious, deliberate, sweat-for-sweat's-sake effort of running, lifting weights, swimming laps, and all the rest.

Either way, the result's pretty much the same: You're fit. You're able to sustain effort over the long haul without getting winded. And you're ready to play hard or work hard at a moment's notice.

But *reaching* fitness isn't enough. Once you're there, you've got to *maintain* it. Let it slip away, and you'll labor twice as hard to get it back. But keep it in trim, and it only takes a little work each day. What's more, there's no alternative to the real work of exercising over an extended period of time. You don't get fit with a quick fix: Running twenty miles in a single day is no substitute for running a daily half-mile for forty days. Nor do you get it by osmosis. Hanging around active people, reading books on fitness, fastening onto this or that diet, soaking up the sports events—these can be worthwhile, sometimes even inspirational. But they just don't cut it when it comes to keeping in shape. In the end, you either work at it or you don't—and nobody's invented anything that takes the effort out of it.

Ethical fitness is much the same. You may come from the most moral, high-minded, right-thinking family in the world—and that's a help. You may have been well schooled and well churched, raised in a community of honest and hardworking folks—and that makes it so much easier to be ethical yourself. You may have taken ethics courses in school, or worked for someone who was a model of uprightness, or gone through ethics training courses on the job—all to the good. You may even have the good fortune to live with a highly moral spouse and work in an environment where your colleagues and superiors are naturally inclined toward honesty, fairness, and a deep respect for one another—which is terrific. But that doesn't *necessarily* mean you're ethically fit.

What is ethical fitness? Start with what it's not. Unlike physical fitness, it's not mentally passive. You can work up a sweat at the gym while your mind is leagues away. Ethics isn't like that. You've got to think about it, reason it through, get the mind in gear and grapple with the tough issues. In other words, you've got to be mentally engaged.

What's more, you've got to care, to be committed through the feelings as well as through the intellect. Ethics is not a blind impartiality, doling out right and wrong according to some stone-cold canon of ancient and immutable law. It's a warm and supremely human activity that cares enough for others to want right to prevail. And it's not mere analysis. It doesn't come from woollying around with apparently insoluble dilemmas or arguing endlessly and inconclusively over case studies. Unfortunately, some ethics training these days does just that. It leaves ethics in the realm of analysis—no conclusions, no resolutions, no ways forward, just a lot of fun talk. Result? "Ethics" becomes an academic, intense, and essentially irrelevant exercise, marginal to the real problems of the world and disengaged from the goal of changing behavior and building a better future. Does it help? Not noticeably. "With that kind of ethics training and a gun," quips Gary Edwards of the Ethics Resource Center in Washington, D.C., "you can rob the Seven-Eleven."

A teacher told us of an experience in which her own ethical fitness was called into action in ways that went far beyond mere analysis and demanded new ranges of intuition and humanity. She had begun her teaching career, she said, in a large midwestern metropolis, where the schools had the typical problems and advantages of well-educated, affluent, suburban America. She had then moved with her husband to a rural district not far away, where family and parental values were much more conservative and where the community seemed more caring and more involved in schooling.

As a first-year teacher in this new high school, she was assigned a task no other teacher wanted: advisor to the junior prom. The rules she was to enforce included a provision that any junior in good standing from that particular high school could attend the prom. Those who wished to bring dates from other classes or schools, however, had to submit forms and get the advisor's permission. All went as planned during the year until, close to prom time, the advisor received an application from a girl asking permission to bring to the prom, as her date, her lesbian partner from another town.

The advisor had strong feelings about the need for tolerance and for respecting the rights of the individual. She was also, however, deeply concerned about the feelings of her newly adopted community—and about the consternation that would arise if this girl and her partner were seen marching across the gym floor together in the Grand Promenade. She called in the student to discuss her concerns. But the student threatened to sue the school if she was discriminated against on grounds of sexual orientation or if her right of free association was abrogated.

The advisor was now well aware that the situation could engulf her own reputation as a professional. If she allowed the student and her date to parade through the gym, she might well find herself without a job the following year. But if she refused the request and plunged the school into a lawsuit, she might find herself similarly unemployed. Clearly this situation had the potential to inflame an entire community. So she asked her superior, a head teacher in the system, what she should do.

The head teacher, a man with years of experience in that community, agreed that the situation was delicate. Taxpayers, he said, would indeed be outraged if their school was seen to sanction such behavior. And since the school system was dependent upon the goodwill of the taxpayers to provide its annual funding, it was essential to avoid such outrage. On the other hand, the entire school budget could be blown apart by legal fees if the student chose to sue. Yet his suggestion for a solution astounded the advisor. She was told to approve the application. Then, a week before the prom, she should arrange for another student to get into a fight with the lesbian. The administration would then have grounds for suspending her during the week of the prom, thereby removing her "good standing" in the school and rendering her ineligible to attend the prom. Result: The potential for community outrage would be averted, the student would have no grounds for a suit, and the year would end more or less peacefully.

In telling us this story, the advisor, a young married woman whose family values squared well with those of the community, indicated her distaste for lesbianism. She also found herself resenting the student's efforts to subvert the entire prom, shifting it in what she saw as selfish ways from an occasion for enjoyment by many into a platform for promoting the narrow social agenda of a few. But she knew that the head teacher's suggestion was unfair and ultimately dishonest, and that she herself could take no part in such a scheme.

So she again called the student in and, like the trooper at the steel-truck wreck, sought a third way through her dilemma. Always endeavoring to be truthful in her comments and assessments, she complimented the student for her maturity and social concern. She pointed out that many, perhaps even most, of her fellow students were hardly up to her level of sophistication—and that, for this girl and her partner, such company for the whole evening of a prom would probably be pretty dull. Then, drawing on her background in the metropolitan school district, she suggested that the student and her friend might instead want to celebrate the evening of the prom having dinner at one of the fine restaurants in a nearby city instead of attending the dance.

To her great relief, the student quickly agreed, thanked her for the idea, and withdrew the prom application for her friend—leaving the teacher with the distinct impression that the student herself had been searching for a way to avoid the inevitable unpleasantness of attending the prom without surrendering her own sense of individuality.

What went on here? Not a lot of deep, cold analysis, but a richly human dialogue. The advisor's solution took account of two central and conflicting principles: respecting the self, and honoring the community. And it sought a way forward based on finding the nearest right under the circumstances. Perhaps school districts should permit homosexual dating at proms. Or perhaps they should clamp down firmly and explicitly on such behavior. That's not the point. At issue, here, are the feelings and attitudes of a student and an advisor, both of whom could have produced deep and lasting damage in their community and to their own careers and lives had they not been sensitive to the need for balance, compromise, and rationality.

One can of course argue—as the student might have—that the need here was not for compromise but for a blunt and militant confrontation designed to change attitudes toward homosexuality, and that only an assertive presentation of the facts of homosexuality could ever cause the community to face up to its alleged blindness and bigotry. But one can also argue—just as reasonably, from the community's viewpoint—that homosexuality is a self-destructive perversion of the natural childbearing processes whereby communities perpetuate themselves, and that communities need to protect themselves from impulses that, if made universal, would render humanity obsolete within a generation. In the end, the issue here did not need to turn on these arguments. It turned on the advisor's perception that the student really seemed willing to avoid confrontation if only her views could be credited. Seeing that—and correctly dismissing the head teacher's suggestion as a right-versus-wrong temptation—she was able to negotiate a solution. No one else could have done it just then: It was hers to do. It needed her ethical fitness—not sooner or later, but right at that moment.

Defining Ethics: Morals and Manners

Then what is ethics? The word derives from the Greek word *ethos,* meaning "custom," "usage," or "character." Standard definitions of *ethics* have typically included such phrases as "the science of the ideal human character" or "the science of moral duty." And *moral,* derived from the Latin *mos, moris* ("manner," "custom," "habit," "way of life," "conduct"), typically describes whatever is good or right or proper. What's *good*? Here a host of other words arise, like *virtue, value, worth, principle, integrity, rectitude, nobility, praiseworthiness,* or (if the context is theological) *righteousness.* The problem, of course, is that every attempt to pin down these words cycles back to phrases like "that which is intrinsically moral" and falls into a vortex of circular definition.

This process of definition is the stuff of academic discourse. And while it comprises a perfectly valid exercise, it is of little use to those seeking ethical fitness. Why? Two reasons. First, most people already have a working understanding of good. They may not be able to provide an airtight definition of the term, but "they know it when they see it." Nor should that phrase be held up to ridicule: Most of us spend most of our lives among concepts—like "a loving wife" or "a really great day"—that we can't precisely define but can certainly recognize. Even our environments raise similar definitional problems these days: Anyone who asserts that only what is firmly definable is practically useful has never tried to determine exactly where "the dining room" becomes "the living room" in a modern, open-plan home—or where dusk becomes dawn in an Alaskan summer.

The second reason to avoid overloading on definitional problems is simply that, at bottom, ethics is not about definitions. Nor is it about footnotes and philosophers, dry tomes and dusty arguments, and all the paraphernalia of logic and linguistics. It's about the inner impulses, judgments, and duties of people like you and me. To say that is not to console the yahoos or lobby for an ostrich-minded anti-intellectualism. Nor is it to dismiss philosophical theory as irrelevant—a point that will become obvious in later chapters, which draw on the traditions of moral philosophy. It is, instead, to acknowledge that for ethics to be practical and applicable it must be understood as the stuff of daily life. Daily life, after all, marches in a constant parade of judgments, many of them moral in nature and most of them shaped not only by our reasoning but by our intuitions. "All that a philosophic theory can do," writes Michael Hooker, an academic philosopher who now occupies the eminently practical role of president of the University of Massachusetts, "is capture human intuition. . . . Philosophers can't inform your intuitions. Your intuitions provide the raw data with which they work. It is for that reason that *you don't need to know philosophical ethics in order to engage in moral debate or in order to resolve moral dilemmas*" (italics added).

That said, however, two definitional points are worth observing:

- There is little to be gained by trying to distinguish rigidly between *morals* and *ethics*. Some think of the former as personal and the latter as institutional. Others see the first as restricted to sexual matters (as in the old euphemism "He was brought up on a morals charge") and the second as covering all other right-and-wrong matters. Still others define the latter as the scientific study of the former. In practice, many philosophers seem comfortable using the two terms more or less interchangeably.
- It *is* worth distinguishing, however, between *morals* and *manners*. Certain unpleasant behaviors—dressing shabbily, talking in loud and boisterous ways, picking one's nose in public—may offend the canons of good taste. But they are not necessarily immoral. Driven to the extreme, of course, they may become so—as in the case of loud talk that damages reputations or provokes violence. Such manners may also be associated with other behaviors classified as immoral—which is no doubt why teenagers in torn jeans and soiled bandannas are more likely than well-coiffed matrons to be stopped at the border by drug-busting customs agents. But ill-mannered people can be perfectly moral. The reverse is also true: The perpetrators of some of history's most egregious immoralities were among the most impeccably mannered members of the Third Reich and the imperial courts of Europe.

But it is not always easy to distinguish morals from manners—as evidenced in the experience of the president of a Midwestern grant-making foundation. Like many philanthropies, hers supported the arts in her community. Among its many grantees was an African-American professional theater company. When she was invited one evening to the opening of one of the company's new plays—written by, directed by, and acted by African Americans—she was happy to accept. And when she learned that the one part written for a non-African-American actor was that of a Japanese, she was especially interested—since she herself is a Japanese American.

When she saw the performance, however, she was appalled. The Japanese character struck her as an excessively negative racial stereotype. The audience, however, loved it: Whenever the Japanese appeared on the stage, they guffawed enthusiastically. To her, it was an exceedingly painful case of irresponsible writing, exacerbated in the production by the inability of the nonprofessional Japanese "actor" to elevate the role.

On the face of it, her dilemma involved her professional obligations. Should she tell the head of the theater company her concerns, or should she keep quiet? As a private citizen, she felt she had every right to speak up. But knowing how foundation personnel are treated in the non-profit community—with a kid-glove delicacy bordering at times on fawning obsequiousness—she was well aware that her comments would be given tremendous weight. To speak up on this matter, in fact, could radically change the internal dynamics of the theater group, with the very real possibility of damage to the reputation of the playwright, the director, and the entire company. And that would constitute, in her mind, an abuse of her power and influence.

Yet not to speak up—to let this serious flaw persist—would be to abet the spreading of a stereotype. It could reinforce elements of racial enmity that she felt were already stirring within the black community. What's more, she was in a peculiar position. It would take an ethnic Japanese, she felt, to be sensitive to the damage being done by this otherwise amusing performance. But given that this company played extensively to black audiences, few Japanese Americans would ever see the production. And very few of them would be in a position to lodge a significant protest. If she didn't speak up, who would?

The moral question she faced, then, was one common to us all: When, in the face of a perceived injustice, do we speak up to correct obvious wrongs, and when do we remain silent to protect ourselves and others from abuse? Behind this issue, however, another lurks. Many theatergoers apparently saw this as a case involving not morals but manners. Indeed, the Japanese character elicited laughter because, as in so many comedies, he seemed starkly at odds with society's expected manners and customs. But the laughter, she felt, was not simply a gentle amusement over an individual's foibles or misfortunes; it betrayed a subtle, harsh scorn for an entire race.

For the mostly black audience, her objections would be seen as far too heavy and overstated, given the lightness of the part. For her, the situation was morally offensive: She saw a serious question of values where others saw only a question of manners.

Defining Ethics: Obedience to the Unenforceable

Like most other terms in ethical discourse, this term *manners* lends itself to various definitions. One of the most interesting comes from an early twentieth century English jurist, John Fletcher Moulton, first baron of Bank and for many years a lord justice of appeal. What he called "manners" we would call "ethics." His phrase for it remains one of the more useful and astute definitions of ethics ever devised: "obedience to the unenforceable."

In his short piece titled "Law and Manners," published posthumously in *The Atlantic Monthly* in 1924, Lord Moulton distinguished "the three great domains of human action" as positive law, free choice, and manners. The domain of law, he observed, is characterized by "laws binding upon us which must be obeyed." He might have called it obedience to the *en*forceable, where punishment—or at least some reasonable fear of it—results from disobedience.

At the opposite end of the scale lies his third domain, that of free choice. It includes all actions where "we claim and enjoy complete freedom." It is the region where "spontaneity, originality, and energy are born," and where "the great movements which make the history of a country" begin. While it may be smaller than the domain of law, it is deeply significant, embracing (in many Western cultures, at least) such vital questions as whom you choose to marry and what religion you will follow.

Between them, says Moulton, lies a

> *large and important domain in which there rules neither positive law nor absolute freedom. In that domain there is no law which inexorably determines our course of action, and yet we feel that we are not free to choose*

as we would. . . . It grades from a consciousness of a duty nearly as strong as positive law, to a feeling that the matter is all but a question of personal choice. . . . [I]t is the domain of obedience to the unenforceable. That obedience is the obedience of a man to that which he cannot be forced to obey. He is the enforcer of the law upon himself.

Because this ethical middle ground lies "between the region of absolute choice and the region of positive law," it is constantly at risk of encroachment from both sides. On one hand, Moulton worries about pressures to "enlarge the sphere of positive law"—to make laws, as he says, "to regulate everything." On the other hand, "there is a growing tendency to treat matters that are not regulated by positive law as being matters of absolute choice."

For Moulton, however, the true test of worth lies in the scope of this ethical middle ground. "The real greatness of a nation, its true civilization," he writes,

is measured by the extent of this land of obedience to the unenforceable. It measures the extent to which the nation trusts its citizens, and its existence and area testify to the way they behave in response to that trust. Mere obedience to law does not measure the greatness of a nation. [Such obedience] can easily be obtained by a strong executive, and most easily of all from a timorous people. Nor is the license of behavior which so often accompanies the absence of law, and which is miscalled liberty, a proof of greatness. The true test is the extent to which the individuals composing the nation can be trusted to obey self-imposed law.

Moulton's article—which the editors of *The Atlantic Monthly* described as "the verbatim record, by an accurate reporter, of an impromptu speech" he made at the Authors' Club in London—was reprinted, they said, "because of its pertinent interest for present-day Americans." The editors were astute: America in 1924 had ample reason for concern about its ethics. The First World War had ended only six years earlier, yet already Benito Mussolini's fascists had taken power in Rome and Adolf Hitler had gone to prison after his attempted Beer Hall Putsch in Munich. None of this seemed to matter much to a newly isolationist United States. Well launched into the age of Prohibition and skyscrapers, jazz and flappers, the nation had just endured the infamous Teapot Dome oil scandal, in which for the first time in its history a sitting cabinet member (Secretary of the Interior Albert Fall) had been sentenced to prison. Radio and the movies were bringing new sources of urban influence into previously isolated towns and villages: The first radio station had opened in Pittsburgh in 1920, and Hollywood was already busy projecting the loose morality of its stars across the nation. America's great expatriate poet, T. S. Eliot, had already encapsulated the mingled boredom and horror of modern life in *The Wasteland,* and the nihilistic paintings of the Dadaists had already sought to expose the futility and meaninglessness of all that was once thought moral. Many connected the "revolution in morals" with Sigmund Freud's ideas, and saw them bearing fruit in a rapidly rising incidence of divorce. What's more, Henry Ford's invention of mass production—which would triple the number of cars by the end of the decade and add significantly to the mobility of the nation—guaranteed further challenges to the fixity of community values that had traditionally formed a bulwark against immorality. Not surprisingly, a vigorous new character education movement sprang up, seeking to tighten the ethical slippage by ensuring that, even if families and communities failed to teach ethics, the schools could provide a moral backstop.

It was, in other words, an age not unlike our own—a point noted by James Leming, who in studying the history of character education has observed that "with striking similarity to the 1920s, the 1980s and 1990s have been a time of feverish activity with regard to character education." Little wonder, then, that Lord Moulton's words speak to us today with freshness and relevance in at least three areas:

• **The relation of ethics and law.** Moulton's observations make it clear why the old adage "If it ain't illegal, it must be ethical" is so deeply flawed. Ethics and law, as Moulton knew, are as different as the unenforceable from the enforceable. To be sure, law is a kind of condensation of ethics into codification: It reflects areas of moral agreement so broad that the society comes together and says, "This ethical behavior shall be mandated." But Moulton's distinctions also make something else clear: When ethics collapses, the law rushes in to fill the void. Why? Because regulation is essential to sustain any kind of human experience involving two or more people. The choice is not, "Will society be regulated or unregulated?" The choice is only between unenforceable self-regulation and enforceable legal regulation.

An example helps here. As recently as the 1950s, you didn't throw litter from a car window simply because "people don't do those things"—because it was the "wrong" thing to do. Now you don't toss litter because there are substantial fines for so doing. What was once (in Moulton's terms) a second-domain issue of ethics has shifted to a first-domain issue of law. You need only count the number of new laws emerging each year from state and federal legislative bodies to realize how powerfully Moulton's worry about the encroachment of law into ethics is playing itself out. Given his distinctions, of course, one could almost have predicted this encroachment: Surely a powerful indicator of ethical decay is the glut of new laws—and new lawyers—spilling onto the market each year. If, as the survey data related in the previous chapter suggests, our ethical decay is severe, the age of hyperregulation cannot be far behind.

• **Ethics and free will.** If excessive regulation stifles, however, excessive license dissipates. Hence the need to distinguish, as Moulton does, between ethics and free will. Here the danger arises from a misplaced feeling that, if it ain't free will, it must be oppressive legalism—that the only alternative to what he calls the "spontaneity, originality, and energy" of free will is the dead weight of heavy-handed legislation. Fortunately, there's another alternative. The noble desire to flee from hyperregulation does not require that the pendulum bang back to the opposite extreme. The domain of obedience to the unenforceable provides a golden mean between the two—with enough obedience to mitigate the selfishness that can come with freedom, but enough unenforceability to permit real creativity.

It was the failure to recognize this ethical middle ground, in fact, that led to one of the most miserable of humanity's failed experiments: the seventy-year attempt to impose communism in the Soviet Union and, later, Eastern Europe. During a visit to what was then called Leningrad in 1989, I heard a Russian Orthodox churchman explaining why the Soviet Union had little tradition of volunteerism and charitable giving, with few organizations even remotely resembling the foundations and non-profit organizations of the United States. He explained that, in the eyes of the state, Soviet man was perfect. All attempts to provide anything beyond the state's beneficence, therefore, obviously implied a distrust in the state—and so were essentially treasonous.

The problem, of course, is that the state saw only two domains: law and free will. Committed to the command economy of the former, it dreaded the individualism of the latter. And well it should have: The individualism of writers like Aleksandr Solzhenitsyn and scientists like Andrei Sakharov presented grave dangers to the state's own sustainability. Believing that everything that was not law was free will, the state refused to approve any movement away from law, even toward a middle ground of "obedience to the unenforceable." Everything that mattered was simply enforced. How well it was enforced

The Golden Mean

"Whoever cultivates the golden mean," wrote the Latin poet Horace, "avoids both the poverty of a hovel and the envy of a palace." With the words "golden mean" (*aurea mediocritas*), Horace gives a popular name to a concept defined some three centuries earlier by the Athenian philosopher Aristotle in his *Nicomachean Ethics*.

For Aristotle, the essence of excellence is "virtue," which he describes as a balance between conflicting states. Moral virtue, to be excellent, "must have the quality of aiming at the intermediate" between an excess and a defect. He provides several examples:

- In matters concerning one's confidence, *courage* is the mean between *cowardice* (the defect) and *rashness* (the excess).
- In questions of honor, there is an intermediate quality of *proper pride* that lies between the defect of *undue humility* and the excess of *empty vanity*.
- In the "giving and taking of money," the defect of *meanness* (or stinginess) and the excess of *prodigality* (or wastefulness) are extremes of an intermediate he describes as *liberality*.

The intermediate, as he says, is always "a mean between two vices." But how does one find that mean? To ask that is to ask how to become virtuous. Since the highest good for Aristotle is human happiness, virtue lies in achieving the greatest happiness—not only for oneself but for the community. The way to happiness is through the golden mean. Such qualities as appetite, anger, pity, and pleasure "may be felt both too much and too little," he says; but "to feel them at the right times, with reference to the right objects, toward the right people, with the right motive, and in the right way, is what is both intermediate and best, and this is characteristic of virtue."

For Aristotle, then, the golden mean is based largely on his empirical understanding of what virtuous people would do in a given situation. This sense of the rightness of action and feeling, he says, is "determined by . . . that principle by which the man of practical wisdom would determine it." But it is also rooted in rationality. Since moral virtue is, he says, "a state of character concerned with choice, and choice is deliberate desire, therefore both the reasoning must be true and the desire right, if the choice is to be good." In that way, the golden mean is a more intellectual construct than the Golden Rule, with which it is often erroneously confused. Both, however, have long provided guidelines for ethical decision-making.

remains in question: Even in the depths of Soviet oppressiveness, religion continued as an underground activity, families reached out to help one another, and the age-old Russian habits of compassion and generosity persisted in whatever was left of private life. Yet Moulton would probably not have found it surprising that today's Western businessmen and scholars, attempting to set up relations with the former Soviet and East Bloc nations, regularly comment that they find a profound ethical vacuum, a piratical and licentious atmosphere of "anything goes."

• **Ethics as a measure of national strength.** The Communist experiment also bears out Moulton's insistence that a nation's strength lies in the size of this ethical middle domain. Having hardly any such domain, the Soviets ultimately failed. History, of course, is littered with similar relics: The stories of numerous Old Testament kingdoms and of imperial Rome bear witness to the fact that without ethics societies simply perish. Seeking to explain why, many turn to theology, observing that broken law (in this case, divine law operating in the moral realm of human experience) brings penalties. Others explain the fact through economics. A society lacking ethics, after all, has two choices. It can follow the example of Italy in the 1980s, where parasitic bribery and corruption threatened to suck the lifeblood from the economy while justice stood helplessly aside. Or, following the Soviet example, it can run to excess in its laws, inventing regulations everywhere and setting up vastly complicated and massively expensive enforcement mechanisms to police every conceivable interaction. The sheer effort of hiring officers to stand behind every bush—or of creating the byzantine network of informers through which the Kremlin kept track of its own citizenry—clearly drains so much labor and capital from productive enterprises that little is left with which to sustain a nation.

What really dooms states, however, is lack of trust. Lawyers are well aware that any contract, however well crafted, can be broken unless some smattering of ethics and goodwill remains on each side. So too with treaties: Witness the dozens of broken cease-fire agreements that litter the terrain of the former Yugoslavia because of battles over Bosnia-Herzegovina. In a society lacking ethics, trust drains away faster than rainfall in the desert. And without trust, there is no basis for agreements of any sort, from the smallest promise to wake up your houseguests in time for their plane tomorrow morning to the largest multinational handshake launching a billion-dollar merger. Without trust, in other words, there is no way for any sort of human relations to be sustained.

Joseph Conrad, in *Heart of Darkness*, gets at this point in his references to the concept of *restraint*. His masterful and multifaceted short novel, published in London twenty-two years before Moulton's death in 1921, describes the impact of Africa upon colonial Europeans who ventured into its vast interior. It focuses on the story of the elusive Kurtz. Setting himself up as a kind of cannibal king, Kurtz abandoned his European manners and morals and took up the ways of the jungle to excess. "He was hollow at the core," says Conrad's narrator, Marlow, noting that he "lacked restraint in the gratification of his various lusts." Again and again, images of and references to lack of restraint echo through the novel, until it becomes obvious that, for Conrad, the moral core of humanity involves a complex system of inner restraints—Moulton's obedience to the unenforceable—without which there is nothing but a heart of darkness within.

Far more than the story of a journey or a man, Conrad's novel is a parable of a modern society abandoning its restraints—its ethical middle ground—and plunging into the kind of rapacious mercantile colonialism that characterized so much of nineteenth-century Europe. Not surprisingly, then, it speaks powerfully to our own age, in which excesses of greed, coupled with racial intolerance and worldwide economic adventurism, combine with lack of restraint to produce a particularly ominous ethical cocktail. Conrad makes negatively the point Moulton makes positively: that national greatness is measured by inner restraint, moderation of desires, and modesty in approach.

Defining Ethics: Deliberate Lawbreaking

Before leaving Moulton's distinctions, we need to raise one more issue: the ethics of civil disobedience. Law and ethics are not the same. Yet it should go without saying that obedience to law, while it is usually a *necessary* condition for ethical action, is not sufficient to guarantee it. Individuals who merely obey the letter of the law may or may not be ethical. That point is nicely made whenever the Ethics Committee of the United States Senate determines that because one of its members has broken no regulation, he or she is to be considered ethical. The widespread cynicism over some of the committee's determinations suggests that there is little public faith in that misnamed body, which appears to have no interest in "ethics" as Moulton would define it, but only in laws or regulations that may have been violated.

Obeying the law, then, is not enough to earn the "ethical" label. But must law always be obeyed for ethics to be in force? No. The standard of civil disobedience—propounded by Henry David Thoreau in 1849, developed by Mohandas K. Gandhi in India in the 1920s, and used so effectively in the Civil Rights Movement in the United States in the 1960s—urges that unjust laws be disobeyed. So firmly has that concept become established that it has now become a law of its own: The failure to disobey orders that called for Jews to be killed in Nazi Germany led to the acceptance, at the Nuremberg trials, of the principle that one has a moral and legal obligation to refuse to obey immoral laws.

Yet the concept of civil disobedience, as practiced by such nonviolent practitioners as Martin Luther King, carries with it a further stipulation: that those who for moral reasons disobey the law must do so consciously and with full willingness to suffer whatever penalties their disobedience brings. Civil disobedience, then, has a moral imperative. But it is not restricted to major social movements—a point demonstrated in the case of Kurt Werner Schaechter, a retired French musical instruments salesman interested in tracing his Jewish ancestry. Researching his family's past in the national archives at Toulouse in 1991 (archives that remain closed to the public), he found his mother's deportation papers, indicating that she had been shipped to Auschwitz in 1944 with the full complicity of the French collaborators. Knowing that there were many similar cases of French Jews sent to extermination by the Vichy government—and knowing that such revelations would be particularly unwelcome for a society that still prides itself on the history of its resistance movements during the Occupation—he illegally smuggled more than twelve thousand documents out of the National Archives, photocopied them, and smuggled them back in again. He later released copies to the press. His point, of course, was not simply to break a 1979 statute limiting access to these documents. His goal was to expose past crimes. Nor did he try to hide his actions or flee from punishment. The French government, perhaps embarrassed by his revelations and hoping to keep his story in low profile, took no legal action against him.

The ethical imperative to break unethical laws, then, is not restricted to issues of great moment. Nor need it involve highly public efforts. Even the most isolated ethical situations can involve elements of deliberate lawbreaking. That point was made in a dilemma shared with us by a seminar participant who told about her son's canoe rescue in the woods of Maine.

The story began with three friends in their early twenties going fishing one cold spring day on a small and nearly deserted lake. The woman's son, John, was a good fisherman and an able outdoorsman. And while he didn't know this particular lake, his two friends had fished there before. So he had no doubt that they knew what they were doing.

As the three of them set off in the canoe, however, the wind came up with unexpected strength. They paddled to the far shore, where they let John off to fish from some rocky cliffs. The two others set out to cross the lake. Busy fishing, John paid little attention to their whereabouts until, sometime later, he realized that his friends were nowhere in sight. Climbing the cliffs for a better look, he saw something that made his heart sink: the shirt of one of his friends, floating by itself in the middle of the lake. There was no trace of the canoe or its occupants.

Abandoning his fishing gear, John set off on a run around the lake, back to a spot where he remembered having seen a settlement. On the shore was a canoe, apparently belonging to one of the cabins. Without stopping to ask permission, John dragged it to the water and was about to set off when its owner charged out of a nearby cottage, demanding to know what he was doing. Explaining breathlessly, John asked the man to come with him and help save his friends. To his amazement, the man refused. He said he felt it was too dangerous to venture out into a situation where the two of them might be drowned trying to save the other two.

So John, with his permission, set out alone in the canoe—paddling with difficulty, the bow swinging like a weathervane in the absence of a second paddler. Before long, he spotted his friends on the shore opposite the cliffs. On reaching them, he learned that their canoe had indeed swamped in the middle of the lake. Unable to right it and empty the water, they had swum for shore, hoping to get there before the chill water numbed them entirely. One of them, large-boned and husky, had apparently come through in good shape. The other, slightly built and wiry, was suffering from hypothermia and nearly delirious when John arrived. The two boys managed to get him into the canoe, back to the car, and over to a local hospital, where he recovered as a result of their quick action.

One postscript: On their way back across the lake in the borrowed canoe, the three friends met its owner coming toward them—in a rowboat. He told them that his wife, on hearing that he refused to go to their rescue, had so shamed and berated him for his cowardice that he got out the rowboat and came to help.

There's a lot behind the owner's dilemma—his grounds for refusal, his wife's evident objection to those grounds, and his failure to offer the much more stable rowboat in the first place. For now, however, think about John's use of the canoe. He apparently felt that, given the emergency, he had a "right" to take the canoe without asking. Was he stealing? He probably saw it as borrowing. Given what the whitecaps had done to his friends and might do to him, however, the canoe might never be returned—and the end result would be the same as theft. Was he right to take the law into his own hands—to be, in that sense, civilly disobedient? Most of us would probably say,

"Yes." The immediacy of the need, the severity of the threat, and the probability that he could make a real difference in the outcome all argued for expediency—despite the fact that wisdom ("It's much too dangerous out there") and legality ("That's not your canoe") argued against it.

Fitness? John had it, not only physically but ethically. What's more, he acted upon his convictions in the face of danger. We call that moral courage—although, had he drowned, we would be tempted to call it foolhardiness. Unlike the state trooper and the prom advisor, he saw no third way forward—although the rowboat might have provided one. Even so, he read the situation accurately and, with no time for analysis, responded immediately.

It may not be too much to say that his wiry friend is alive today because of John's ethical fitness.

This sort of fitness is no luxury item. From the smallest personal experiences to the broadest international relationships, it's part of our survival kit for the future. At the very least, it diminishes suffering and averts lawsuits. At its best, it saves lives. It frequently has no time for analysis—although it reflects the thoughtful preparation that has gone into creating it.

That's what this book is about. Not an emergency manual for extremities, it is instead intended as a vehicle for reflective dialogue. It is meant to be absorbed quietly without the pressure of a looming ethical dilemma—so that, when the moment for action arrives, the thinking has already been done, the impulses internalized, and the intuitions prepared to lead to resolutions that make the world a better place.

Chapter Four

Core Values

In his short poem "Traveling Through the Dark," the twentieth-century American poet William Stafford finds in a commonplace situation the elements of a powerful moral dilemma:

> Traveling through the dark I found a deer
> dead on the edge of the Wilson River road.
> It is usually best to roll them into the canyon:
> that road is narrow; to swerve might make more dead.
>
> By glow of the tail-light I stumbled back of the car
> and stood by the heap, a doe, a recent killing;
> she had stiffened already, almost cold.
> I dragged her off; she was large in the belly.
>
> My fingers touching her side brought me the reason—
> her side was warm; her fawn lay there waiting,
> alive, still, never to be born.
> Beside that mountain road I hesitated.
>
> The car aimed ahead its lowered parking lights;
> under the hood purred the steady engine.

I stood in the glare of the warm exhaust turning red;
around our group I could hear the wilderness listen.

I thought hard for us all—my only swerving—
then pushed her over the edge into the river.

"Traveling through the dark," Stafford's narrator had no way to foresee the moral dilemma he was to encounter. When he came upon it, what was he to do? Was he capable of saving the living fawn in the mother's belly, there in the darkness of that wilderness road? Or would it die whatever steps he took, since the mother was already dead? The poem sets up a central question: Did the narrator do the right thing? At least he faced up to it—and "thought hard for us all" in the process. But was that the best he could do? Stafford leaves that for us to decide.

Stafford's anecdote raises another question, less obvious but just as compelling: Why did he stop? There is no law that says, "You must stop on narrow roads and remove potential hazards from the path of other motorists." In fact, there are plenty of reasons not to do so. Stopping at night on narrow roads, we're told, is dangerous. You might get hit by another car, or set upon by animals attracted to the carcass. At the very least, you might get dirty. Besides, there's nothing you can do anyway. This is a job for the authorities. And you've got somewhere else to get to.

But most of us would also see a moral imperative here—to save other motorists, to try to help injured animals, to take responsibility for your surroundings even though you have no obligation to do so. That imperative, apparently, is what drove Stafford's narrator. Given his own life-protecting principles, he had to stop. It's not that he sought out this dilemma. He may well have wished it had never happened—which, had he been driving some other road that night, it might not have. But he wasn't, and it did. So he stopped—not because he was compelled to do so by external forces, but out of obedience to an unenforceable, internal, and apparently powerful set of principles. He stopped because of his values.

Lord Moulton's definition of ethics as "obedience to the unenforceable" helps us understand such obligations. But it leaves open the fundamental question that remains at the heart of any ethical consideration: What is one's duty to the unenforceable? What *is* the unenforceable? What, in the end, is right?

Efforts to answer that question in practical terms often result in statements about qualities or characteristics that ought to govern one's life. They frequently take shape in codes of ethics or statements of principles—brief listings of the core moral values by which one should live. Notice that key phrase: *core moral values*. What, exactly, does it mean?

A *value*, says the *Oxford English Dictionary*, is "that which is worthy of esteem for its own sake; that which has intrinsic worth." It is not something valuable only as a means to reach some other worthy thing: It is an end in itself. Diligence and truthfulness, for instance, are very fine traits. Diligence, however, is not usually seen as "worthy of esteem for its own sake," but as an important characteristic of those who wish to accomplish things. What they choose to accomplish may be wonderful or terrible: Just as diligent firemen contribute to society's well-being, so diligent con men detract from it. Diligence is a kind of *operational* or *instrumental* value, worthwhile because of its effects rather than in and of itself. So the question "Why be diligent?" can properly be answered, "Because it leads to other worthy goals or values." It's less common to answer the question "Why be truthful?" that way: Truthfulness is much more easily seen as something that has "intrinsic worth." That, after all, is what the tired but accurate phrase "Virtue is its own reward" seeks to communicate.

The kind of "core values" that many codes of ethics embody, then, are the ones that are intrinsically worthwhile. And they are *moral* values—a point worth exploring. Society, after all, has all sorts of values that do not lie in the moral realm:

- **Political values.** There are profound differences, going straight to the level of "intrinsic worth," that separate conservatives from liberals. For some, the phrase "deregulation" is so hallowed that to ask "Why deregulate?" is to pose a silly and even offensive question. Deregulation, they say, is worthy in itself. Others, just as fervently, assert the same about regulated markets. These views can be in vehement opposition. Yet neither is in and of itself "moral": Both conservatives and liberals can be highly moral individuals.

- **Economic values.** There is a world of difference between those who say, "Always buy the best, even though it costs a little more," and those who say, "Always shop at yard sales and try to find the bargains." The malls of America, in fact, recognize the polar distance between Wal-Mart shoppers and the Neiman-Marcus crowd. These opposed values, however, are not moral but economic: Neither side is immoral, unless their values get pushed to an excess of opulent indulgence on one hand or miserly bargain-driving on the other.

• **Culinary values.** All of us have tastes that are neither immoral nor moral, but simply expressions of individual leanings and desires. There is nothing inherently unethical about a Tex-Mex taco that is remedied by choosing Chinese egg rolls. That's not to say there are no moral issues raised by food: Vegetarianism typically elevates eating to a matter of conscience, selecting carefully on the basis of values that go far beyond taste. In matters of taste, however, the values are not usually moral: When, at age five, I heard my mother assert (in words that have somehow stuck with me ever since) that "lettuce, by and large, improves the taste of any sandwich," I found myself in the presence of strongly held values, though she was not laying down a moral decree.

Moral Values, Lettuce Values, and Codes of Ethics

The world, in fact, is full of lettuce values. Useful as they are, they make no attempt to answer the question "What is right?" That task typically falls to a code of ethics. A brief look at a half-dozen such codes reveals their similarities and points toward their usefulness:

• **The Ten Commandments.** This great statement of God's law, recorded in the Bible (Exodus 20:1–17) and described as handed down from God to Moses on tablets of stone, stands as the central list of precepts for Judaism and Christianity. It falls naturally into two parts. The first four Commandments define God's relation to man. They prohibit the worship of more than one god, the creation of graven images, the taking of God's name in vain, and the breaking of the Sabbath. These four—especially the second and fourth—are explained in some detail. The final six, by contrast, are direct, simple imperatives: Honor your parents, don't kill, don't commit adultery, don't steal, don't give false evidence or lie, don't envy or covet. All ten are predominantly phrased in the negative, establishing prohibitions against behavior instead of asserting what must be done.

• **The Boy Scout Law.** In contrast to the Ten Commandments, this statement is positive in its syntax. In fact, it is not even a set of commands. It does not say what Scouts should *do*, but defines what they *are*.

A Scout is:
Trustworthy
Loyal
Helpful
Friendly
Courteous
Kind
Obedient
Cheerful
Thrifty
Brave
Clean
Reverent

Some of these values are perhaps less moral than instrumental—"friendly" people, after all, can be decidedly immoral, while some highly moral individuals (some of Europe's Calvinists, for instance, or America's colonial Puritans) have habitually been more somber than "cheerful." But many of these terms, like kindness and trustworthiness, direct us toward such great moral values as love and truth. There are, it should be added, some anomalies bordering on the comical when this Law is contrasted to the Girl Scout Law:

A Scout is:
Trustworthy
Loyal
Useful
Friendly
Courteous
Kind to Animals

Obedient
Cheerful
Thrifty
Clean in Thought, Word, and Deed

Boys, it is found, must be kind—while girls need only be "kind to animals." And while boys are "helpful," girls are simply "useful." Like a time bomb on the doorstep of feminism, this issue has already prompted a revision now in the works.

• **The West Point Honor Code.** Among the most concise of ethical codes, the U.S. Army's statement takes just thirteen words to define the Academy's standard: "A cadet does not lie, cheat, or steal, or tolerate those who do." Picking up on prohibitions from the Ten Commandments, it passes them through two screens: Not only does this code regulate one's own action, but it requires attention to the actions of others. Just what "tolerate" means, of course, has provided food for thought for generations of West Pointers. Is it enough to turn up one's nose and walk away from cheaters and liars, or must one vigilantly spy out and report every infraction?

• **The Rotary Four-Way Test.** The linchpin of Rotary International's ethical practice, this code takes form in still another syntax: a series of questions. "Of the things we think, say, or do," this test asks,

1. Is it the TRUTH?
2. Is it FAIR to all concerned?
3. Will it build GOODWILL and BETTER FRIENDSHIPS?
4. Will it be BENEFICIAL to all concerned?

The moral values embraced here—truthfulness, fairness, friendship, and helpfulness to others—are posed as a test not only of speech and action but also of thought. That's a tough test. It recalls Jesus' injunction that simply obeying the letter of the Commandment against adultery was not good enough, but that "every man who looks at a woman lustfully has already committed adultery with her—in his heart." In like manner, the Rotary test reaches back past behavior to motive.

• **McDonnell-Douglas Code of Ethics.** Typical of many corporate codes, this one comes to life in nine bullet points requiring employees to be:

- Honest and trustworthy in all our relationships;
- Reliable in carrying out assignments and responsibilities;
- Truthful and accurate in what we say and write;
- Cooperative and constructive in all work undertaken;
- Fair and considerate in our treatment of fellow employees, customers, and all other persons;
- Law abiding in all our activities;
- Committed to accomplishing all tasks in a superior way;
- Economical in utilizing company resources;
- Dedicated in service to our company and to improvement of the quality of life in the world in which we live.

That it bears strong resemblance to the Boy Scout Law is no accident. While he was CEO of the firm, Sanford McDonnell took up scouting with his son—and then realized that his company lacked a code of ethics. So in 1983 he assembled a task force of executives to draw one up. "I told them I wanted them to devise a code of ethics for McDonnell-Douglas," he recalls, "that wouldn't look like the Scout Oath and Law but nevertheless would cover all the points." The only item missing: reverence. "I didn't feel that we could use our influence," he explains, "to leverage our employees into adopting our religious faith."

• **The Minnesota Principles.** Proposed by the Minnesota Center for Corporate Responsibility in 1992 as a guide to international business activities, this statement includes a preamble and a six-part statement of "Stakeholder Principles" that cover relations with customers, employees, owners/investors, suppliers, communities, and competitors. But the heart of it, under the heading of "General Principles," sets forth four core moral values:

Proposition #1: Business activities must be characterized by fairness.

We understand fairness to include equitable treatment and equality of opportunity for all participants in the marketplace.

Proposition #2: Business activities must be characterized by honesty.

We understand honesty to include candor, truthfulness and promise-keeping.

Proposition #3: Business activities must be characterized by respect for human dignity.

We understand this to mean that business activities should show a special concern for the less powerful and the disadvantaged.

Proposition #4: Business activities must be characterized by respect for the environment.

We understand this to mean that business activities should promote sustainable development and prevent environmental degradation and waste of resources.

Corporate Ethics Codes: A Growing Trend

Do corporate executives think ethics matters?

Yes, indeed, according to surveys by the Conference Board, a New York–based association of major corporations. One measure: the prevalence of corporate ethics codes. Once regarded simply as a means to "deflect cyclical outbursts of public distrust of business institutions," writes Conference Board researcher Ronald E. Berenbeim, corporate ethics initiatives "now enjoy a broad base of support within individual companies."

The Conference Board's 1992 survey of 1,900 corporations (with 264 companies responding) in the United States, Canada, Mexico, and Europe, titled "Corporate Ethics Practices," finds that:

- **Codes are most common in the United States.** Some 84 percent of U.S. respondents have corporate ethics codes, while only 58 percent of non-U.S. firms have them. A parallel study by the Institute of Business Ethics in London found that 71 percent of its sample of United Kingdom companies had codes of ethics in 1991—up from 55 percent in 1987.

• **Chief executive officers are commenting "openly and often" on business ethics.** Among respondents in the United States, 31 percent of CEOs spoke out on ethics in the prior year; in Europe, traditionally more reticent on the subject, the figure was a surprisingly high 40 percent.

• **Ethics is increasingly popular in corporations.** Nearly half (45 percent) of the respondents' codes of ethics had been enacted since an earlier Conference Board survey in 1987. Financial firms, however, are still much less likely (57 percent) to have codes than companies in other industries (82 percent).

• **America and Europe have different views on codes.** In the United States, where codes tend to be seen as legal documents, the corporate legal counsel is often central to the drafting process. In Europe, where the code is more often viewed as a social compact between the company and its workers, boards of directors play a central role—and are far more apt to bring employee representatives into the drafting process.

• **Ethics training is on the rise.** Some 25 percent of the respondents have set up new ethics training programs, ethics committees, or ombudsman's offices in the last three years.

Why this flurry of interest? The Conference Board cites four concerns:

• **Global management issues.** Companies operating internationally "want to determine their company's 'core' values while simultaneously showing respect for local customs and practices."

• **Total quality management.** TQM, which typically requires of workers "a core of shared commitments and values to develop and to achieve a high standard of production," depends on ethics for its success.

• **Workforce diversity.** Corporations are concerned about minority representation. In addition, they find that in an era of downsizing, "new and less experienced workers and managers are now responsible for decisions"—and need an ethical handle on decision-making.

• **Inadequate education and training.** In addition to deficiencies in science, math, and literacy, graduates of public secondary education lack ethical literacy.

Those four ideas—fairness, honesty, respect for human dignity, and respect for the environment—square well with the central moral ideas found on numerous corporate codes of ethics developed in recent years.

What, then, characterizes a code of ethics? First and most notable, it is brief. Unlike rule books, law codes, or policy manuals that explore the finer points of operational values, codes of ethics usually bring into focus a core of moral values that is concise and easily memorized. The longest one cited here—the Boy Scout Law—has only twelve elements. It is also, I suspect, one of the most widely memorized codes in the world: In nearly every executive ethics seminar I've conducted, at least one of the participants has been able to reel it off by rote.

Second, a code is not usually explanatory. Occasionally it becomes wordy, as with the efforts of McDonnell-Douglas and the Minnesota Center to surround their key terms with synonymous and related words. But the very brevity of a code requires condensation. The prize in this category, of course, goes to the Ten Commandments: Two of the world's best-known commands, against killing and stealing, take but four words each. That doesn't mean these concepts are easy to define: far from it. They do, however, raise a standard that, once definitions are clear, leaves little room for waffling.

Third, a code can be expressed in a number of forms. It can be positive or negative, a definition or an exhortation, a set of single words or a series of elaborated sentences.

Fourth, it centers on moral values. While it may occasionally include values that seem more instrumental than ultimate, it typically leaves aside the lettuce values drawn from realms of taste, politics, economics, and other hotly debated but morally neutral realms of human experience.

And what good is a code? One answer became clear in the now-famous Tylenol tampering case. In 1982, executives at Johnson & Johnson received a chilling report: Several poisonings had been reported in the Chicago area, linked to Tylenol capsules laced with cyanide. Within the first twenty-four hours, two things were clear: There was a need for prompt action to prevent further poisonings, and there was no obvious way to determine whether the capsules had been adulterated by a disgruntled employee, contaminated by a flaw in the manufacturing process, or subjected to tampering after the product had been shipped. Also clear was the context: Tylenol produced $100 million annually for Johnson & Johnson, a company that, under the leadership of chairman James Burke, had recently revitalized its long-standing Credo, or code of ethics, through a series of meetings with executives.

J & J's action was swift, extensive, and highly visible. In a sweeping recall, it removed all forms of Tylenol—not just the capsules—from every shelf in every store. Then, through a well-orchestrated campaign to inform the public of its concern for safety and through various incentives to attract customers, it reintroduced the now-tamper-proof product. Within eighteen months, it had regained its market share.

What role did the company's Credo play? A large one, according to Harvard Business School professor Laura L. Nash, who cites this case as one involving a leadership style that ultimately puts ethics ahead of marketing. "Having personally interviewed the three top officers involved," she writes, "I am certain that no textbook marketing analysis could quantify or even identify the factors that informed their strategy. *From an economic and public relations standpoint, one could have made a very reasonable argument for keeping the product on the shelves:* The contamination was not the company's fault, and did not appear to have originated from a J & J facility; this was an isolated incident, the result of aberrant behavior; the benefits of the product to the majority of the public vastly outweighed the injuries that might occur if the product remained on the shelves."

Nash further notes that, within those first twenty-four hours, more than two hundred decisions had to be made. What held those decisions on an ethical track, apparently, was the firm's Credo. This page-long statement has four parts—arranged in what J & J employees understand to be priority order—covering the company's responsibility to customers, to employees, to communities, and finally to stockholders. It begins, "We believe our first responsibility is to the doctors, nurses and patients, to mothers and fathers and all others who use our products and services." Unlike some corporate codes that hang numbly on walls or circulate to impress the public, this one had been kept alive—so much so that, when the time came for rapid-fire decision-making up and down the corporate ladder, there was little need to ask "What's the company line?" or "Should we stonewall this one?" The Credo, and the commitment of the chairman to its implementation, was understood to be the standard: While stockholders' profit mattered, public safety mattered more. "As one manager later told me," Professor Nash writes, " 'Tylenol was the tangible proof of what top management had said at the Credo challenge meetings. You came away saying, "My God! You're right. We really do believe this. It's for real. *And we did what was right.*" ' "

We did what was right. There are few statements in life that resonate with greater long-term satisfaction. There are few things more worthwhile than being able to look yourself in the mirror each morning and say, "Yes, I've done the right thing." To the extent that right-doing emanates from careful attention to a code of ethics—crafted not in the heat of the moment but well ahead of time in the coolly reflective recesses of an organization's collective thinking—such codes are clearly worthwhile. They can help companies and individuals prosper—even while, as in the Tylenol case, they can probably save lives. Put simply, they matter.

Brainstorming for Universals: The Core Values

But do the codes of ethics mentioned here, however much they may help individual corporations, have much in common? Aren't the codes of Johnson & Johnson and McDonnell-Douglas quite distinct—and both rather different from the Minnesota Principles? Does each organization simply arrive at its own code as it wishes, with little regard to any common, overarching principles? Are there, in fact, any such principles? Is there any set of moral values so widely shared by humanity that it might constitute a universal code?

These questions sweep in their wake a long train of answers—from the roaring *No* of nihilists and skeptics to the pulpit-pounding *Yes* of fundamentalists and evangelicals. Between, however, lies a quieter realm of rational discourse that points strongly toward such universality.

One such universal principle appears to be the injunction against killing. "There is no group that thinks it right to kill an adult, healthy member of the society who has committed no crime and whose death is not required by the welfare of the group," writes philosopher Richard B. Brandt. His assertion is part of his summary of the findings of anthropologist Edward Westermarck, whose classic 1906 study, *The Origin and Development of the Moral Idea,* surveyed ethical standards in a variety of social groupings. Westermarck, despite his strong preference for what he elsewhere called "ethical subjectivism," also found, says Professor Brandt, that

> *"there is no group in which marriage or sexual intercourse is approved between members of the immediate family, with the possible exception of some royal families and with the further exception of some important ritual occasions. There is no society in which kindliness, sympathy, hospitality, or regard for others and their rights is disapproved."*

Coming from an anthropologist, that might sound surprising. The long tradition of that field, after all, has often held that various and diverse habits, ideals, and lifestyles have equal moral validity, and that whatever any one society chooses to do is "right" simply by virtue of their doing it. But by 1959 Brandt was able—and apparently pleased—to report that "anthropologists have come to find much more common ground in the value systems of different groups than they formerly did." He notes anthropologist Clyde Kluckhohn's observation on the topic:

> *Every culture has a concept of murder, distinguishing this from execution, killing in war, and other "justifiable homicides." The notions of incest and other regulations upon sexual behavior, of prohibitions upon untruth under defined circumstances, of restitution and reciprocity, of mutual obli-*

gations between parents and children—these and many other moral concepts are altogether universal.

Since World War II, in fact, one corner of the debate on the universality of moral concepts has grounded itself firmly in political theory and practice. The Universal Declaration of Human Rights, promulgated in 1948 by the United Nations and since upheld and extended in the 1975 Helsinki Final Act of the Conference on Security and Co-operation in Europe, used the consensus-building and universalizing structure of these multinational bodies to agree on a set of core principles that numerous nations could affirm. The 1948 document, in particular, "assumed the existence, in some sense, of common moral standards for judging nations and governments," says philosopher Alan Gewirth of the University of Chicago. Indeed, such assumptions have crept into public policy debates that reach well beyond that document. "A common morality," continues Professor Gewirth, "is also invoked not only in contemporary appeals for human rights but also in the agonized concern over such ongoing problems as homelessness, poverty, drug addiction, AIDS, and other human afflictions."

But is there any universalizable code, any set of moral values or rules that could stand as a guide in contemporary life? Addressing that question frontally, philosopher Bernard Gert gives an unequivocal "Yes." "The ten rules listed below," he writes in *The Moral Rules: A New Rational Foundation for Morality*, "are the basic or fundamental rules of morality":

The First Five

1. Don't kill.
2. Don't cause pain.
3. Don't disable.
4. Don't deprive of freedom or opportunity.
5. Don't deprive of pleasure.

The Second Five

6. Don't deceive.
7. Keep your promise.
8. Don't cheat.
9. Obey the law.
10. Do your duty.

Coming to the question from a different perspective, German theologian Hans Küng examines the commonalities of the world's religions. There, he finds that "five basic commands to human beings[,] which also have countless applications in the business world and in politics, hold in *all* the great world religions:

1. Do not kill;
2. Do not lie;
3. Do not steal;
4. Do not practice immorality;
5. Respect parents and love children."

There is, then, a well-argued theoretical basis for a universal code. But is there any evidence that people from various cultures actually share a common core of principles? Setting out as a journalist to explore that question, I recently completed interviews with twenty four individuals from sixteen countries, chosen because they represented clearly ethical thinking in the eyes of their peers. Some, like Nobel Laureate and former president of Costa Rica Oscar Arias, are well-known international figures. Others, like Dame Whina Cooper, a Maori activist born late in the last century on the dirt floor of a rural cookhouse in New Zealand, are well known only within their own country. Still others, like Buddhist monk Shojun Bando, are known within smaller circles. To each of the interviewees, I put the same question: If you could formulate a global code of ethics for the twenty first century, what would be on it? Their responses are reported at length in my book *Shared Values for a Troubled World: Conversations with Men and Women of Conscience.* The common ground that emerged is represented by the following list of core values derived from those interviews:

- Love
- Truth
- Fairness
- Freedom
- Unity

- Tolerance
- Responsibility
- Respect for life

As a piece of journalism, this list makes no claim to socially scientific validity—something that must await more rigorous reporting based on survey data from numerous countries. It does, however, garner support from each executive ethics seminar I conduct. In these seminars, participants are typically asked to develop, from the thin air of a brainstorming session and the background of a few readings, a list of shared values for their group. If the participants are all from a corporation that has yet to develop its own code of ethics, we set out to create one. Otherwise we adopt a convenient fiction, pretending (for example) to be a local school board that wants to carve a list of moral values above the door of the local high school as a statement of common belief. However we do it, the results are astonishingly similar: Group after group, without prior knowledge of earlier groups' findings or of the eight values from my global interviews, arrives at a nearly identical list. Some want to include words like "creativity"—which, I try to suggest, seems out of place on a list of *moral* values since, were it there, every honest and upright but ploddingly unoriginal individual would have to be defined as *immoral.* Others agonize over the finer distinctions among such words as *honesty, integrity,* and *trustworthiness.* But I have yet to find a group that did not include on its list some word for love, for truth, for tolerance, for responsibility, and for fairness.

Is there, then, a fundamental core of shared values? Those who say no face a monumental burden of proof: how to explain, in the face of congruences like the ones examined here, a "mere coincidence" so intercultural, repeatable, and persistent as to be nearly miraculous.

Ethical Relativism and the Mother's Uncle Syndrome

Over lunch on a tree-canopied patio in Palo Alto in 1989, Stanford University professor Ronald A. Howard explained to me how he addressed his students' occasional skepticism about this "mere coincidence" of universality. They would regularly come at him, guns drawn, over the question of moral relativism—insisting that all ethics is relative, situational, subjective, negotiable, and up for grabs by whoever wants to lay down the definitions. That, after all, is not an uncommon thesis—although, as Professor Howard's fellow Stanford faculty member John W. Gardner notes, it is "hard to live by." Even those who theoretically claim that there is no objective truth, says Professor Gardner, "conduct their lives as though they do believe in something. A scholar of my acquaintance who stoutly asserts that there is no basis for moral values was overcome with moral outrage when a colleague stole one of his ideas and published it without giving him credit."

So when Howard's students took up this line, he would engage them in a little thought experiment. Imagine, he told them, that I'm going to parachute you into a country somewhere in the world, and you haven't any idea where it is. As soon as you get out of your parachute, I want you to walk up to the first person you see, take away whatever he or she is holding, and run away with it. Then see what happens.

With the possible exception, he explains, that you have landed in front of a Buddhist monk and taken away his begging bowl—and that his only response is to sigh, "Ah! That's karma!"—you will have run squarely into the universal concept of property rights, codified in the Western world through the commandment "Don't steal." You didn't bring that precept with you. You didn't impose it on the culture from the perspective of your Judeo-Christian, free-enterprise, democratically individualistic heritage. You found it. And you will find it in any culture in which you land. On this issue and on the question of killing—two fundamental principles that address what Howard calls "crimes of violence against people and property"—he finds "an amazing universality of agreement in nearly every culture."

Since our conversation, I've used Professor Howard's example in various public talks—after one of which an anthropolgist leaped to his feet and, with obvious excitement, asserted that he knew a culture "where it was okay to steal." Further questioning elicited an admission that his statement was a bit too broad: It was only acceptable, in certain situations, to steal from your mother's uncle. Still, he insisted, there you are: How can you talk of universal moral values when there are obvious exceptions? Isn't it only right, then, to abandon the concept of moral universals and return to ethical relativism?

There's an answer to his question, it seems to me, in the realm of physics. In hundreds of ways, physics is a science of universals. Yet again and again we hear it said that, since Einstein proved all things to be relative, there is no more reason to think there are universal *moral* fundamentals than there is for thinking there are universal *physical* absolutes. But that logic comes apart not only under the force of historical understanding—since Einstein's theory of relativity clearly was not meant to extend into social, political, and philosophical realms—but also in the face of physical reality. Physics, in fact, is replete with "absolutes": The speed of light, the acceleration due to gravity, the fine structure constant, Avogadro's number, Planck's constant, and *pi* are just a few. If physics were merely situational, we might expect each research team to determine its own daily values for these constants—setting *pi* at 3.14 only in certain cases, and using 2.95, say, in other circumstances—with obviously confused results.

In fact, most physicists still work comfortably in the regime of laws identified by Sir Isaac Newton some three centuries ago. There is, however, a realm of physics where these constants have little bearing. It is called quantum mechanics, and it talks of such things as "particles with no size, a 10-dimensional space, an observer-created reality, a multitude of parallel universes, and a world where probability replaces certainty." It is highly theoretical and, to the layman, most bizarre, for it holds that matter simply isn't real, solid, and tangible in the ways we've always thought it to be. Case in point: a phenomenon known as quantum tunneling, in which it has been discovered that particles fired with great velocity at an impenetrable object are found to "show up"—there's really no other word for it—on the other side. They don't do it all the time. But there is enough chance that they will do so, with what physicists call "a small but nonnegligible probability," that certain measurement instruments are now commercially available based on this technology.

And that, says University of Chicago astronomer David Schramm, is what makes the quantum world so interesting. If single particles can do that, so can groups of particles—with much lower but still "nonnegligible" probabilities. Groups of particles include such things as baseballs—or people. Quantum mechanics makes it clear that a baseball or a body, hurled at a wall with terrific force, has a probability, minuscule though it is, of passing right through unscathed. "If I threw a ball against the wall," says Schramm, "the probability is much, much higher that the ball will bounce back than that the ball will go penetrating through the wall. But the probability of its going through the wall is not absolutely zero."

Does that mean, then, that people should conduct their daily affairs according to the facts of quantum mechanics? Should we, as we approach a traffic jam on the freeway, simply accelerate into the cars ahead in the hope of tunneling through? Hardly. "In principle," says Princeton University physicist David Gross over lunch in a faculty dining room, "there is some nonnegligible probability that I'm located on the other side of the room. But that probability is so small that one would have to wait many lifetimes of the universe for me to jump over there and back again." The exceptions of quantum mechanics notwithstanding, most of us—and most physicists—still act in accord with the old constants of the Newtonian order. Edward W. Kolb, a physicist at the Fermi National Accelerator Laboratory in Batavia, Illinois, put it about right when he observed that "when I'm driving over a bridge, I don't worry about the probability that I'm to tunnel through the bridge instead of drive over." Then, pointing out that even those who puzzle over quantum physics must lead ordinary lives, he notes that "you have to mow your lawn, whether you know the origin of the universe or not."

There's an analogy here to the moral realm. Just as we don't abandon the entire Newtonian order in the face of a few quantum exceptions, so we need not abandon the entire framework of basic, shared precepts or prohibitions—against stealing, for instance—simply because of a mother's uncle somewhere. Yet the mother's uncle syndrome—the notion that all ethics is relative—remains a pervasive and undermining concept in popular philosophy these days:

• In our schools, it would keep us from articulating a core of common values to transmit to the next generation by asking, "But whose values will you teach?"

• In our corporations, it would keep us from identifying a code of ethics, on the assumption that there are no shared values to identify and that any code would be little more than an imposition of somebody's values on others.

• In our social and civic life, it would keep us from recognizing that the prevalence of stealing in certain inner-city areas does not necessarily mean that the residents there espouse a different moral code that approves of stealing—that somehow "they like it that way."

• In our international life, it would keep us from understanding that thuggery and bribery, despite their commonality in some cultures, do not render obsolete the widespread moral prohibitions against force and fraud.

The British philosopher Walter T. Stace put it well a half century ago when, in the course of a ringing rejection of ethical relativism that has become something of a classic, he addressed the practical consequences of such a view:

> *If men come really to believe that one moral standard is as good as another, they will conclude that their own moral standard has nothing special to recommend it. They might as well then slip down to some lower and easier standard. It is true that, for a time, it may be possible to hold one view in theory and to act practically upon another. But ideas, even philosophical ideas, are not so ineffectual that they can remain for ever idle in the upper chambers of the intellect. In the end they seep down to the level of practice. They get themselves acted upon.*
>
> *. . . Certainly, if we believe that any one moral standard is as good as any other, we are likely to be more tolerant. We shall tolerate widow-burning, human sacrifice, cannibalism, slavery, the infliction of physical torture, or any other of the thousand and one abominations which are, or have been, from time to time approved by one moral code or another. But this is not the kind of toleration we want, and I do not think its cultivation will prove "an advantage to morality."*

So there are core values that have a real, practical claim to universality: So what? What difference does that fact make in our lives?

One answer comes from the experience shared in one of our seminars by a young insurance agent who was working for a small firm in her hometown. She was at her desk one day when a young man appeared with whom she had gone to high school. The son of a wealthy local businessman, he had just bought an expensive high-performance car and needed coverage.

She asked him the routine questions any insurance provider would use in determining whether to accept or refuse him. He gave generally satisfactory answers. By one answer, however, she was troubled. When she asked, "Have you ever been convicted of operating under the influence of alcohol?" he answered "No." She was fairly sure she recalled a newspaper story a few years earlier about his conviction for drunk driving. So she queried him in more detail—without, however, mentioning the reason for her concern. He maintained his position that no such conviction had ever been on his record.

After he left, her conscience troubled her. So she took up the matter with her boss, the owner of the agency. He brushed it aside, counseling her not to be so worried—since, after all, she really had nothing to go on but a hazy and possibly inaccurate memory of the

Situation Ethics

What journalists of the 1960s called the "new morality" received its most systematic popular expression in a little book called *Situation Ethics*, published in 1966 by American Protestant theologian Joseph Fletcher. "The new morality, situation ethics," he wrote, "declares that anything and everything is right or wrong, according to the situation." He took issue with ethical systems based either on "legalism" or "antinomianism"—the first clinging rigidly to explicit codes and directives, the second embracing an existential anarchy with no rules or principles. As a kind of middle way, he proposed an approach aimed at "a contextual appropriateness—not the 'good' or the 'right' but the *fitting*."

His thesis predictably scandalized both the Protestant and the Catholic camps, who saw it as a kind of superutilitarianism that provided justification for doing (in the language of the time) "whatever turns you on." Page by page, Fletcher gleefully fueled their fires. Claiming that ethics should be pragmatic, relativistic, positivistic, and personal, he insisted that there is no such thing as conscience—noting that "there are no 'values' in the sense of inherent goods," that "everything has its price," and that "only the end justifies the means; nothing else." Fletcher's views, especially when seen in conjunction with Sidney Simon's initial work on values clarification published the same year (see box, pp. 219–220), lent weight to arguments against the teaching of ethics in the schools: His critics wanted no such casuistry polluting young minds, while Fletcher himself argued that there was no "system" of ethics that could be taught.

In fairness to Fletcher, his thesis is less existential than his detractors claim. He insists on one moral absolute: Christian love, which he describes as "binding and unexceptionable, always good and right regardless of the circumstances." Other laws and principles are "only *contingent*, only valid *if they happen* to serve love in any situation." Lacing his book with quotations from the Bible, especially Paul's writings, he spends much of his effort amplifying the Christian concept of love—noting, for example, that because it is not sentimental, "love wills the neighbor's good whether we like him or not." In that way, then, love replaces law, since "love and justice are the same, for justice is love distributed."

Fletcher did not invent situation ethics. In fact, he traces it to earlier twentieth-century European thinkers, including Dietrich Bonhoeffer, Karl Barth, H. R. Niebuhr, and Paul Tillich. In 1956, "*Situations-ethik*" (as the Catholic Church termed it, picking up the German word used by these earlier thinkers) was banned by the Catholic church from parochial schools and seminaries. As used today, the term applies to the view that the rightness or wrongness of an act is determined only by the morality of one's own motives or intentions in a given situation.

newspaper story. Then he reminded her of what she took to be the real reason for his unwillingness to pursue the matter: This young man's father was a major client of the agency and a longtime friend. She urged her boss at least to share her concern with the insurance provider. He refused to do so, insisting that she had already done all she was legally required to do to determine that this customer would be a good insurance risk.

So against her better judgment, she submitted the forms. The young man was insured. Three days later, on a high-speed drive at night with some friends after a bout of drinking, he skidded off the road into a tree. He and one of his companions were killed.

A case of conflicting values? Yes, indeed. In our seminar, the young agent articulated them: her desire to pursue the truth on one hand, and her boss's desire to retain this family's business on the other. Also figuring here: her desire to do her job conscientiously, building for the long haul, versus her boss's desire to move efficiently and without unnecessary entanglements through the short term. Her telling of the tale, however, suggests that her boss didn't see that this was, at heart, a moral issue until its fatal consequences appeared.

Could a code of ethics have made any difference? Not by itself. No mere scrap of paper framed beside the boss's trophy case could have altered those circumstances—unless it had been presented, discussed, and revisited regularly by the entire staff with the full backing of the boss. If *that* had happened, however, much might have changed. Such a code would almost surely have focused on the need for truth-telling—and perhaps on the need for diligent efforts to uncover all relevant aspects of each case and develop free and trusted communications with clients and providers. It might have adjusted, however slightly, any underlying relativism in the boss's thinking—away from the notion that "truth" is merely subjective, and toward the conviction that integrity requires the consistent application of standards even when strong personal and financial ties are at stake. It might have given the agent a better way of talking with her boss. It might have inched the dialogue toward the side of further investigation. It might have been, in the long run, exactly what the customer needed—however much he would have resisted it at the time. It might, in the end, have meant that two young men would still be alive today.

Codes of ethics, then, provide us with shared reference points. They also give us small beacons of certainty in a troubled world—allowing us to dismiss out of hand issues that might, in other circumstances, grow into agonizing dilemmas. Where all things are relative, after all, everything requires debate and decision. That is why sports referees typically require clear out-of-bounds lines on courts and athletic fields, rather than simply a crumpled shirt tossed in each corner. It's not because they are priggish perfectionists. It's because they want to prevent the bigger issues of playing the game and moving toward a conclusion from getting overwhelmed in a mass of petty squabbles about whose foot was where. If the code of ethics is in operation, a good deal of energy once given to such debates can be released for productive work. Where the option of lying, cheating, or stealing is effectively eliminated through an inner self-regulation, for example, it may not occur to an employee to "get back" at his or her superiors through deception or fraud. Nor, if the code is running properly, should there be as many reasons to want to "get back" as there otherwise might be.

Abortion, Riots, and the Values-Tactics Ladder

But there's another, more global reason to aspire to shared values: It is here, on this level, that we have the best opportunity for creating consensus. That fact shows up in relation to what I call "the Values-Tactics Ladder."

In any organization, four words frequently bubble around without much clarity:

- Values
- Goals
- Plans
- Tactics

Here an example helps. Suppose we've established a code of ethics for our local high school and nailed it above the door. It has on it the word *honesty*. Along the way to establishing that code, nearly everyone in our community has bought into the importance of putting that word on our list. But how does it translate? What does it mean? How can we make it operational in our school?

Well, we might observe that there is far too much cheating in the school and propose that our goal—the second step down on our ladder—ought to be to reduce cheating dramatically. Most of the community would probably buy into that, too. Some might demur, of course, asking whether it is really the *most important* goal we could address. But the consensus would probably be fairly broad.

So, moving down still another rung on the ladder, we ask what plan or strategy might best reach that goal. How do we reduce cheating? The answer that comes back might be, "Throw the book at cheaters! Clamp down on them with fierce determination—detentions, expulsions, letters home, failing grades, and all the rest!" Here consensus will get seriously frayed, as perhaps up to half the community says, "Wait a minute: The kids who are the real problem cheaters have already been hammered in all kinds of ways. More punishment won't do it. They need care, counsel, and attention."

But you persist, moving down to the bottom, tactical rung. Through what tactic, you ask, can we fulfill our plan of getting tough on cheaters? Why not close down all the public schools—since they have wimpy attitudes on punishment, anyway—and force all kids to attend private schools, where we can really control them? Here consensus dissolves as the vast majority flees to other options.

The point of this intentionally exaggerated example is that it is much easier to get agreement on the level of values than on the level of tactics. Note this: The very people who fled in horror from the final, tactical suggestion remained firmly in favor of the fundamental value of honesty. Another way to say it: We rally around the highest vision we can find of our future direction, even though we don't always agree on the means for getting there. That point was driven home to me in a conversation I had in Washington with several top Republican strategists shortly after George Bush lost the 1992 presidential election. This distinction between values and tactics, they agreed, explained the difference between Bush and former president Ronald Reagan. Reagan was generally able to talk about shared values, articulating a vision for the nation that appealed broadly to a majority of the electorate. Many voters disagreed with his tactics on particular issues—sometimes violently. Yet Reagan was able to articulate a core of values they liked, and it was that articulation that kept them loyal when it came time to vote.

But Bush, said one of these strategists, was never able to talk successfully about values. When he tried, he voiced such unfortunate phrases as "the vision thing." The one point at which he was successful came when, at the 1988 Republican convention, he called for "a kinder, gentler nation." The effect of that speech, said this strategist, was dramatic. Polling data that showed voters drifting away from Bush turned around, and Bush won the election—only to lose four years later when, his tactics and plans unable to please the voters, he seemed incapable of rallying them to a vision of the nation's shared values.

The point, here, is not to chastise Bush but to provide insight into leadership styles. Leadership, especially in democratic organizations and nations, is not about tactics, micromanagement, and fine detail. It is about articulating shared values and developing a vision for the future—since that, after all, is how consensus is built and gridlock broken.

How can a focus on values bring practical insights into today's pressing problems? Look at two very different kinds of contemporary issues—the abortion debate, and the 1992 Los Angeles riots—that cry out for understanding and resolution.

The Abortion Debate

On its face, abortion raises some of the most fractious and intransigent arguments ever to confront Western society's civil life. Dividing friends and communities, it has become the litmus test for many politicians; shattering religious congregations, it is presented as the touchstone of true faith. Even the terms used to characterize the opposing camps—*pro-life* and *pro-choice*—suggest deep fissures in a structure of core values, as though only the former side has any interest in life and only the latter any concern about choice.

At bottom, however, this is less a debate about values than about definitions. How so? Imagine that you've brought before a television studio audience the most thoughtful, articulate, and vehement pro-lifers you can find, and confronted them with equally reasonable, skilled, and committed pro-choicers. Then imagine, in violation of every canon of inflammatory journalism, that you begin by asking *not* why they hate each other, but what they have in common. You can imagine a conversation that goes something like this:

Do you all think life is important? Each side answers "Yes"—since that, after all, is what fires their convictions with such force.

Then do you support murder? Not at all, insists each side, since murder destroys the sanctity of life.

But do you all place high regard on the concept of freedom of choice? Yes again, they all say, since that is fundamental to individualism and democracy.

What about children—do they matter? Of course, say both sides, for without them there is no future worth discussing.

But what if children aren't wanted: Should they be killed or abandoned? No way, everyone asserts, since that would be the highest offense against our respect for life.

And what about the woman's role in society? Vitally important, say all concerned, and steadily progressing toward the desired state of full legal equality with men.

So women, like men, have a right to freedom? Indeed they do, say both sides, lest we go spiraling backward into an appalling loss of human rights and reverse decades of progress under the law.

Ah, yes, the law: Should it be obeyed? Certainly, all parties agree, since without that groundwork you have mere anarchy.

What about unjust laws? Change them, all agree, not through violence and vigilante tactics but through rational discourse in legislative and judicial channels, holding open the option of civil disobedience but always respecting the rights of others to dissent.

How about raising families—shouldn't women pay attention to that? Indeed they should, both assent, just as much as men should, and with full participation of schools, churches, and governments.

Finally, what of religion—does that have a role here? It surely does, all sides agree, since to say otherwise would be to infringe dangerously on First Amendment rights, and since worship and faith, combined with charity and mercy, are powerful contributors to the health and well-being of our communities.

Then where, pray tell, do you all disagree, given that you hold in common all these fundamental values?

On just one issue, they will say: the definition of the point at which life begins. One side defines it as beginning at the point of conception—and that to end it with an abortion is to murder. The other defines it as developing within gestation, and that to destroy a fertilized embryo in its early stages amounts to little more than trimming a fingernail. Between these definitions there is, admittedly, a great gulf fixed, with powerful and deep-rooted feelings on both sides. But if the pro-life side were suddenly convinced that life had not yet begun by this or that week, they would have no more difficulty allowing the woman an abortion at that time than they would in letting her decide to clip her nails, since they feel strongly about individual choice. And if the pro-choice side could be persuaded that life began at conception, they would have no interest in ending that life, since "choice" does not imply that individuals ought to be allowed to decide whether or not to commit murder. What keeps these sides apart? Not their values, which line up with remarkable congruence. What separates them is their definitions.

It has been said, perhaps truly, that the abortion debate will drop from political view within the next decade or two, as the French abortion drug RU-486 or its equivalent makes its way into the hands of women. There will continue to be efforts to prohibit it. But the history of America's Prohibition movement earlier in this century, and the record of humanity's relentless desire to make use of whatever technologies we invent, give little reason to think that something the public widely wants can long be legislated out. Legalization of abortion, however, will only shift the ground of the debate from a public confrontation involving courts, doctors, and abortion clinics to a personal wrestling involving women in the privacy of their own homes. The legal question, in other words, will be resolved, but the moral issue will remain. No drug, and no law, will solve the central question of when life begins.

In fact, argues philosopher Michael Hooker, that question is "*conceptually* undecidable." To explain, he turns to an engagingly simple analogy. He imagines having a large glass urn full of marbles—so many marbles that anyone looking at it would say, "My gosh, that's a lot of marbles!" Suppose you begin removing the marbles, one by one, until there are so few marbles left that anyone looking on would say, "Goodness, there are hardly any marbles in there." Question: Which marble was it that, when you took it out, caused the onlookers to shift from a state of saying "a lot of marbles" to a state of saying "hardly any marbles"?

"Obviously, there was no single marble," says Hooker. In that regard, he explains, fetuses are like urns of marbles. "There is no point in the life of a developing human being when you can say, 'Yes, at that point it becomes a human being.' There is no discrete event. . . . There *is* no 'moment of conception.' It is a continuum of biochemical events. The concept that there is a moment of conception is unintelligible. It cannot be made real when you reduce it to the level of molecular biology."

Values, then, certainly inform both sides of the abortion debate. But it is not, broadly, a debate over values. True, the debate will remain in the moral realm simply because the question "When does life begin?" can find no solution in the scientific realm. But the numerous shared values that unite both sides of this issue are, in the end, much more pervasive than the single definition that divides—illustrating once again that, however much we may fragment over details, we can still find common ground as a nation at the level of values.

The Los Angeles Riots

On April 29, 1992, a lower court acquitted the four white Los Angeles police officers who had been videotaped beating black motorist Rodney King. That afternoon, South Central Los Angeles erupted in riots. A day later and $700 million in damages poorer, the nation began assessing the impact. Over the next week, I recall, the language of the news analysts and commentators gradually shifted. They had begun by seeing this situation as a breakdown of law and order. Several days later they were admitting that something more was at stake here—that there had been a fundamental collapse at the level of social and legal policy. By the end of the week the issue had sunk home in all its force. This, they were saying, was not simply a question of crime or an issue of policy. It was a moral meltdown. The values of American society—not simply among the rioters, but within the entire nation—were sadly awry and needed realigning.

That was a powerful and healthy recognition. It helped remind us that a community depends on a common core of values—and that when these values drain away, communities exist only in name. Because such core values cannot be imposed, even by government, this assessment of the underlying problem facing Los Angeles helped turn the nation from seeking an elusive governmental "fix" at the policy level and toward a much-needed period of soul-searching.

But how can such soul-searching be made practical and productive? It is one thing, after all, to hand-wring over the lapse of morality. It is something else altogether to take clear-eyed, positive action in the arena of values. Bearing in mind that consensus begins with values, the following six steps offer at least an outline of a way forward in Los Angeles and other frayed communities:

Step 1: Identify the moral voices in the community. These may or may not be the rich, the powerful, or the political. Whatever their background, however, they will represent the most ethical individuals in the community—people whose peers would say, "Now, *that's* an ethical thinker!" Remember that *community* means those who interact around a core of interests and values. It is not simply a geographic definition: Some of the most important players may live thousands of miles from one another.

Step 2: Assemble these voices and define common values. This values-definition process, already in use in many corporate-management settings, seeks to *find* (not to *impose*) the fundamental, shared values of these men and women of conscience—moral attributes such as honesty, equity, peaceful resolution of conflict, and respect for the future that they most want to honor. A useful question to start the discussion is, "If you all could arrive at a shared code of ethics for this community, what would be on it?"

Step 3: Perform a values audit for the community. The point here is to compare the values identified in Step 2 with the actual values found in the community. How different are the values practiced on the street from the values most often held up as exemplary? If there are great points of divergence, it may be worth asking whether the community really does live in a moral vacuum, or whether instead an ethical majority has been silenced by fear.

Step 4: Perform a values audit on social, legal, and economic policy as it affects the community. By refining Step 3, this step asks, "To what extent are the desired values of this community created or reinforced by governmental or corporate policy? Is this a positive or negative reinforcement? Do our laws enhance or degrade the community's values?" While it is true that government plays (or should play) only at the margins on values questions, lawmaking clearly can skew or support sound values.

Step 5: Create a process for a Values Impact Statement to accompany all proposed policy changes. We're all familiar with environmental impact statements, required by law to discover the possible bad effects of any intended change in the physical environment. We need to ask similar questions about laws that intend to change the community. Will this new law force families apart or keep them together? Will it reward honesty or duplicity? Will it open new avenues of greed? Will it benefit some at the expense of many? Will it promote or ameliorate violence, hatred, apathy, and low self-esteem? Will it not only *be* fair but *look* fair? Will it help confirm the relevance of moral values or reinforce a steely values-neutrality? The basis for such assessments, of course, will be the shared values arrived at by the stakeholders and refined by community and policy audits.

Step 6: Build coalitions to support the above steps. It has been wisely said that nothing can be steered until it moves. The process leading to a values impact statement must be given momentum—

not by a handful of leaders, but by a grassroots campaign. Why? Because values are not for specialists. They are part of each individual. In this process, there are no outcasts, no have-nots: Everyone has a conscience, and all have something to contribute. The coalitions that arise around this process, in fact, may well form a new pluralism—a community of conscience based not on special interests but on the force of shared values, centered on a few core truths and radiating outward into families, schools, places of worship, and the entire nation. Oddly enough, such coalitions may arise most readily out of the intense heat of Los Angeles–like situations, where the need is most felt and the moral outrage most strong.

Are there many Los Angeles–like situations? In conversation after conversation around this country, I hear more and more despair over inner-city life. These are no longer tales featuring the poor-but-honest working family. These are tales where family does not figure at all, where gangs replace grandma, where the only values are those of survival and self-defense. They are tales of implosions waiting to happen in a values-neutral environment ignored or walled off by the rest of society. They cry out for an understanding of the role of values and vision in our local and national leadership—and for the development of processes and programs that can bring values to bear before the violence bursts.

Conclusion: Pausing for Icarus

Are we willing to pay attention to such moral issues? In his masterful poem "Musée des Beaux Arts," the English poet W. H. Auden raises that question. Titled with the French words for "Museum of Fine Arts," the poem refers to the paintings of the Old Masters, centering on a work by the Flemish painter Pieter Brueghel the Elder, *Landscape with the Fall of Icarus*. The Old Masters, says Auden, understood that even the most intense suffering takes place in a context where bystanders seem indifferent and unconcerned. His poem ends with a startling image of the mythical Icarus, who used wings of feathers and wax made by his father Daedalus and flew too close to the sun, whereupon the wax melted and he fell into the sea.

> In Brueghel's *Icarus*, for instance: how everything turns away
> Quite leisurely from the disaster; the ploughman may

Have heard the splash, the forsaken cry,
But for him it was not an important failure; the sun shone
As it had to on the white legs disappearing into the green
Water; and the expensive delicate ship that must have seen
Something amazing, a boy falling out of the sky,
Had somewhere to get to and sailed calmly on.

All of us, it seems, have "somewhere to get to." Yet all of us, like the narrator in William Stafford's poem, are in some ways "traveling through the dark," unaware of the moral dilemma that may arise around the next curve. How can we best be prepared? What is it that keeps us from sailing calmly past? What is it that causes us to swerve just enough to see that a moral issue is at stake—and then, if necessary, to pause and engage it?

The answer, I think, lies in a recognition of our core values. The issue may involve a local insurance agency failing to make decisions that could save a life—or an international corporation struggling through a fatal case of product tampering. It may center on intense policy debates over abortion—or grim eruptions of hatred on inner-city streets. It may be as personally engaged as a decision to roll a dead deer off a highway—or as philosophically rich as a classroom thought experiment involving a parachute and a foreign culture. Whatever the issue, it will only seem important in proportion as we are willing to recognize and activate the moral values lying at the core of our thinking. Without a clear sense of our core values, we may simply sail on by. With it, we pause and at least try to help.

With an understanding of this common core, then, we're better prepared to turn to the toughest choices individuals ever make—those between right and right.

Chapter Five

Right Versus Right: The Nature of Dilemma Paradigms

Peter was not a sexist—not in his own eyes, and not (as far as he could tell) in the eyes of his female colleagues. Heading a laboratory specializing in the analysis of hazardous waste, he employed both female and male professionals. Chemistry had always seemed perfectly gender-neutral to him: He knew plenty of women who were excellent scientists and laboratory technicians, and it had really never occurred to him to discriminate.

But in the mid-1980s his company asked him to set up a special laboratory to deal with one of the nastiest and most toxic substances known: dioxin. Using all the standard precautions and then some, he established a very promising operation. Only in one area did he depart from orthodox procedures: Deliberately, he sought to hire chemists who either were males or were females over childbearing age. The reason: The best literature of the day suggested that mothers exposed to dioxin experienced a higher-than-usual incidence of spontaneous abortions, birth defects, and neurological disorders in the children they bore. The studies all focused on women: Peter found nothing in the literature to suggest that exposure by men led to deformities in the children they subsequently fathered.

Coming as it did on the heels of extensive publicity about the dioxin contamination of Times Beach, Missouri, in 1982—a town evacuated at the recommendation of the Centers for Disease Control in Atlanta—the establishment of the lab proved to be the right thing at the right time. It was clearly a success. Then one day Peter was informed that a bright young scientist from another division of the company had requested a transfer into his lab. There was only one problem: Camille, the scientist, was a married woman in her late twenties. She was scheduled to leave the company in the next six months to further her education. Meanwhile, she very much wanted a stint in the dioxin lab for the sake of her résumé: There were few women with such backgrounds, and she felt this experience could significantly help her career.

Somewhat warily, Peter invited Camille for an interview. Trying to be as delicate as possible—to elicit information without asking unduly personal questions—he discovered that she did indeed intend to have children. He also learned that she was adamant in her insistence on working in his lab—and that she was prepared to take legal action against the lab if he did not hire her. Other than the gender issue, Peter could see no reason to refuse her: Given her excellent record, she was just the kind of employee Peter would ordinarily love to attract to his team.

The dilemma, for Peter, arose out of his core values. Deep in his conscience were two things he cared dearly about. One was the sense of gender equity, coupled with a deeply held belief that mature, thinking adults like Camille ought to be allowed to make their own decisions. The other was a profound concern for the sanctity of life—the very feeling that had impelled him into environmental work in the first place—coupled with a special sense of care for infants and small children who depend on the decision-making of adults. On one hand, he knew he should give Camille the job, not only for the sake of her own interests but to further erode the gender barrier. On the other, he knew he should prevent her from perhaps causing irreparable harm to her children for the sake of immediate professional gain. Both impulses, he felt, were right. But he couldn't do both.

Nor was Camille inclined to help him in his decision-making. She made it clear that, were she *not* hired, she would sue the company for discrimination. Yet if he *did* hire her, and if her children subsequently suffered deformities, he also knew the company could be legally liable for failing to protect her. The lab took stringent measures to ensure the safety of its workers. But was he certain they were enough? Dioxin was a new chemical; how could *anyone* be sure? He *was* sure, however, that there was no legal document she could be asked to sign that would absolve the lab of its responsibility for her and her children's safety.

Either way, the company was over a legal barrel.

In the end, Peter refused to approve her transfer—insisting that, if she were to join his lab, the move would have to be authorized over his head. Ultimately, the company president approved her transfer. And she proved to be very good: She did excellent work, liked her job, and left as planned after six months.

Were there any later complications? None that Peter knew of. But he did learn—as the nation has since learned—more about dioxin. The latest research suggests that it is not nearly as toxic as once thought, that the shutdown and disincorporation of Times Beach was probably unnecessary, and that a chemical once identified by the Environmental Protection Agency as "the most toxic man-made chemical" is in fact only a weak carcinogen requiring high levels of exposure to cause any harm.

Do Men and Women Have Different Moralities?

Ever since Kohlberg constructed his stages of moral development based on studies of boys (see pp. 50–51), questions have arisen from female researchers about the validity of his work. Do women develop moral judgment in different ways?

To find out, Harvard University educational psychologist Carol Gilligan conducted in-depth interviews for three different projects—with 25 college students, then with 29 women contemplating abortion, and finally with 144 men and women in nine age brackets from six to sixty. Her aim, she writes in *In a Different Voice*, was to understand "women's identity formation and their moral development in adolescence and adulthood."

Her book is a rich and honest tapestry of analytical discussion interwoven with the narrative voices of her subjects, and it suggests multiple conclusions. Among them:

- Men tend toward an "ethic of justice" that views morality as a question of rights, while women gravitate toward an "ethic of care" that emphasizes responsibilities. For men, what matters most is equality, with everyone treated the same. Foremost for women, however, is "the premise of nonviolence—that no one should be hurt."

• Women find greater moral worth in networks and lateral relationships, while men tend to focus on hierarchical chains of command. Strength, for example, has different meanings for men and women: While men equate it with assertion and aggression, women see it as nurturance and interdependence.

• These perspectives are so fundamentally different that they produce separate modes of thinking about resolutions. For men, resolving dilemmas tends to lie in "formal and abstract" expression, while for women moral problems are more naturally resolved in ways that are "contextual and narrative."

• Given these different perspectives, the development of moral judgment among women is significantly different from that of men. From the abortion study, Gilligan finds that "the sequence of women's moral judgment proceeds from an initial concern with survival to a focus on goodness and finally to a reflective understanding of care as the most adequate guide to the resolution of conflicts in human relationships."

The contrast to Kohlberg is instructive. To be moral, for Kohlberg, is to rise to the sixth stage of development, a moral consciousness that adheres to justice and equality based on universal moral principles. From the perspective of the women Gilligan interviewed, by contrast, "a moral person is one who helps others; goodness is service, meeting one's obligations and responsibilities to others, if possible without sacrificing oneself."

All of that information, however, had not yet come to light. Because he was acting on the best information available to him, and because his own core values were so strong, Peter faced an ethical dilemma of the right-versus-right sort.

His dilemma lends itself to analysis from the perspective of the four paradigms introduced in Chapter One:

- Justice versus mercy
- Short-term versus long-term

- Individual versus community
- Truth versus loyalty

The names used here are less important than the concepts:

- The point behind the justice-versus-mercy paradigm is that fairness, equity, and even-handed application of the law often conflict with compassion, empathy, and love.
- Short-term versus long-term, or *now versus then,* reflects the difficulties arising when immediate needs or desires run counter to future goals or prospects.
- The individual-versus-community paradigm can be restated as *us versus them, self versus others,* or *the smaller versus the larger* group.
- Truth versus loyalty can be seen as honesty or integrity versus commitment, responsibility, or promise-keeping.

Call them what you will, these four patterns help us describe the basic issues at the heart of so many ethical conflicts—the clashing of core values that makes it hard for good people to make tough choices.

That clashing of values constitutes a *dilemma.* Here several definitions are in order—not to prescribe, restrict, or discount other definitions, but simply to clarify ways in which these words can be most helpful. To deal in ethics, after all, is to deal largely in the ways we talk to each other: The problem, as one of T. S. Eliot's characters spluttered in a moment of verbal frustration, is that "I've gotta use words when I talk to you." Indeed so. If ethics seems at times fuzzy around the edges, part of the problem lies in our definitions. The answer does not lie, as I've argued above, in intense exercises at razor-sharp definitional distinction. But neither does it lie in vagueness—particularly about such words as *dilemma.* The word is from the Greek: The prefix *di-* means "two," and the word *lemma* means "a fundamental proposition, a basic assumption taken for granted." While popularly used to describe a situation posing two unpleasant or negative alternatives, the original meaning of *dilemma* carries no negative connotations. As the word is used here, it describes any situation that pits one deeply held lemma against another. I use the term *ethical dilemma*, then, to stand for those right-versus-right situations where two core moral values come into conflict—distinguishing such dilemmas from the right-versus-wrong issues that produce what can usefully be called *moral temptations*.

The other term needing a word of definition is *paradigm*, from the Greek prefix *para-*, meaning "beyond" or "aside from," and *deigma*, meaning "example." The word literally means "pattern" or "model." It is typically used to describe an overall concept, framework, or thought process that is widely accepted (especially in intellectual communities) as an effective way to explain complex phenomena or sets of data. Animals facing winter, for instance, can be categorized through several paradigms, one of which is migration. This paradigm, drawn literally from the concept of a group of people leaving one homeland for another, makes sense of a great variety of observations concerning birds, mammals, fish, butterflies, and even retired Americans with homes in Florida. By extension, it also lets us talk about the movement of ions toward an electrode and the shifting of atoms from one position in the molecule to another. What connects all these things? Not their particular details: Ions, hummingbirds, Floridians, and refugees don't seem, on the surface, to have much in common. Here as elsewhere, the paradigm emerges only as we strip away particulars and get down to central ideas—in this case, an idea regarding the movement of groups.

So it is with our dilemma paradigms. What helps us classify our dilemmas into four sets has little to do with the descriptive elements of the experience. It is not the presence of dioxin in Peter's story that helps us spot the most relevant paradigm, nor is it the fact that he is a scientist, nor even that his problem arises from a legal issue concerning potential gender discrimination. No, what matters here are the core values that drive his decision-making. To see what they are, try running his story through the four paradigms:

• **Justice versus mercy.** This one seems to fit best. On one hand, Peter is keenly aware of the elements of fairness, equity, and justice. Despite the fact that science tells him of undeniable differences between males and females, he clearly does not want to discriminate on the basis of gender. Following the dictates of justice, he should hire Camille.

On the other hand, his sense of mercy urges him to sit down with her and try to talk her out of her decision—not for his sake, nor even for her sake, but for the sake of those yet to be born. His compassion and respect for life finally drive him to take a stand that is professionally difficult, surely unpopular, and probably illegal. How much easier, after all, simply to go with the flow, hire her, and hope for the best. That would not be "wrong." It's just that his conscience wouldn't let him do it: Following what he sees as the dictates of compassion, he can't take her into the dioxin lab.

• **Short-term versus long-term.** This paradigm seems relevant in two ways. First, it helps us see the dilemma Peter faces as extending through time. It is proper, he might well say, to honor Camille's short-term rights without concern for the longer-term consequences—which, as it turned out, would prove to be negligible. It's right, in other words, to hire her. But isn't it also right to honor the long-term health of her children—and his company? Contemplating the dreadful "what ifs" of this case, shouldn't he help insure against them by not hiring her? Wouldn't it be right to establish a long-term precedent to the effect that, if the best scientific research of the day declares a high level of gender-related risk, that gender (whether male or female) should be treated differently from the other?

This paradigm illustrates something else as well: Dilemmas have actors. For Peter, the short-term-versus-long-term paradigm might not seem as powerful as its justice-versus-mercy counterpart. If we take Camille as the actor, however, the situation changes. Justice versus mercy doesn't seem to fit: Because she has no reason to see the situation in that light, she's not torn between a sense of fairness and a feeling of love. But she *is* caught on the horns of a short-term/long-term tension, just as he is. Her own best interests in the immediate future might well be to put "dioxin experience" on her résumé. But should she trade that advantage for the prospect of caring for a deformed child in the long-term future—a child who could conceivably require so much attention that she might no longer be able to work as a chemist at all? Or is that "prospect" overly remote in the face of available facts? All of us balance risks against benefits every day, and often choose to endure certain levels of risk—in the foods we eat, the cars we drive, the places we work, and in dozens of other ways. Is this any different?

Notice that the assessment of risk turns on a crucial factor: knowledge. To the extent that Camille is an expert chemist, she possesses that knowledge. She is fully capable of rendering professional judgments on the probability of her coming into contact with toxic substances—and finding ways to protect herself with everything from specially designed hoods to cutting-edge robotics. But Peter, too, is a chemist, and has his own set of professional judgments. In this case, they both got it wrong—Peter for thinking that dioxin was highly dangerous (it proved not to be), and Camille for thinking experience with it would matter greatly on her résumé (which might no longer be the case as dioxin loses its "most dangerous toxic" status). The point is that the resolution of dilemmas often depends on the knowledge we have—a subject we'll revisit later in more depth.

• **Self versus community.** Take Peter as the "self" here. His instinct, perhaps, would be to avoid entanglement—to approve her hiring, make no fuss, and not get himself embroiled in a sticky problem. But would that be best for the community—the lab as a whole, the community in which Camille would live and (maybe) raise a deformed child, or ultimately the universe of female chemists of child-bearing age? Probably not: Honoring the needs of the self conflicts with honoring those of the community. Here, however, another problem arises. This paradigm can be argued from a different slant. Maybe the demands of the self would urge Peter to take a firm line at the outset to avoid complications down the road—not hire her, not have anything to do with her, in order not to complicate his own life with long-term legal problems. But it might also be true that the demands of the community—especially the community of women who, after centuries of discrimination, are only now beginning to move into such male-dominated arenas as professional science—would urge him to hire her, as a way of helping build the kind of equitable, fair society in which he would like to live.

This paradigm, while it fits, seems less helpful than the earlier ones. Why? In part, I think, because the process of analysis reveals that neither side of the "self" argument—avoiding entanglement by simply going with the flow and hiring her, or avoiding long-term legal hassles by not hiring her—rings with the true metal of high moral character. In the end, they both strike us as overly selfish, rather than genuinely self-aware and self-interested.

Should it worry us that, when this self-versus-community paradigm is applied, the two sides can be argued in such different ways?

Not really. The purpose of *analyzing* dilemmas through these paradigms is not to *resolve* them at this point. That comes later, through the application of our three decision-making rules. At this stage we're simply trying to understand the fundamental, core values that are in conflict—so that when we finally apply the resolution rules, the conflict needing resolution will have been stated as clearly as possible and will stand out in bold relief.

• **Truth versus loyalty.** This paradigm, so powerful in many cases, seems out of place here. Neither Peter nor Camille faced or ducked any objective and obvious "truth." And neither seemed driven to make decisions based on strong feelings of loyalty. Had Peter known what we now know about dioxin, and had he chosen to ignore or obscure it, truth would certainly have been involved. Even there, however, the paradigm would not really have fit: The case would then have been pretty clearly a right-versus-wrong issue, to which these paradigms simply don't apply.

And that's an important point. One clear value of paradigm analysis lies in its ability to help us distinguish right-versus-right dilemmas from right-versus-wrong temptations—as the following example makes plain.

Randy, an American living in the capital city of a South American country, managed one division of the Latin American office of a multinational manufacturing corporation. Like many South American nations, this one was eager to develop its own domestic electronics industry. So far, the quality of this fledgling industry's products had been very poor. To protect it, the government had slapped high tariffs, ranging up to 100 percent of the value, on imports of computer equipment. It was widely known, however, that this nation's customs officials were grossly underpaid and were given great freedom to collect bribes as a means of supplementing their incomes.

As he prepared for a vacation with his family back to the United States, Randy was approached by his boss and given an assignment. His office, which frequently made sales presentations, needed a high-quality color printer to prepare sharp-looking documents. The boss, from looking at catalogues put out by U.S. firms, knew exactly the printer he wanted and how much it should cost. So he asked Randy to buy one and bring it back with him on the plane. He also asked him to buy a couple of bottles of expensive whiskey to use as bribes at customs. He assured Randy that he would be reimbursed for whatever he spent—happily so, since even the most expensive liquor would cost but a fraction of what he would otherwise pay in duty.

What should Randy do? Does he bring in the printer, or doesn't he?

As you run this example through the paradigms, you may notice something peculiar. The paradigms don't really seem to fit. It's easy to see that the self (or the small group constituting the firm) and the community (or the larger group comprising the nation) have differing claims. But it's hard to see that there are "right" claims on both sides. Nor does this seem to be a justice-versus-mercy challenge or a short-term/long-term standoff. The closest candidate might seem to be truth versus loyalty, where loyalty to his boss would urge him to buy the printer while truth would urge him to obey the law. But how, then, do you articulate the two rights here? Is it "right" to break the law? From a Yankee perspective, these laws may seem unjust. But is that sufficient reason to flout them? To be sure, there are cases where lawbreaking may be in order, as in civil disobedience. But Randy was apparently not willing to go to jail for his beliefs; and he surely was not interested in bribing the customs officials in the full glare of publicity, so that all could see what he was doing.

In fact, it's difficult to see this case as a situation of right versus right—for the simple reason that it's probably not. Many observers, looking in from outside in an unbiased way and with no self-interests at stake, would classify this case as right versus wrong. Moral courage, they would say, compels Randy to find a way to refuse to carry out his boss's request—to do what's honest even when asked to do what's expedient. Our efforts to apply the paradigms will often alert us early on to a right-versus-wrong issue: If none of the paradigms fits, the reason may be that it's not an ethical dilemma at all, but simply a moral temptation.

Paradigm #1: Truth Versus Loyalty

With that as background, let's look more deeply into the first of our four right-versus-right paradigms, truth versus loyalty.

Truth, to most people, is conformity with facts or reality. Loyalty involves allegiance to a person, a government, or a set of ideas to which one owes fidelity. Those are deceptively simple definitions.

But they are valuable insofar as they distinguish between the objective and the subjective, the idea of a reality apart from an observer's bias and the concept of a personal feeling of attachment that depends on the presence of a personality. It is in this tension between the objective and the subjective that some of our most piercing dilemmas arise.

But what is truth? The question is perennial. "This is why I came into the world, to bear testimony to the truth," Jesus explained. "Truth!" Pilate snorted. "What does truth mean?" Jesus assumed, apparently, that his hearers understood there to be such a thing as truth. Pilate challenged that very assumption, and philosophers before and after him have grappled with the implications of his question. Is there an objective truth? Or is truth only what we make of it? Even quantum mechanics takes up the query, describing an observer-created reality that effectively voids the distinction between objective and subjective.

Pilate's question is intricate, fascinating, and complex. For those wanting to pursue some practical form of ethical fitness and resolve day-to-day dilemmas, however, it may not require deep attention. If we are struggling to resolve a truth-versus-loyalty dilemma, it is probably not because we are engaging in profound epistemological ruminations about whether or not there is any such thing as truth. It is probably because we see fairly clearly that truth, which means *this*, tells us to act one way—while loyalty, which means *that*, urges us to go another way.

Then what does truth mean in the everyday experience where dilemmas arise? It is true, we say, that I've been to town today—if in fact I've moved myself physically into a nearby municipality smaller than a city. But what if I've simply walked up the road to get some milk from the rural grocery store? If my wife and I understand "town" to mean any place where I can get needed supplies, then I'm truthful if I tell her I've been there. I might, nevertheless, be challenged in court if it were proved that I *said* I went to town when *in fact* I went only to the local store.

Truth in human experience, then, turns in great part on what we all agree to be truth. It is, as Walter Lippmann quoted approvingly from Charles S. Pierce, "the opinion which is fated to be ultimately agreed to by all those who investigate." Such agreements can depend entirely on language. In saying that water is wet, wood comes from trees, and ants are insects, we are making statements that are true simply by definition: That's what we mean when we say "wet," "tree," or "insect." But most agreed-upon truths go beyond the definitional and depend on our knowledge of the world around us. We gain this knowledge in several ways. Much of it comes from empirical investigation, meaning that it's founded not on assumption, guesswork, or opinion but on experiment or experience growing out of the observation of phenomena. Some of it may come through intuition or feelings. And some may come from logical deduction based on what we take to be overriding realities. So if we say that the car needs fixing because it wobbles when we drive it, we hold that to be a true statement based on experience. We may also observe that we won't have it fixed over at Harry's Service Station, since he's a sleazy glad-hander who talks a good game but doesn't know much about cars—a statement given such wide credence in town, especially among those who've taken their cars to Harry's, that it's generally seen as "true." We may also say that every time we wash the car it rains—a statement based more on superstition than careful record-keeping, but so clearly congruent with our recent experience that we let it stand as the truth.

In practice, the truth that most often figures in truth-versus-loyalty dilemmas is based on accurate reporting of the world around us in terms that most would use to report it themselves. Typically, the world gets misreported in three ways. When we say things happened that did not, we are not being accurate. When we deliver only partial accounts that hide salient details, we are not being complete. And when we obscure an important truth with other truths that miss the mark, we are not being relevant. The laws of evidence require that we be accurate, complete, and relevant—a set of characteristics familiarly summarized in the courtroom query "Do you swear to tell the truth, the whole truth, and nothing but the truth?" Truth, then, is reflected in our statements about the world. But "when we undertake to deceive others intentionally," writes Sissela Bok in her masterful book on lying, "we communicate messages meant to mislead them, meant to make them believe what we ourselves do not believe." She goes on to define a lie as "any intentionally deceptive message which is *stated*." Her definition provides a useful test, in fact, for the application of this truth-versus-loyalty paradigm: If the dilemma arises in our experience because we are asked to make *statements* that violate truth, the truth-versus-loyalty paradigm is probably relevant.

For many people, this truth-versus-loyalty paradigm will seem the central issue on the ethical horizon—perhaps the only one. Ethics, they will say, is all about truth-telling: With it, you have the essence of a moral life, and without it there is no hope for ethics. Bok's insights support the latter claim. The effect of truth-telling, she says, is to promote trust, without which there is no possibility of a moral society. "Trust in some degree of veracity," she writes, "functions as a *foundation* of relations among human beings; when this trust shatters or wears away, institutions collapse." Yet while truth-telling is indeed a sine qua non of an ethical life, it is not the whole of it. Frank and brutal truth-telling can accompany murderous tyrannies, loveless marriages, unjust societies, and irresponsible apathies.

Loyalty, by contrast, focuses not on statements of fact but on perceptions of allegiance—"the willing and complete identification of his whole self with his cause," as the philosopher Josiah Royce defined it. It may arise for reasons that are monetary (he pays me, so I'm loyal to him), or emotional (she's the love of my life), or tribal (he's one of us), or political (he represents my ideas in the legislature), or intellectual (I'm convinced that the earth orbits the sun, and will not even investigate alternative explanations), or in various other ways. But it typically involves a fidelity to a person or concept that is sufficiently strong to resist the intrusion of contrary opinions or facts. It requires, as George P. Fletcher writes in *Loyalty: An Essay on the Morality of Relationships*, "the rejection of alternatives" that would undermine the loyal relationship. "Some of the strongest moral epithets in the English language," Fletcher observes, "are reserved for the weak who cannot meet the threshold of loyalty: They commit adultery, betrayal, treason." At its best, loyalty accounts for the patriotism that caused colonists during the American Revolution to give their lives for the infant idea of a new nation, and for the heroism that still causes individuals to endanger themselves to save others during hurricanes and floods. In its middle ranges, it can keep marriages together even in the absence of love, keep children caring for aging parents who are difficult and ungrateful, keep an employee hanging on to an unpleasant job until someone can be hired to take his or her place. At its worst, loyalty accounts for some of the most horrifying excesses of the century, perpetrated by those with allegiance to Hitler, Mao, Stalin, Saddam Hussein, and so forth. But it typically involves some component of responsibility, dedication, and honor. It also involves some recognition that there are obligations, even of the most elusive sort, that must be fulfilled.

Then is it truly a "right" quality? Many say yes. A 1993 survey for *Industry Week* found that 96 percent of the respondents believed loyalty was an important factor in the organization's success or failure, while 87 percent of the respondents felt there was less loyalty between companies and employees than there was five years earlier. Clearly, loyalty matters—which is why truth-versus-loyalty dilemmas are not simply matters of right versus wrong.

To see why, take another example—one drawn from a survey done for the Girl Scouts by the Lewis Harris Organization. There, five thousand children from elementary through high school were asked to respond to various hypothetical situations. One was as follows: Your best friend has just bragged to you about vandalizing the school building. The next day the principal asks you point-blank, "Did your friend do it?" What do you say?

Most respondents—you can almost see them squirming in their desk-chairs over the question—said they would lie to protect their friends. And most adults, looking at the results, are appalled that the majority of these kids are willing to lie. But the problem is more complicated than that. Ever since these children have been able to walk and talk, they've been told one way or another that loyalty is a very good thing and that they must be loyal to their friends. Yet in almost the same breath they've been instructed that truth-telling is very important and that they must never lie. This situation puts them squarely into a right-versus-right dilemma of the truth-versus-loyalty sort. There are ways to help them sort it out, of course: You can help the older ones, at least, understand that some of the worst crimes of this century have been committed by people who put military loyalty above objective truth. But you won't sort out this dilemma by pretending it doesn't exist. The principal who tells the child, "Don't you know loyalty is a terrible thing, and that you should always tell the truth?" flies in the face of one of that child's most salient convictions, which is that loyalty is *not* a bad thing, and that there may be times when you had best *not* tell all the truth.

If that sounds like thinly veiled ethical relativism, consider the following case. You're an American caught in the Iraqi invasion of Kuwait City at the outset of the Gulf War in 1990. As the Iraqi soldiers are sweeping down the streets in house-to-house searches, your Kuwaiti friends take great pains to hide you in their attic. The knock comes. Your friends open the door. "Have you any Americans hiding in your house?" they are asked. Hearing the question, you dearly hope they will put loyalty above truth—at least this once.

Have they done wrong in telling a lie? Few would say yes. In fact, this situation opens up higher realms of philosophical inquiry, in which arguments can be made that your friends' answer, while appearing untruthful in its immediate context, actually maintained a greater truth by saving a life. Does truth require you to answer accurately every question, especially when the purpose of the questioner is to harm the innocent? Does truth-telling, in other words, always serve the ends of truth? It is not necessary to drive this argument into such realms of metaphysics, or to quibble over fine meanings of the word *truth*, in order to observe that there are indeed circumstances—usefully summarized under the heading of "loyalty"—where the immediately apparent claims of truth-telling may be less right than some higher formulation of truth. Questions of harsh, frightening, or harmful bluntness also fall into this category—as Emily Dickinson makes clear in her poem beginning, "Tell all the Truth but tell it slant":

As Lightning to the Children eased
With explanation kind
The Truth must dazzle gradually
Or every man be blind—

Being truthful is one thing. Telling all the truth on every occasion, however, is something else.

Truth Versus Loyalty: Three Examples

So how in practice does this truth-versus-loyalty paradigm operate? Consider the following three examples:

• **The letter of reference.** As an executive in a mid-sized manufacturing firm, Cal finds himself often thrown together with Harry, who works for a unit he oversees. He and Harry live in the same community, their children attend the same school, they are both committed to their families, and they often show up at the same social functions. What's more, they are both devoted golfers and play together fairly regularly. Over the years, they've built a particularly firm friendship, made all the more pleasant by the fact that their spouses are very close to one another.

One day, to Cal's deep dismay, he hears that Harry has been implicated in some financial irregularities at work. The issues, while serious, leave room for doubt: There is reason to think Harry got ensnared by regulations, though he may afterward have tried to cover up that entanglement by being less than forthright. Yet after what Cal observes to be a careful audit and investigation, Harry is let go from his job.

Coming to Cal, he asks for a letter of reference.

What is Cal to do? Truth compels him to describe Harry as financially risky—a label that will be difficult if not impossible to shake off in the business world and could prevent Harry from ever holding another responsible job. Loyalty urges him to focus on the many other strong characteristics that he knows Harry to possess and to downplay the financial issues. Both are right, and he cannot do both.

• **The board chairman's question.** In his position as the number two in a loan organization, Andrew was appointed directly by the board of directors, as was the president. The organization, a non-profit with some $10 million in assets, had a good record of dispensing loans to families in need. It proved to be a very attractive entity to a similar and slightly larger organization, whose principals approached the president and suggested a merger.

For some months the talks between the organizations continued, with the president as the chief negotiator for Andrew's side. The board of directors was aware of the activity. As the situation seemed to be approaching a decision point, however, the board got cold feet and one day instructed the president to cease and desist in his negotiations, explaining that from now on all contacts with the other organization should flow through the board.

Several days later, the president told Andrew he had invited the senior officers from the other loan organization to town for a day-long site visit, where they could examine the loan files and learn about the procedures of this organization. Andrew was taken aback: Was not this in direct violation, he asked, of the board's directive? The president admitted it was, but asserted that he was tired of being run around by the board. He told Andrew that he was going ahead with plans for what seemed to him a very good merger, not only for the two organizations but for the client base they served. And he asked Andrew to be present for the day-long meeting.

Andrew's initial dilemma was clear. As an appointee of the board, he had more than the usual commitment of a number two to an organization's governing board. Yet he knew that, were he to cross the president on such a matter, his tenure in the organization could be short-lived. What's more, he liked and respected the president. What to do?

He explained to the president that, while he did not feel he could stand in his way, his conscience would not let him participate. So they agreed that he should work at home on the day of the visit. The day came, and Andrew was at home when, early in the afternoon, the phone rang. It was the chairman of the board, who asked why Andrew was at home.

Now the dilemma was immediate. It was right, Andrew knew, to support his president, show the kind of loyalty that he knew the president would show him in similar circumstances, and not play the tattletale. What's more, it would have been easy to create an explanation that was acceptable and unrevealing—pleading, for example, a health-related problem. Yet it was right to tell the truth—especially when the question was a legitimate one, coming from an individual who had every right to know what was happening.

• **The counselor's boyfriend.** As a counselor on sexually transmitted diseases in a social service agency for women, May discovered to her horror that she herself had two such diseases. Knowing she had had no sexual relationships with anyone but her longtime companion, she reasoned that the diseases could only have come from him. Confronting him with her concerns, she accused him of transmitting the diseases to her—in effect charging him with promiscuity, since he could have contracted the diseases only through sexual relations with others. He denied it adamantly, refusing even to submit to medical testing. She subsequently ended their relationship.

Some months later, a young woman May did not know came in for counseling after having contracted a sexually transmitted disease. In their discussion, the client revealed the name of her boyfriend. To

May's astonishment, it turned out to be her own former boyfriend—a fact apparently unknown to the young woman.

May's dilemma: Does she maintain her professional demeanor and give no hint that she knows anything about the man? Or does she warn the young woman of what she knows?

On one hand, it is right to do the former. Her loyalty to her profession requires her to avoid personal involvement with her clients and to provide them with objective counsel untainted by bias of any sort. That requirement seems even more compelling where powerful feelings are involved. Were May to reveal her own past relationship with the man, she might raise serious questions in the mind of her client about her reasons for doing so—including, perhaps, a suspicion that she was seeking vengeance on her former lover by trying, possibly through false accusation, to destroy his current relationship.

Yet it is also right to warn the client of something May knows, almost certainly, to be the truth. This man, in her professional opinion, is dangerous to the health of her client. Were her client alerted, she could avoid further infection from other diseases. The truth, coupled with her deep compassion for her fellow beings, urges her to tell the client what she knows and prevent further suffering—something she would do in any other human situation where speaking up about dangers could save lives. Can there ever be any reason, she asks herself, not to tell a lifesaving truth for another's benefit?

As these three dilemmas show, truth-versus-loyalty dilemmas are familiar to us all. While they may not always rise to the levels of complexity and tension suggested here, they turn up frequently in our experience, especially at those points where honesty is at issue. They are just the sort of examples that cry out for an application of the resolution principles. Before turning to these principles, however, we need to consider the three remaining dilemma paradigms. Then we need to ask why we've found only four.

Chapter Six

Three More Dilemma Paradigms

As the discussion of truth versus loyalty in the preceding chapter shows, right-versus-right dilemmas are commonplace. They are so because the two opposing elements of the dilemma show up on just about everybody's code of ethics. That's fine when there's no conflict. But in situations where these right ideas pull in opposite directions and cannot easily be reconciled, you've got a serious ethical dilemma. In similar ways, the three remaining paradigms—individual versus community, short-term versus long-term, and justice versus mercy—raise profound ethical dilemmas that go straight back to our core values.

Paradigm #2: Individual Versus Community

Of the forces shaping history, none is more potent than the two pitched together in the next of our right-versus-right paradigms: the assertions of individualism and the claims of the community. Individualism underlay the entire process by which the American frontier became a nation. But community stood for everything the new nation longed to become. These days, as the exports of American culture spread around the globe, a tension between these poles that was once confined within the boundaries of the United States is spilling over into other nations. To understand why this dilemma remains so challenging, look briefly at the roots of these two opposing forces.

"Individualism is a calm and considered feeling which disposes each citizen to isolate himself from the mass of his fellows and withdraw into the circle of family and friends; with this little society formed to his taste, he gladly leaves the greater society to look after itself." With these words, Alexis de Tocqueville, that sharp-eyed and intuitive commentator on the America of the 1830s, focused attention on the recently coined word *individualism.* The force he described, however, was not new. America's "other" Tocqueville, the French settler J. Hector St. John de Crèvecoeur, had earlier praised the thrust of individualism. "We are all animated with the spirit of an industry which is unfettered and unrestrained," he wrote in 1782 in *Letters from an American Farmer,* "because each person works for himself." A powerful force in the conscience of a young nation, individualism took shape notably in the life of Benjamin Franklin, the son of a soapmaker whose initiative and industry made him a kind of model American. That model quickly came to frame the political thinking, not only of the new republic, but of much of the budding understanding of capitalism. "It is not from the benevolence of the butcher, the brewer, or the baker, that we expect our dinner," wrote Adam Smith in *The Wealth of Nations,* "but from their regard to their own interest." By the end of the eighteenth century, write Robert Bellah and his colleagues in *Habits of the Heart,* "there would be those who would argue that in a society where each vigorously pursued his own interest, the social good would automatically emerge."

Not surprisingly, that pursuit of individual interest quickly came into conflict with the claims of the community—which, whether they took shape in the military ethos of General Washington's Continental Army or the oppressive Puritanism chronicled in Nathaniel Hawthorne's *The Scarlet Letter,* seemed intent on corralling individualism. Just as Thoreau's retreat to Walden Pond was self-consciously designed as a flight from the social world of Concord, so the very title of Walt Whitman's "Song of Myself" speaks reams about the growing literary preoccupation with an internal mind that must create rather than an external world that must be recorded. In his 1841 essay "Self-Reliance," Ralph Waldo Emerson set forth the opposition of individual and community in no uncertain terms: "Society everywhere is in conspiracy against the manhood of every one of its members," he wrote, adding that "whoso would be a man must be a non-conformist."

With the spread of American influence in the twentieth century has gone, inevitably, the spread of individualism. As the technologies of rapid long-distance travel and instant communication broke apart the confining nature of communities, so the automobile put significant power into the hands of single individuals. And as cinema and then television focused intense attention on personalities—making it permissible, for the first time in history, to stare close-up for an extended time and without embarrassment at another's face through the agency of a larger-than-life screen—the claims of individualism gathered even more force. Add to that the ravages of communism from the 1930s onward, and the fear it engendered in democracies everywhere, and individualism rose supreme. The "Red Scare" that swept the United States after World War II, culminating in the anti-Communist hearings led by Sen. Joseph R. McCarthy in 1954, proved that you had better assert individual values loudly and firmly—since any hint that you favored a more communal approach tarred you instantly with the brush of "comrade" and "fellow traveler."

By the mid-1980s, however, the climate had changed significantly. When financier Ivan F. Boesky proclaimed in the 1985 graduation speech at the School of Business Administration at the University of California at Berkeley that "greed is healthy," he stood as the unanointed spokesman for an era in which economic individualism had transmuted itself into public selfishness. By 1989, as the Berlin Wall collapsed, the perversions of community carried out under the banner of communism began to come to light. And as it became acceptable again to affirm the power of community, new voices arose to give meaning to the concept.

One of the most thoughtful belongs to John W. Gardner, founder of the citizen lobbying group Common Cause and former secretary of health, education, and welfare. In his 1990 book *On Leadership,* Gardner identifies eight ingredients of successful communities:

- "*Wholeness Incorporating Diversity,*" allowing groups to "face and resolve differences" without fragmenting;
- "*A Shared Culture,*" in which "norms and values are explicit"

and there are "many opportunities to express values in relevant action";

- "*Good Internal Communication,*" through which people "believe that they can have their say" in the presence of "neutral convenors" such as churches and universities;
- "*Caring, Trust, and Teamwork,*" by which members are nurtured and protected, leading to "a feeling that when the team wins everybody wins";
- "*Group Maintenance and Government,*" including formal governing mechanisms and nongovernmental leadership opportunities;
- "*Participation and the Sharing of Leadership Tasks,*" encouraging "individual involvement in the pursuit of shared purposes";
- "*Development of Young People,*" through which successor generations "learn to take some responsibility for the well-being of any group they are in"; and
- "*Links with the Outside World,*" lest the community be tempted to "draw boundaries to protect its integrity" and ignore relations with "the larger communities of which it is a part."

Relating these ideas to leadership, Gardner notes that "Skill in the building and rebuilding of community . . . is one of the highest and most essential skills a leader can command." Implicit in his argument is the fact that such building and maintenance engages the self-versus-other paradigm: "The good community," says Gardner, "finds a productive balance between individuality and group obligation."

That balance is also the concern of Amitai Etzioni, cofounder with William Galston of the Communitarian movement and author of *The Spirit of Community: Rights, Responsibilities, and the Communitarian Agenda*. It is through community, he writes, that "we find reinforcement for our moral inclinations and provide reinforcement to our fellow human beings." He continues:

> *When the term* community *is used, the first notion that typically comes to mind is a place in which people know and care for one*

> *another—the kind of place in which people do not merely ask "How are you?" as a formality but care about the answer. . . . Our focus here . . . is on another element of community, crucial for the issues at hand:* Communities speak to us in moral voices. They lay claims on their members. *Indeed, they are the most important sustaining source of moral voices other than the inner self.*

Etzioni's distinction—between the community and the "inner self"—speaks directly to the dilemma presented in the individual-versus-community paradigm. Notice that, for him, both the inner and the outer voices are "moral." Both, in other words, are right: The dilemma is a true one, pitting core moral values against one another.

For a participant in one of our seminars, this self-versus-other dilemma came home when, as an undergraduate thirty years earlier, he sat in a philosophy class discussing the morality of suicide. Was there ever, his professor asked, a circumstance in which suicide could be justified on moral grounds? After much debate, the class said, "No." So the professor, who had served in World War II as a pilot, shared with them his own experience.

Shot down over Germany, he was taken to a prison camp and interrogated by the Nazis. As it happened, he had no useful information to give his captors. His duties lay outside the strategic planning functions of the military, and he knew little about such things as troop deployments or planned air raids. So after rigorous questioning that included painful physical torture, he was returned to his quarters.

One night some weeks later a new prisoner arrived—one of his close friends, who like him had been shot down in the plane he was piloting. As they talked, the friend asked about the nature of the questioning and torture he was scheduled to undergo the next morning. The professor told his class that, in explaining to his friend what he would encounter, he withheld some of the more grisly features of his ordeal. Still, he could see his friend becoming more and more agitated. Finally the friend confided his concern: He had a very low threshold for pain. He said that, subjected to torture, he knew he would break down and talk. What's more, he had extensive knowledge about troop movements and planned raids. If he talked, the Nazis would put that knowledge to good use; the probable result would be numerous casualties on the U.S. side. He could see no alternative, the professor told his class, other than his own death. Yet so great was his aversion to pain that he lacked the will to commit suicide.

Instead, he asked his good friend to kill him before morning.

Starkly on the table, then, were the alternatives of the self and the community. Among the highest claims of the individual is the right to exist, to avoid death. But the community—in this case, the U.S. military personnel whose lives would be endangered if his friend talked, and in some sense the entire nation that stood behind them—also had a right to survive.

In a military context, some of the noblest actions involve individual self-sacrifice for the sake of the group: From that perspective, death was indeed a highly moral choice.

Yet how could it be moral to take the life of a friend?

Perhaps a more familiar version of the self-versus-community dilemma happened to Julia, who thirty-five years ago launched a small metal-plating firm. Over the years it grew steadily, until by the mid-1960s it had an extensive laboratory of its own. From the beginning, Julia had insisted on the proper disposal of large amounts of chemicals used in the plating process. But the laboratory, following the standard practices of the day, simply dumped its small amounts of used solvents "out the door." In the 1970s, as new regulations came in and as the plant's once-rural neighborhood was turning into housing developments, the lab invested in more sophisticated recovery equipment and stopped this practice.

Recently, in breaking ground beside her plant for a state-of-the-art day-care center for use by employees and the public, Julia came upon a disturbing discovery. Samples of groundwater showed low-level contamination from some of the hazardous solvents regularly used in the lab. The levels were within acceptable limits. But given the newly heightened environmental consciousness, the plant's neighbors were becoming increasingly concerned about its activities. Many of them drew drinking water from wells not far from the new construction. Some of them, in fact, were Julia's employees.

For the sake of the community, should she share the test results with her neighbors, at the same time launching an investigation to confirm (she hoped) that their wells were not threatened, that there was no current pollution, and that the source was a long-ago-curtailed activity? Or would that fuel worries—and perhaps provoke so much hysteria that the construction of the much-needed day-care center would be delayed or stopped, thereby harming not only the company but numerous individuals in the community who expressed a real need for such a facility?

Still another form of the self-versus-community dilemma arose for Bill, the head of a small liberal-arts college. Among the small staff of administrators with whom he worked closely was Maud, a single woman in the comptroller's office whose loyalty to the school knew no bounds. In twenty years of service, she had held a number of different positions. Yet she never quite proved suited to any of them. Big-hearted with her fellows and careful in her tasks, she was nevertheless a slow, deliberate worker unable to grasp the newer technologies and easily flustered by changes in routine. Bill had several conversations with her about her work, each ending in tears on her part. He knew that, six years away from retirement, she had little accumulated savings and no family. Her life seemed completely wrapped up in the school.

Bill was also aware, however, that with increasing costs and a leveling of enrollments, he had to make adjustments to his staff. It was clear to all involved that Maud's work could be nearly eliminated by new computer equipment. It was also clear that there was no obvious position into which she could be moved, and that her salary was a significant drain on the budget. The requirements of the community made it plain that she should be released. The needs of the individual, however, urged Bill to keep her in place for another six years.

Each of these three dilemmas registers the tension between the individual and the community—a tension we'll examine further in the following chapters.

Paradigm #3: Short-term Versus Long-term

In one sense, this dilemma paradigm is the most familiar of all. It comes upon us every day in dozens of ways. Every time I take a dollar from my wallet, for example, I'm bucking the tension between these two poles. Should I save this dollar so my daughter can go to college in the future? Or should I spend it so that she can eat and have clothing and shelter right now? To ignore the latter is ultimately suicidal: Without due attention to the needs of the moment, moments do not accrue and there is no future. Yet to overlook the future is foolish: Living for the moment leaves nothing to live on when the next moment arrives.

As a personal dilemma, short-term versus long-term strikes home in other ways as well. Do I snack now and ruin my appetite for a long-delayed but excellent dinner? Do I sign up for an evening course leading to a new career, or spend my evenings this month with my children? Do I speak up firmly, right now, about a wrongdoing in my community, or wait to let correction come in some other, maybe gentler, way? In the personal dimension, this paradigm also sends deep roots into religious and theological thinking. Common to most theologies is the concept of self-denial, usually linked to a promise of blessings in a temporal or spiritual future. Yet most religions place emphasis on immediate acts of individual kindness and care—sometimes to a point that strikes outsiders as a reckless abandon of self-concern, but usually with a deep faith that reward and restitution come to those who do God's will. Do I give what little I have today to help others have better tomorrows? Or do I (to borrow symbolism from the airlines) put on my own oxygen mask first so that I can then help the child beside me put on hers—attending first to my own survival, lest I fail to survive to help others in the future?

This paradigm also extends beyond personal concerns. It rings a dominant theme across modern society in at least two larger and more institutional ways:

• **Economics.** Every quarter, the typical corporation reports a bottom line. Because that figure needs to be positive, there is plenty of pressure to have it reflect a substantial profit—and to distribute as much of that quarter's earnings as possible to stockholders. But because the company must attend to its future, there is plenty of pressure to invest in new equipment, staff, research, and product development. The tension between these opposites is constant. Few firms are so immune to economic fluctuations that they remain serenely committed to long-term investment in tough times. Yet the increasing awareness of the dangers of short-termism—particularly its ability to erode a company's quality, leadership, and competitive edge—is moving a number of firms toward greater efforts at strategic planning and future-oriented thinking.

Figuring into the short-term/long-term equation are the developments of modern capitalism and its market economy. Here the voices of concern are largely raised against the domination of the short-term. In *The Illusion of Choice,* Andrew Bard Schmookler observes that "over time there has been a shift from values emphasizing productiveness to values that promote consumption. The asceticism of the Protestant Ethic was ideal for the accumulation of wealth. But as the productive power of the economy expanded, some believe, the continued growth of the system depended on assuring a sufficiency of *demand* for the goods produced." Quoting historian Daniel Horowitz, he notes that the trend began in earnest about a century ago. "In the late nineteenth century," writes Horowitz, "a shift started from self-control to self-realization, from the world of the producer, based on the values of self-denial and achievement, to the consumer culture that emphasized immediate satisfaction and the fulfillment of the self through gratification and indulgence." The result, according to Daniel Bell, was that "by the 1950s American culture had become primarily hedonistic, concerned with play, fun, display, and pleasure."

Such worries are shared by William H. Donaldson, chairman and chief executive officer of the New York Stock Exchange. From Donaldson's perspective, this short-term/long-term paradigm is at center stage. "There is a close connection," he says, "between moral and ethical capitalism and the issue of short- versus long-term behavior and professional standards of business." Building on sociologist David Riesman's term "transaction mentality," Donaldson notes that there is "an important difference between a transaction-based mentality"—looking only at "the expediency of the short-term profit opportunity"—and "a business mentality that fosters long-term relationships beneficial not only to clients or customers but to others involved with, and dependent on, a corporate enterprise." Noting Wall Street's recent emphasis on "putting transactions above relationships," he observes that "it is not unfair to call the 1980s the transaction decade."

• **Environmentalism.** One of the most visible generators of short-term/long-term dilemmas is the environmental movement. Pitting conservation against development, the protection of a global future against the needs of the present moment, environmentalism raises some of the most challenging dilemmas of our day. Many of them center on the inexorable thrust of population growth for a world already carrying 5.5 billion people. With a net global population expansion of roughly a million people every four days—almost all in the developing world, and mostly in urban areas—the world will add about eighty cities the size of metropolitan New York between 1990 and 2025. Simply feeding and sheltering these people puts tremendous, immediate strains on the environment—so much so that pressures for short-term development (of jobs, farmlands, forest industries, housing, and new cities) often outweigh the demands for careful attention to our long-term future.

Yet the recent growth of environmentalism has been little short of spectacular. A movement committed almost entirely to long-term thinking, it is both global and large: Some two hundred million people in 140 countries turned out for Earth Day in 1990. "The problem," as Harlan Cleveland notes in *Birth of a New World: An Open Moment for International Leadership,* "is not the management of the global commons. It is the management of human behavior in the commons. . . . The road ahead is littered with ethical choices, to reconcile what's efficient with what's prudent and fair." And, he might have added, to reconcile short-term demands with long-term investments.

Because the warnings in both economics and environmentalism are all against short-termism, it might seem as though all short-term/long-term dilemmas are nothing more than right-versus-wrong temptations. Is it not always right, we might ask, to favor the long-term over the short-term? No. In fact, attention to the short term is so important, and so natural a human response, that we sometimes forget to give it the intellectual attention it deserves. Self-denial, after all, is not the same as self-immolation: Even as one defers gratification, one must attend to present needs. While there is great wisdom in John Galsworthy's observation "If you do not think about the future, you cannot have one," it is also true that if you do not think about today you may not be around to think about any future. Perhaps Winston Churchill struck the proper balance between future investment and immediate nurturing when he commented that "there is no finer investment for any community than putting milk into babies."

Sometimes, as Churchill suggests, consumption and investment are one. More frequently, however, they are at odds. That was the case with Paolo, who was working in a specialty engineering position with a large company in Pennsylvania when a smaller but fast-growing and well-regarded company offered him a more senior position and a substantial increase in pay. Paolo was honored: While the recession had put a damper on jobs in his profession, the smaller firm made it clear they were very impressed by his work and were keen to have him join them.

But Paolo's family, after several moves in the last ten years, were at last happy where they were. His wife, having just finished a major renovation of the hundred-year-old house in which they lived, had recently taken a position with a local advertising agency. And their two teenage children, after some initial disruption traceable perhaps to racial discrimination (like him, they were dark-skinned), enjoyed school and were well integrated into a pleasant circle of friends. Since the smaller firm was a five-hour drive from their home, Paolo knew that changing jobs would require them to sell the house and move, with all the immediate turmoil involved in such a transition. Yet he also knew that an increase in salary would benefit his family as he contemplated the costs of college education in the not-too-distant future. It was right, he could see, to respect the needs of the short term and not put his family through yet another uncertain period of adjustment. Yet it was also right to respect the needs of the long term and lay up greater financial security for his family and professional satisfaction for himself.

A similar short-term/long-term debate coursed through Jon's mind when he was given two tickets. These were not just *any* tickets: They admitted him and his wife to a fund-raising dinner sponsored by the city's opera company, at which their most famous prodigy—whom the papers hailed as "the new Caruso"—had agreed to sing. The dinner was to kick off a new capital campaign to renovate the opera house, a project for which there was much enthusiasm in the city. Selling at five hundred dollars each, the tickets were much in demand. And here they were, on his desk.

Jon, of course, knew why they had come. As a program officer for a private charitable foundation, Jon worked closely with arts organizations throughout the region. The opera company was the recipient of long-standing and ongoing support from his foundation, totaling well into the millions of dollars. As program officer, Jon reviewed the opera company's grant applications and made recommendations to his board of trustees concerning funding. He knew the company was planning to submit a very large grant proposal to the foundation to help launch this capital campaign.

Jon's foundation had a standard policy against paying for fund-raising events—a policy Jon had helped draft as a way of reducing the potential for conflict-of-interest situations and avoiding floods of small requests from every non-profit organization in the city. In this case, however, there was no request for funds: The tickets were free. Jon, who loved his work in part because he was an avid fan of opera and the arts, was keen to hear "the new Caruso." He also felt he had a professional reason to go—not only to hear the announcement of the campaign (though of course he could read about it later), but to gauge from conversations with his network of acquaintances at the event the prospects for such a campaign's success. He clearly did not want his foundation to make a major gift for a project doomed to failure from the start. There were, in other words, some compelling short-term reasons for him to accept the tickets.

But he felt he must also honor the long-term issues here. This was clearly a substantial gift. Would he be accused of taking a payoff to influence his consideration of the new grant proposal? Would his judgment, in fact, be compromised by his attendance—by paying more attention to the personalities and glitter of the evening than to the substantive issues of the proposal? Would he set up a dangerous precedent for the future, signaling an expectation that organizations seeking largess had better provide special perks for their funders? Would his attendance make it harder, rather than easier, for him to do his job well in the future?

For Pun, a researcher in a marketing firm, the now-versus-then question came suddenly, without warning, and had all the potential for ending her career. When, some weeks before, Alex had called Pun to ask for some demographic analysis of a particular market segment, she had happily complied. Alex was a longtime customer in a large corporation. She had done similar work for him for a number of years, always to the satisfaction of both sides. It seemed a routine assignment. She completed it quickly, then sat down with Alex to explain her findings and conclusions. The results, she explained, were subject to varying interpretations; but she felt from discussions with her own superiors that she had provided the most reasonable analysis.

So she was not concerned when, a week later, Alex invited her to observe the presentation he was making to his own senior management on these results. Knowing she had no role to play beyond listening, she went. Ten minutes into his presentation, however, she knew something was amiss. Alex was using her research in a subtly selective way—and was driving toward a conclusion that was the opposite of hers. What's more, she could see the senior management warming to his presentation: His analysis squared with their preconceptions and seemed to confirm them in a direction they wanted to go. In another ten minutes, Alex would be finished. Shortly afterward, management would vote, and the corporation could be launched down a path that, she felt, might cause them to spend millions on a market that was nowhere near as robust as he had led them to believe. Should she interrupt and correct his presentation?

Everything in the short term argued, "No." To do so would embarrass him in front of his peers and superiors. It could do lasting damage to their friendship, and perhaps limit future contracts between her firm and his corporation. It could, in fact, put her own job in jeopardy: Some months ago, she had taken issue with a line of reasoning of one of her superiors based on her own research, and had been politely but firmly told that many valid conclusions were possible other than her own. She did not want a reputation as a troublemaker. Besides, as a single mother, she very much needed her job to support her daughter and felt herself fortunate to be working in a position that exactly fitted her skills and interests.

But she could see the dangers ahead. The corporation's long-term reputation in this market niche could well be affected by this afternoon's decision. If, in two years, the product line had failed, would the collapse be traced back to Alex? To her firm? To her? Would his job be on the line? Would the long, carefully cultivated relationship between these two organizations be endangered? And would her own reputation for accurate analysis be impugned—making it harder, in the future, for her to develop in this job or to find other work in her profession? Would she be faulted for failing to speak out when a warning was most needed?

Paradigm #4: Justice Versus Mercy

You've just caught your son smoking, in direct violation of the rules of the high-school baseball team, on which he's the star pitcher. He's scheduled to pitch the play-off game tomorrow. Do you tell the coach to bench him, or do you lecture him and forgive him?

You're grading a set of final exams, and one ordinarily good student gets a 59 and fails the course. He pleads extenuating circumstances, and you're sure he's telling the truth. Do you round him upward to a passing grade of 60, or stick by your system?

You're on the governing board of a private prep school whose headmaster, with a history of alcoholism, has been caught drinking with some of his students. Do you vote to dismiss him to protect the school and the community, or do you seek to keep him on and help him reassemble his life?

If these questions trouble you even a little, you're experiencing a dilemma as old as literature and as timely as tomorrow's fashions. The claims of justice urge us to stick by our principles, hold to the rules despite the pressures of the moment, pursue fairness without attention to personalities or situations. That's why the eyes of Justice, as personified in painting and statuary, are typically covered—blind to outward circumstances, so that she can judge only according to an even-handed impartiality that cherishes equality and plays no favorites.

Mercy, by contrast, is never blind. The claims of compassion urge us to care for the peculiar needs of individuals case by case and to seek benevolence in every way possible. Mercy impels us to love without condition or restriction—beyond all regulations or constraint of laws, and sometimes in violation of them. Recognizing that each person is unique and each circumstance new, mercy attends to the specifics of the experience and the differences among individuals.

Most codes of ethics embody some form of justice or fairness, along with some form of love or compassion. The tough dilemmas arise when the two are pitted against each other—as they seem increasingly to be as humanity develops. In some ways, in fact, this justice-versus-mercy paradigm has not always been as powerful as it is today. The original meaning of justice, writes Robert C. Solomon in *A Passion for Justice,* "lies in the realm of the personal passions, especially in our sense of vengeance." In Homer and in parts of the Old Testament, he notes, justice is seen as "simply self-assertion, the unqualified insistence that one's honor and integrity must be defended, and that any offender deserves the worst. . . . The idea that justice should be tempered with compassion and mercy was still a millennium away. . . . " By the end of the Old Testament, however, the idea of balancing the two was clearly dawning: "What doth the Lord require of thee," asks the prophet Micah (6:8), "but to do justly, and to love mercy, and to walk humbly with thy God?"

But what does it mean to "do justly"? What is justice? For philosopher John Rawls, it is "the first virtue of social institutions, as truth is of systems of thought." Explaining this comparison, he notes that "a theory however elegant and economical must be rejected or revised if it is untrue; likewise laws and institutions no matter how efficient and well-arranged must be reformed or abolished if they are unjust." A just society, he continues, is one in which "the liberties of equal citizenship are taken as settled; the rights secured by justice are not subject to political bargaining or to the calculus of social interests."

Then what about mercy? Not surprisingly, the primacy of justice in social systems leads Rawls to define love and benevolence merely as "second-order notions." The reason: Love, which "seeks to advance the other person's good," is fine as long as only one person is in focus, or as long as all those who are loved have similar claims to justice. "The difficulty," he says, "is that the love of several persons is thrown into confusion once the claims of these persons are in conflict." It is in the adjudication of these claims that justice must rise above mercy.

Is justice, then, the supreme condition, brooking no alternative? Are all dilemmas that fall under this paradigm really only versions of right-versus-wrong temptations in which *justice* is right and *mercy* wrong? Not according to so eminent a theologian as Reinhold Niebuhr. "The relationship between love and justice has been the major problem for Niebuhr in his elaboration of a social ethic," writes D. B. Robertson in *Love and Justice: Selections from the Shorter Writings of Reinhold Niebuhr.* In Niebuhr's writing, "love is the final or highest possibility in man's relationship to man," Robertson observes, adding that "it is the peak of the fulfillment of man's nature as a social being."

Niebuhr himself puts it this way: "[An ethic] must give guidance not only in terms of the ultimate possibilities of life, for which sacrificial and forgiving love is the norm, but must also come to terms with the problem of establishing tolerable harmonies of life on all levels of community." For Niebuhr, however, this "forgiving love" must take precedence over the "tolerable harmonies" of justice—since, as he writes, the "desire for justice is one form of love," and justice itself is simply "an approximation of brotherhood under conditions of sin." Niebuhr admits that living love is not easy, and he spends plenty of energy excoriating what he calls "moral idealism." Yet he leaves no doubt that the standard must ultimately be love.

The point, here, is not to resolve the argument in favor either of love or of justice. It is to recognize that each has strong claims upon us, and that these claims create powerful and sometimes wrenching dilemmas. Consider the following real-life situations:

• **Detox or detention.** As principal of a small public high school, Allen took great satisfaction in his girls' teams. The year before, in fact, the girls' basketball team at his school had won the state championship. Things looked even better this year: Four of last year's starters were back again as seniors this year.

But one November day, several weeks before the team was officially allowed to form and begin practices, these four girls left school at nine o'clock in the morning, walked downtown to a bar, got smashingly drunk, and returned to school in time to catch the buses home at 2:30. There was no hiding their condition. No sooner had they set foot in the building than the entire school erupted in controversy. Within minutes the principal's office was packed with faculty and staff in a frenzy of argument. One side insisted that the girls be suspended immediately, given significant detention when they returned, and kicked off the team—or, since there was no official team as yet, at least be prevented from playing on it once it convened. Justice, they said, must be done: These girls must be made clear examples to the student body.

The other side called attention to the circumstances of the case, noting that to get drunk and *then to return to school* was a transparent cry for help. Was no one aware, they asked, of the miserable domestic conditions of these children, several of whom came from abusive homes where alcoholism was prominent? These kids did not need suspension and detention: They needed detox clinics and professional counseling. Mercy, they said, must take precedence here; if the school was to set an example, let it be an example of caring.

Justice and mercy: The principal had to make the call, and he could not apparently satisfy both sides at once.

• **Clawing back the bonus.** As head of a large teaching hospital, Rick oversaw some two thousand employees. As a non-profit organization, the hospital depended on fund-raising and gifts for part of its revenue. Some of these funds were distributed each year as bonuses to employees who, having reached the top of the salary range for their position, deserved recognition for excellent performance. Such payments typically amounted to about 4 percent of the base salary.

One of the employees in that category was Bea, who for years had been Rick's executive secretary. One day shortly after the bonuses had been awarded, she approached him with her paycheck in her hand and a look of concern on her face. The problem: There was too much money in her check, even including the bonus, and she suspected the payroll department had made a mistake. On investigation, she was proved right: In calculating the bonus, payroll had mistakenly included into the base salary some of the amounts provided as benefits, and then made the 4 percent calculation. The overpayments were not large, ranging from a low of one cent to a high of $300. But since 301 employees had been awarded bonuses that year, the total overpayment was more than $13,000.

Seeking advice, Rick was urged by his human resources department to ignore the problem and let the employees keep the overpayments. These were all dedicated, long-term employees—just what you would expect from a group that had received merit bonuses. Besides, it was the hospital's fault. These employees trusted payroll to calculate accurately, and would have no reason to check the figures. To ask them to repay it would not only seem small-minded but could cause real hardship, since some of his employees might already have spent it. Such a move might also cause undue embarrassment and overload to an otherwise well-functioning payroll department that had made an innocent mistake.

But Rick saw, too, that there was a principle involved in the issue. As a non-profit executive, he was charged with the proper distribution of funds that had come, in part, from charitable contributions. He felt that he was responsible for handling money others had entrusted to him—other people's money, in fact—and that he had an obligation to oversee it according to his highest sense of principle. It was not the amount that mattered; $13,000 would hardly make a ripple in the hospital's $200 million annual budget. It was simply not fair, he felt, to distribute others' money accidentally rather than according to a predictable and even-handed policy. However much he wanted to be compassionate to his employees—especially to Bea, whose integrity he hardly wanted to punish by reducing her bonus—he felt that justice needed to be done.

At that point, however, the hospital's attorneys advised against the recall, citing the risk of an employee lawsuit and noting that, under state law, the hospital could not withhold money from future paychecks to make up for past overpayments. Rick acquiesced, and the recall was never requested. It was, he told us, a sound business decision, though not a great moral decision: Even though the law dictated the outcome, the situation remained an ethical one in Rick's eyes.

• **Speeding into motherhood.** Linda, expecting her first child, went into labor shortly after lunch one weekday afternoon. Her husband, Walt, was home at the time. The contractions seemed to be coming close together as they rushed to the car in great agitation: This had never happened to them before, and while they had been told what to look for, they hardly knew what to expect or how to control their emotions.

They were flying through the suburbs on the way to the hospital when, in his rearview mirror, Walt saw the blue flashing lights of a police cruiser. Looking at his speedometer, he saw he was going eighty miles an hour. Looking around him, he saw small children playing on the street and sidewalks as they walked home from a nearby school. As he braked to a halt, it suddenly hit him that, for the sake of his own family and a child he was eager to love, he was endangering the lives of other children and the happiness of other families. For him, the issue was clearly of the self-versus-community variety, and he saw that he had acted more out of selfishness than out of consideration for others.

But what was the dilemma for the policeman? Still unaware of the circumstances, he was sitting in his cruiser, routinely calling in the license number to headquarters as the seconds turned to minutes. Even when he had taken in the entire situation—a perspiring and gesticulating husband and his obviously pregnant wife—what was he to do? Clearly, he needed to escort them to the hospital, which he did. But then what? Was Walt to be let off scot-free, despite the significant dangers he had posed to the community? Was justice being served by allowing an individual to take the law into his own hands whenever there were extenuating circumstances—even when to do so posed significant risks? Clearly Walt would have been severely penalized had a child run out in front of his car and been hit. Should the mere fact that he had escaped such an outcome, however narrowly, mitigate his punishment? Or is there a principal of uniformity here requiring the officer to impose some sort of penalty regardless of the consequences? Everything in Walt's case—his genuine nervousness, his efforts to do good, his wife's obvious discomfort, the warmth and support we feel for motherhood—argued for mercy. But everything in the legal structure—the need for fairness, the requirement for protecting the innocent, the obligation to enforce standards—argued for justice.

It was the patrolman's call, and he couldn't do both.

Are There Only Four Paradigms?

As the patrolman's dilemma reminds us, several different paradigms can be embedded in a single situation. While this case seems particularly suited to illustrating the justice-versus-mercy paradigm, it also has elements of self-versus-community, especially if Walt is identified as the principal actor in the dilemma. Given the time pressures involved, it may lend itself to a short-term/long-term analysis; and given the tension between Walt's allegiance to his wife and what he knows to be the traffic laws, there may even be an overlay of truth-versus-loyalty here. The point is not to determine a single paradigm to the exclusion of all others. It is to allow the analysis to clarify the fact that there is a right on either side of the issue, so that we understand just why the dilemma is so real, compelling, and difficult.

But might there not be a fifth or sixth paradigm? Why are there only four? Why, in analyzing hundreds of real-life dilemmas in our seminars, have no other paradigms surfaced that appear able to stand as equals to these four?

It was the British author C. P. Snow, in his 1959 book *The Two Cultures and the Scientific Revolution,* who popularized the now-famous opposition between scientific and humanistic thinking. In fact, the distinction is not new. The split—between the penchant for observing and measuring the objects of the physical universe on one hand, and the impulse to tell stories and discern the mentalities of the observer on the other—is probably as old as humanity. Plato, recognizing the division between the philosopher and the poet, launches the two-culture debate and finds, in the end, that the perception of absolute truth is most nearly manifested in mathematics. His pupil Aristotle—author of one book titled *Poetics* and another titled *Physics*—recognizes

The Potter Box

Of the efforts to systematize ethical decision-making, one of the more intriguing is the so-called Potter Box. First formulated by Ralph B. Potter in a 1965 dissertation at the Harvard Divinity School dealing with Christian responses to the nuclear threat, it uses a quadrant to chart the flow of ethical decision-making.

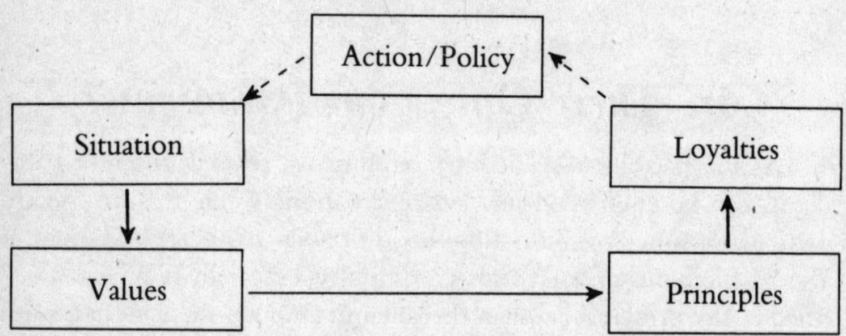

Clifford Christians, illustrating this process in *Media Ethics: Cases and Moral Reasoning,* uses the case of two competing newspapers covering a fire that guts a cinema specializing in gay films. Dead in the fire: a prominent minister, a politician, and a banker. One paper prints their names; the other does not.

How might these papers arrive at their respective decisions? The process starts by assessing the *situation:* What are the facts of the case? The first paper sees it as a situation in which several local leaders died. The other sees the event as a community disaster like many others. Next step: Determine what *values* are called into play. The first paper, standing on journalistic credibility, fears that its reputation will be tarnished if it selectively withholds any relevant information—especially when it routinely prints the names of disaster victims. The second paper, aware that revelations of homosexuality are potentially embarrassing, fears that damage will be done to individuals who may or may not be gay. The third step is to adduce the relevant *principles* at work. For the first paper, the maxim is "Always tell the truth," while for the second it is "Always protect the innocent." Last step: Determine where *loyalties* lie. For the first paper, they lie with the general readership, while for the second they lie with the survivors and their families.

Structurally, the left side of the Potter Box (situation and values) is designed to deal with a description of what *is*, while the right (loyalties and principles) deals with what *ought to be*. The upper half (situation and loyalties) can also be seen as concerning social phenomena, while the lower half (values and principles) concerns analytical and philosophical phenomena.

Useful as it is as a guide to thinking, the Potter Box in fact leans heavily toward utilitarianism, emphasizing *loyalties* rather than *principles* as the final arbiter in the decision-making process. It also leaves unclear the relation of such overarching ethical principles as Kant's categorical imperative or the Golden Rule to this process. In that the process is intentionally circular, however, it allows for a reiteration of ideas through several cycles of discussion, in hopes that a consensus will eventually form around a particular action or policy.

different mental methodologies at work, emphasizes ideal types that transcend the merely physical, and attributes to art and literature the highest capacity to fulfill what nature has left undone. Yet it is the medieval Roger Bacon—the founder of English philosophy whose knowledge of chemistry and mathematics led him to recognize the value of deductive reasoning, establish a scientific method, and invent spectacles—who has been called the last man to know everything, the last man to bridge the two cultures.

In the centuries since, science and the humanities have parted ways. So firm is the division, in fact, that our universities routinely sanctify the split by broadly dividing academic programs into the sciences (chemistry, physics, biology, mathematics) and the humanities (literature, language, history, philosophy)—with the hybrid social sciences (sociology, anthropology, psychology, political science) blended uneasily from the two. The line of demarcation follows the division between objective and subjective—variously described as truth and fiction, method and imagination, reality and desire, thought and feeling, the referential and the emotive, the outer and inner life. The scientific method, at its most rigorous, seeks to exclude from its calculations the personal side of experience and focus on an objective world existing apart from human observations of it. The humanist, by contrast, inquires into motives, responses, and observations: Recognizing that an observer is present in all observation, the humanist focuses on the mind that assesses in an effort to grasp the complexity of the world. Even as the best practitioners on both sides strive to bring the two poles together, the dichotomy remains one of the most powerful structures in twentieth-century arts and sciences. Just as quantum mechanics moves toward an observer-created reality once thought to be the domain of poets and painters, so various forms of photo-realism and modern poetry set out to erase the subjective. "No ideas but in things," insisted the American poet William Carlos Williams, a phrase transmuted by his contemporary, Wallace Stevens, into a poem paradoxically entitled "Not Ideas about the Thing but the Thing Itself." Yet the dualism remains, enforced (in the United States, at least) by the secondary-school system's culminating in a two-part aptitude examination for college students that tests separately for mathematical and literary prowess.

Fundamental to this dualism is the methodology used on each side. Science typically depends on counting and measuring phenomena. The humanities depend on storytelling and understanding character. It needs no special insight to recognize that geniuses at measurement may not know much about character. And there is ample proof that the greatest storytellers sometimes can't count very well. Yet each of these two methodologies is further divided into subsets. To the extent that science concerns measurement, it counts either time (duration, velocity) or space (extension, distance). These two, in fact, make up the space-time continuum central to the general theory of relativity. Yet they are so different that, according to Heisenberg's famous uncertainty principle, you can measure only one or the other, but never both, with any degree of certainty.

To the extent that the humanities involves character, it also takes two approaches, conceiving of human character as uniquely individual but also as a product of the interactions of the culture, order, or organization that supplies its context. So powerful is this subdivision, especially in the social sciences, that entire schools of thought arise to argue the nature-nurture issue—which, essentially, is a debate centering on whether character and behavior are the products of heredity or environment, the results of individual or social factors. Similar debates arise as artists discuss the relation of figure to ground, dancer to dance, and individual interpretation to overall conception.

If much of the above sounds esoteric and irrelevant to the practical issues of resolving immediate ethical dilemmas, that's not surprising.

These dichotomies and their subdivisions are so fundamental to our way of thinking that we take them for granted: Just as a fish would presumably have great difficulty if asked to define water, so we tend to see these ways of looking at the world as so much a part of our intellectual makeup that we fail to distinguish them. But they provide, I think, a framework for understanding how we come to terms with our experience. When we think scientifically, we tend to focus on the measurement of time or of space; when we think humanistically, we tend to focus on character in its uniqueness or in its relation to organizations.

So, too, when we think about dilemmas, we find ourselves dividing as best we can between those situations that challenge us because they involve counting and those that challenge us because they involve character. Of the four dilemmas we've identified, two depend so much on counting that, if we abandon measurement, we have no dilemma left to examine. Short-term versus long-term clearly depends on our ability to measure time, without which the tale embodying the dilemma would be incomprehensible. Similarly, the self-versus-community paradigm requires us to count space or scale: If the smaller group cannot be distinguished from the larger group by some recognized and predictable scheme of measurement, the dilemma ceases to matter.

The other two kinds of dilemmas depend not on counting but on character. The truth-versus-loyalty paradigm will never be analyzed by summing up numbers. The counterpoint to truth, in this paradigm, comes not from measuring some different truth, but from a kind of personal allegiance best understood through the humanist's lens of uniqueness, individuality, and identity. Similarly, the justice-versus-mercy paradigm arises in situations where the greatest emphasis is put on order, organization, and wholeness: The tension is always one in which an established pattern of expectations (justice) is threatened by claims for an exception based on unique circumstances (mercy).

Insofar as there are four broad ways of looking at the world, then, it should come as no surprise that there are four paradigms for human experience that reflect them. Is this an airtight system? Perhaps not. To demand that it is, in fact, would be to invalidate about half of what has just been argued. To insist that the above analysis of the differences between the scientific and the humanistic mind-set is entirely correct—and that moreover there is a direct correspondence between its four parts and the four dilemma paradigms—may well be inexact. The above endeavor, after all, draws its methodology from only one side of the dichotomy—the scientific side, which places high values on formal, exact, schematic reductions. And while an admission of inexactness may trouble scientists mightily, it will come as no surprise to humanists, accustomed as they are to the messy and immeasurable ambiguities of daily life.

In the end, of course, the real question is "So what?" The point is not whether these four paradigms are all that can ever be found. The point is that, however many there are, they will prove useful in cutting through the wealth of contextual detail that surrounds every real-life dilemma. Subjected to paradigm analysis, the essential nature of the dilemma will stand forth. As a result, the core values, central to the internal code of any moral thinker, will become readily visible. So will the tension between them. Insofar as this tension fits a recognizable pattern, it may trouble us less and seem more amenable to resolution. And resolution, not simply analysis, is what this process is all about, and is the subject to which we must now turn our attention.

Chapter Seven

Resolution Principles

In the hurly-burly of daily journalism, ethical dilemmas abound. That's not surprising. The news deals with the real lives of people in real events. A subtle shift of nuance in a news story can lose votes, destroy confidences, threaten livelihoods, and impel revenge. Journalism gone wrong, then, is a highly dangerous thing.

Done right, however, journalism builds bridges, shares knowledge, provokes new revelations, and impels constructive change. A worthwhile news story left unpublished can involve a social and economic price in lost opportunity—and, at times, a tremendous political cost in chicanery undetected and duplicity unchallenged. Little wonder that democracy is so closely tied to journalism. "Were it left to me to decide whether we should have a government without newspapers or newspapers without a government," wrote Thomas Jefferson, "I should not hesitate a moment to prefer the latter."

Good journalism is all about good sources. While that's obviously true for the reporter who gathers the news and writes the story, it's more subtly true for the editor who must decide what issues to follow and what stories to print. Editors typically develop sources at the highest levels of the communities they cover—the political, corporate, cultural, and educational leadership that shapes opinion and sets agendas.

And therein lies a dilemma central to journalism everywhere. On one hand, it is right for the editor to know the community so well, to care for it so profoundly, and to be so much a part of it that nothing important slips past and everything meaningful comes into view. On the other hand, it is right for the editor to stand apart from the fray, evenhandedly weighing the hotly contested claims of the participants and covering them with a cool and dispassionate impartiality. To gather the news, it is right to be deeply committed. Yet to report that same news, it is right to be objectively aloof. What's more, the tension inherent in this truth-versus-loyalty dilemma often develops quickly, on deadline, in a high-stakes game where careers are on the line and only minutes remain to make decisions.

The ramifications of that tension came home with full force to Katherine Fanning when, as editor and publisher of the *Anchorage Daily News* in Alaska, she found herself between the proverbial rock and a hard place. Later, as editor of *The Christian Science Monitor* and president of the American Society of Newspaper Editors, she was one of the contributors to a book on journalism ethics titled *Drawing the Line.* Here's how she begins describing her dilemma:

> *The disconsolate banker was waiting when I returned to the paper after dinner.*
>
> *I knew why he was there. He had just learned that the* Daily News *was preparing to write a story about his son, who was under investigation for arson. The midnight torching and total destruction of the popular Bobby McGee's Restaurant had shocked the city. Now the revelation that the suspected arsonist was the wealthy son of one of Anchorage's most respected families—and himself the owner of a competing restaurant—would stun the community.*
>
> *We had known for six months about the investigation that implicated Frank Reed Jr. Reporter Don Hunter brought in regular reports from confidential sources, but we remained silent while the probe continued, hoping we could verify independently what we were hearing. Now, our sources told us, a grand jury indictment was imminent. We had just learned that the U.S. attorney had sent a letter to Reed advising him that he was the target of an investigation. We had also discovered that the authorities had incriminating tape recordings. Yet no source would speak for attribution, and we didn't have a copy of the U.S. attorney's letter or any other document.*
>
> *The key editors were ready to publish. "Why now?" I asked.*

"Because it's 'on the street.' The competition may have it soon." We had countless hours invested in the story.

Against this backdrop, Frank Reed Sr. had come to say his son had been framed, that he was sure there would be no indictment. If we published now and there was no indictment, we would ruin his son's life, damage his small children, wreck the family.

As I faced the agonized father, my thoughts raced to the time when Frank Reed Sr., one of Anchorage's most prominent civic leaders, had been the only member of the business community who had publicly supported my newspaper during a desperate period of financial instability and conflict with the competing newspaper. He had co-chaired a committee whose work helped keep the Anchorage Daily News *alive. Now he was begging me not to run the story about his son.*

Most of the time I had a pretty good rapport with the newsroom staff. Tonight they were waiting to see what I would do—whether I would be swayed by the wealthy banker's clout. The executive editor was adamant. We should publish in tomorrow morning's paper.

"Why can't we wait until the indictment comes down?" I asked.

"Because we've been sitting on the story for months. We have it confirmed by several sources. And if we don't publish, the competition will."

"What if the man has been framed?"

"Everything indicates he's guilty as hell."

"What's the harm to the public interest in waiting a few days to see?" I also asked if we could get any official to go on the record. "No."

*The story would be attributed only to '*Daily News *sources." We would be asking our readers to trust us that it was true.*

As I tussled with the problem, I felt certain any respect the newsroom and my executive editor might have for me would vanish if I "caved in." In 15 years working together, he and I had never had a confrontation like this.

I turned to reporter Don Hunter. "Why do you think we should run the story now?" I asked.

He hesitated. "I'm not sure. It's on the street."

With only a few hours until deadline, Fanning found herself facing a truth-versus-loyalty dilemma of the first intensity. The dictates of truth suggested publication. But the demands of loyalty urged her to hold the story.

How to resolve it?

For Fanning, as for any of us facing tough choices, that's the paramount question. The resolution process begins with gathering the relevant information, as Fanning did in her step-by-step questioning. It continues by seeking alternatives that might point to a way around the dilemma: Can we get someone to go on the record, or can we agree to hold the story? But when the questioning is done and facts remain stark and unrelenting, the mind seeks direction in something beyond the dilemma itself. That's when we reach out for a moral principle that can lead us toward a resolution.

Three Principles for Resolving Dilemmas

Whether or not we realize it, we're all familiar with three such principles, so widely used that they come readily to mind as simple, colloquial phrases:

1. "Do what's best for the greatest number of people" (which we'll refer to here as *ends-based* thinking).

2. "Follow your highest sense of principle" (or *rule-based* thinking).

3. "Do what you want others to do to you" (or *care-based* thinking).

We don't usually stop to analyze these principles. In fact, we may be so familiar with them that we've never thought about how distinctly different they are from one another. Nor do we typically apply all of them in every situation: We may have grown so attached to one that we rarely turn to the others. But chances are that, if forced to articulate the reasoning we use to resolve a tough dilemma, we'll find ourselves using the logic developed from one or more of these principles. Why? Simply because these principles grow right up out of everyday human experience. True, each has a long history in moral philosophy or religious instruction. But they are not abstract inventions imposed by philosophers or divines. They have worked their way into the teaching and practice of ethics simply because each is such a familiar part of the human thoughtscape.

To be sure, the three principles outlined here are not the only philosophical positions one could bring to bear on this issue. Ethics, after all, is all about the concept of "ought." It is not about what you have to do because regulation compels it (like paying to ride the train) or nature requires it (like eating and sleeping). It's about what you ought to do—have an obligation to do—because it is "right." Not surprisingly, there are those who recognize obligations other than the three suggested here—like maximizing your own self-interest regardless of others, or doing only what your leader says, or acting in the national interest, or following what Joan of Arc called her "voices," or doing whatever feels good. And there are those who recognize no obligations at all, asserting that ethics is wholly relative and situational and that no general rules can exist. These people will no doubt prefer other principles. The three proposed here, however, are among the most widely recognized and commonly used. In our seminars, we've found them to be the most helpful in confronting the choices we commonly face in today's world.

Before applying these three principles to Fanning's tough choice, let's examine them in more detail.

1. Ends-Based Thinking

The first moral principle, which asks us to consider the greatest good for the greatest number, is formally known as "utilitarianism." We commonly know it through the phrase "the greatest good for the greatest number." We've called it the *ends-based* guideline, since it relies so heavily on assessing the consequences or ends of action. The English philosopher Jeremy Bentham (1748–1832), generally credited with developing the first systematic utilitarianism, noted that the measure of the rightness of an action was to be found in the greatest happiness for the greatest number. Focusing on institutions rather than individuals, Bentham was keen to bring a scientific accuracy to the study of morality. Since he saw pain and pleasure as the parameters of happiness, he developed an elaborate scheme to assign relative values to pains and pleasures. His friend John Stuart Mill (1806–1873) further developed utilitarianism by focusing particularly on issues of personal conduct. Refining Bentham's quantitative assessments of pleasures and pains, he argued that "some *kinds* of pleasures are more desirable and more valuable than others," and noted that the highest pleasure lay in the desire for unity with others. "The happiness which forms the utilitarian standard of what is right in conduct," wrote Mill in his landmark essay "Utilitarianism," in 1861, "is not the agent's own happiness, but that of all concerned. As between his own happiness and that of others, utilitarianism requires him to be as strictly impartial as a disinterested and benevolent spectator." A third Englishman, Henry Sidgwick (1838–1900), developed Mill's utilitarianism by introducing three "axioms of the practical reason" under the headings of prudence, benevolence, and justice.

In all of its formulations, utilitarianism is a species of what philosophers describe as *consequentialism*—which, simply stated, is the concept that right and wrong can be determined by assessing consequences or outcomes. Known also as a *teleological* philosophy (from the Greek *teleos,* meaning "end" or "issue"), utilitarianism focuses on the results of an action (rather than, say, the motives behind a behavior or the rule that is followed to arrive at a particular decision). It is generally seen to fall into two broad camps: *act utilitarianism,* which instructs us to take whatever *action* maximizes the good, and *rule utilitarianism,* which urges us to follow whatever *rule* will bring about the greatest benefit. Both, however, are inseparably wedded to an assessment of consequences: You know what's right only by determining what eventually happens.

In practice, modern policy-making is largely founded on utilitarianism. The acid test for most proposed legislation is, "Will it serve the largest possible constituency with the greatest benefit?" Not surprisingly, then, a great deal of policy formulation is based on some sort of future assessment, in which current data is extrapolated to show probable consequences. So, too, utilitarianism in the personal realm depends on a careful weighing of alternative futures to determine the more satisfying. This calculus, taking into account the two central factors of utilitarianism, seeks to determine both the relative levels of benefit in the future (the "greatest good") and the scope of the population (the "greatest number") to whom it will be distributed.

The necessity for performing this sort of calculus opens utilitarianism to serious criticism on both the "greatest good" and the "greatest number" fronts. How, critics argue, can you possibly foresee all the consequences of any personal action, let alone of actions on a broad social scale? Humans are notoriously poor speculators, these critics argue, routinely missing the most important consequences and stumbling into unforeseen problems of their own making. Did our ancestors really understand consequences when they imported African slaves into the American colonies with little thought to future racial inharmonies? Did they have a clear sense of end results when they built nuclear reactors with little concern for nuclear waste disposal or put CFCs into aerosol cans with no understanding of the ozone layer? Then how can we possibly be entrusted to determine the "greatest good"? Nor, they object, are humans any good at understanding the "greatest number," since actions have such unforeseen consequences that they may affect vast numbers of people far beyond those first identified. Finally, critics raise serious practical objections. Taking this theory to its logical extreme, they note that a good utilitarian would have to approve the death of a dozen babies in a medical experiment if the result would be a drug that could save millions of other babies. Similarly, utilitarianism would condone the killing of a few innocent passengers to save an airliner full of people from a hijacking, and it would support the exclusion from Western nations of all Iranian travelers because some might be terrorists—positions that would give grave discomfort to most moral thinkers.

2. Rule-Based Thinking

It is partly because of such objections that the second or *rule-based* principle has such appeal. Asking us to act on our highest sense of inner conscience, it seeks to base action on a maxim or precept that could be universalized. As a form of nonconsequentialism, it is described by philosophers as *deontological* (from the Greek word *deon,* meaning "duty" or "obligation"), since it asks not about the outcomes of an action but about our obligations in performing it. It is commonly associated with the name of Immanuel Kant (1724–1804), the German philosopher, and with his concept of the *categorical imperative.*

That phrase sounds more forbidding than it really is. It describes an imperative (or requirement) that our actions conform to certain large patterns—in other words, that they can be made into universal principles of action. "An action done from duty," Kant wrote, "has its moral worth, not in the purpose to be attained by it, but in the maxim in accordance with which it is to be decided upon." Moral worth, then, depends not on the final purpose of a course of action but on the "maxim" or ethical principle we've used to determine what to do. "What is essentially good in the action," he wrote, "consists in the mental disposition, let the consequences be what they may." For Kant, rightness or wrongness was never to be measured by "the realization of the object of an action" or "the results expected from it," but solely by "the conformity of actions to universal law as such."

So the categorical imperative, as Kant articulated it, is: "I ought never to act except in such a way that I can also will that my maxim should become a universal law." In other words, we should act in accordance with whatever law we would like everyone else in the world to follow in relevant circumstances. It calls upon us, that is, to imagine that by doing the thing we are about to do, we are establishing the type and creating the standard that we want all others to obey from now on. It is perhaps the fullest expression of the adage that we should always live and act according to our highest principles.

Critics of the rule-based approach argue that this guideline is impossibly strict. It commits us, they say, to the absurd rigidities we usually associate with the schoolmarm's refusal to let little Johnny undertake some tremendously creative project because "If I let you do it, I'd have to let everyone do it." To demand universalizability, they argue, is to overlook both the vast varieties of human individuality and the press of unique circumstances in an imperfect world. If we elevate promise-keeping to a universal maxim, what is a child to do when, having promised her dad to stay indoors while he's shopping, she sees that her puppy has broken its chain and is wandering close to the busy highway? Does she honor the promise and let the puppy get hit, or rush outside to save him? To this, of course, the rule-based thinker may well retort that the promise was exacted precisely because of such situations—so that the child, trying to save the puppy, would not also endanger herself. Thinking consequentially, she worries that the puppy may be injured. But her consequentialism may not have extended far enough to calculate the danger to herself—a problem her dad foresaw in asking her to obey the rule regardless of what might come up. Very well, say the critics: Then are you saying that the Kantian, for the sake of obeying a universalizable rule such as "Keep all promises," is willing to overlook an equally powerful rule that says "Prevent killing"? It is on this point of conflicting rules that such an approach is vulnerable.

3. Care-Based Thinking

But what if neither ends-based nor rule-based thinking seems right to us? If we seek something more than what one commentator describes as "the invasive do-gooding of utilitarianism" or "the coldness and severity toward normal human concerns of Kantian theory," where do we turn? The third principle, urging us to do to others what we want others to do to us, is widely known as the Golden Rule. We've called it the *care-based* principle, since unlike the first two it asks us to care enough about the others involved to put ourselves in their shoes. This rule, familiar to students of the Bible, is often thought of as a narrowly Christian dictum. To be sure, it appears in the book of Matthew: "All things whatsoever ye would that men should do to you, do ye even so to them: for this is the law and the prophets." But Jews find it in the Talmud, which says, "That which you hold as detestable, do not do to your neighbor. That is the whole law: the rest is but commentary." Or, as it appears in the teachings of Islam, "None of you is a believer if he does not desire for his brother that which he desires for himself."

Why is this rule "golden"? The word suggests its rank as the first and most valuable rule—"the law and the prophets," as Jesus said, or "the whole law" according to the Talmud. But the label "golden" was applied by Confucius (551–479 B.C.), who wrote, "Here certainly is the golden maxim: Do not do to others that which we do not want them to do to us." Similar formulations appear at the center of Hinduism, Buddhism, Taoism, Zoroastrianism, and the rest of the world's major religions. As philosopher Marcus G. Singer writes, the Golden Rule is "a principle of great antiquity" that has "played a key role in the moral teachings of nearly all cultures and religions and continues to play a key role in moral education." Until recently, however, it "did not receive much philosophical discussion, had been mentioned usually only in passing, and was discussed mainly in works of . . . moral theology."

The Golden Rule partakes of the criterion of reversibility. The test of the rightness or wrongness of an action is to imagine yourself as the *object* rather than the *agent* of that action and consult your own feelings as to the results. Whether the rule is expressed positively or negatively—prompting us to do what we want done to us, or to avoid doing what we don't want done—makes little difference. More important is the point, made by Augustine and others, that the Golden Rule not only sets limits on our actions but encourages us to promote the interests of others. In that sense, the rule is so commonplace as to be almost unavoidable in human experience. "To protest 'double standards'—arbitrary exception making, inconsistent application of judgments when persons and situations are relevantly similar,'' writes Yale University ethicist Gene Outka, and to "attempt to put oneself in another's shoes, to try to identify imaginatively with his or her narrative: when we perform these and similar exercises, we follow the Golden Rule." Even philosopher John Rawls's concept of the "veil of ignorance," a thought experiment designed to level the moral playing field, partakes of the reversibility criterion inherent in the Golden Rule (see box, below).

Critics of the Golden Rule—chief among them being Kant himself, who dismissed it in a famous footnote as "merely derivative of our principle"—protest that it is too simplistic to be a supreme moral principle. "It was never intended as a guide to practical choice independent of all other principles of conduct," writes Sissela Bok, adding that "it has nothing to say about specific choices, nor does it endorse particular moral principles, virtues or ideals." For example,

The Veil of Ignorance

Can there be such a thing as "impartial judgment"? Can ethical decision-makers take a point of view that is *general,* rather than specific to the self-interest of an individual or group? Many philosophers have thought so. Immanuel Kant talked about creating legislation in the "realm of ends." Jeremy Bentham, for all his emphasis on self-interest, noted the "interest of the community." Henry Sidgwick talked of making moral judgments from "the point of view of the universe."

But where does one stand to take that point of view? In a neatly devised thought experiment, Harvard University philosopher John Rawls constructs what he calls "the veil of ignorance" to ensure impartiality.

Imagine, he says, that decision-makers are "situated behind a veil of ignorance" in such a way that they have no idea how "the various alternatives will affect their own particular case." He does not insist that these decision-makers be ideal supermoralists, but imagines them to be completely self-interested. He also assumes them to be entirely rational. Finally, he grants them full access to general knowledge about contemporary society, economic theory, human psychology, political affairs, and so forth.

What they do *not* have, however, is knowledge of anything that might make them different from others. They are ignorant of their own class, social status, or wealth. They don't know their level of intelligence or strength, their aversion to risk, their optimism or pessimism. They know nothing of their own society. They don't even know the generation to which they belong. It is as though they had not yet been conceived, and could be born as any of the world's 5.5 billion humans.

So, as they choose principles upon which to make their decision, they can't take into account the consequences for themselves: They simply don't know who they are. What principles will they use for decision-making? The fairest and most impartial ones available—since any others might ultimately work against them, and since they don't know enough to be able to "tailor principles to [their] advantage."

Like the Golden Rule, Rawls's test is a form of what philosophers know as the "reversibility criterion." It asks us to assume the role of another and base our decisions on that perspective. Here, however, the "other" is purely hypothetical. Rawls's test holds particular value for policy-makers, who as they formulate regulations might well ask themselves, "Will this be fair to me wherever in the world I end up being born?"

---

the rule fails to give guidance in situations where both parties happen to like immoral things. It would approve, apparently, my bribing someone else with the understanding that, were I in his shoes, I would want to be bribed. The rule also produces some practical difficulty of determining the most relevant "other"—the one into whose shoes you wish to fit—whenever a number of players are involved each having different concerns and issues. It remains, nevertheless, a principle frequently and effectively applied to tough dilemmas by decision-makers everywhere—including participants in our seminars.

What happens when we apply these three principles to Fanning's example?

1. Ends-based. The utilitarian calculus begins by asking, "What's the greatest good?" For an editor committed to First Amendment rights and the Jeffersonian importance of the circulation of news, that "good" may well be the story itself. While a small number of people in Frank Reed's family may be well served by refusing to publish the story, the "greatest number" is probably the public. So the greatest good for the greatest number may demand that the public at large, rather than the Reed family, be the focus of attention. From this perspective, the consequences of publishing the story—sustaining the free flow of information, even when some of it is potentially damaging to individuals who may be innocent—probably outweigh the consequences of bowing to pressure and protecting, for the moment, an old friendship and a still-unindicted citizen.

2. Rule-based. Here the thinking process begins with a consideration not of consequences but of rules. What is the highest rule, we may ask, that should be followed here? What, moreover, is the rule that Fanning would like to see universally invoked? How would she like to see all other editors behave in similar circumstances? The rule may be, "Always publish the truth, and let the consequential chips fall where they may"—since, for many people, a world of universal truth-telling, while sometimes uncomfortable, is the healthiest and most sustainable of worlds. But the rule may be, "Always protect the innocent, and let the chips fall where they may"—a rule that, followed here, would lead Fanning to hold the story. Whichever the rule, one point is clear: This way of thinking focuses not on consequences but on the rule itself.

3. Care-based. When we consider doing to others as we would want them to do to us, we quickly recognize that there are several "others" here: The executive editor, the reporter, Frank Reed Jr. But the most compelling "other," for Fanning, is pretty clearly Frank Reed Sr. Putting herself in his shoes, she finds that she, too, could well be convinced of the son's innocence and long to shield him from harm. From this perspective, she may choose to set her sense of individual care and human concern above the other two principles. She could, of course, argue that if she were in his place she would want the newspaper to be tough and unswerving in its commitment to justice. But she would probably be more readily drawn to the argument that, in his shoes, she would want compassion, a listening ear, and a helping hand.

In the end, as Fanning recalls, her decision was apparently based on the second and third of these guidelines. Here's how she concludes her account:

> *A decision could be delayed no longer. "Hold the story," I said, reversing the executive editor. Daggers.*
>
> *My reasoning was simple: Was beating the competition enough reason to risk damaging someone's life and reputation? What public interest was really being served by printing this story before the indictment? It was bad luck that everyone knew I was emotionally indebted to Frank Reed Sr., but that was irrelevant to the principle involved.*
>
> *Would I have made the same decision if the father had been an unknown? I certainly hope so. Would I have taken so much heat? No.*
>
> *A week later Frank Reed Jr. was indicted for arson. This time, my luck was good. We got the story first.*

The highest principle she articulates, here, is that you don't damage someone's life simply to beat the competition. Consulting her motives for action, she recognizes that if the justification for publishing is largely to scoop the other newspaper, that's not good enough. She also sees the decision as one of timing. The question is not "Is this a valuable story?" but "Is this the time to publish it?" The tone of the decision very much reflects her personal and individual care for others—not (she hopes) based on the position of Frank Reed Sr. in the community, but on the common humanity she shares with her fellow citizens.

Applying the Principles: Four Examples

In ethics, as in the rest of life, there are no magic answer systems. The three modes of decision-making described here center on three moral principles. But they provide no detailed formulas for action: You don't stick in the dilemma at one end, turn the crank, and pick up your answer at the other. Indeed, no one expects moral principles to provide that sort of precision. Making ethical decisions depends on judgment, character, moral awareness, perception, discrimination—a whole host of imponderables.

But neither should one assume that those imponderables, if unguided by fundamental precepts and sporadic in their application, will lead to sound decision-making. The task of any sort of conscious reflection on moral choice—including the discussions in this book—is to make explicit what's often left unsaid, to help systematize the fragmentary and order the haphazard. If these three principles help us resolve the right-versus-right choices we face, it is only because they square reasonably well with our own intuitions about the moral life. They work, in other words, because we feel comfortable working with them.

To help bolster that comfort, let's turn to some of the dilemmas raised in earlier chapters and see how these principles apply. To save the necessity of page-turning, the relevant part of each narrative is reprinted here.

1. The Trooper's Dilemma

This case concerned an auto mechanic called to the scene of a wreck on a state highway in Ohio.

> *Arriving at the isolated, wooded spot, he could see immediately what had happened: A large flatbed truck had gone off the highway and hit a tree head-on. On impact, its load of steel had torn loose and slid forward through the back of the cab, pinning the driver helplessly inside. The cab was on fire, in danger of exploding at any minute.*
>
> *As he arrived, so did a state police car. And as the trooper ran to the open cab window, the mechanic could hear the driver inside screaming, "Shoot me! Shoot me!" It was obvious that the trooper could not lift off that load of steel and free the driver. So, with the flames growing in intensity, the trooper slowly removed his service revolver from his holster. Then he paused, reconsidered, and slid the revolver back into his holster. And then, amid the driver's screams, he removed it a second time, paused, and put it back once again.*
>
> *It was at that point in this agonized struggle that the mechanic saw the officer do a remarkable thing. Running back to his cruiser, he grabbed a small carbon tetrachloride fire extinguisher. It was hardly enough to quell the fire. But it was large enough to spray in the driver's face and put him to sleep, which is what he did.*
>
> *Shortly afterward, the cab exploded.*
>
> *(Chapter Three, pp. 57–58)*

The dilemma facing the trooper, it appears, is primarily of the short-term-versus-long-term variety. On one hand, it is right to relieve suffering in the short term—a position arguing for him to shoot the driver. On the other, it is right to preserve life in the long term—a stand that urges him never to kill another person, no matter what the circumstances. Seen this way, the dilemma also fits the justice-versus-mercy paradigm, with mercy urging him to put the driver out of his misery and justice requiring strict adherence to the laws prohibiting murder. Either way, the trooper has a tough choice to make—because he holds deeply felt core values that are directly in conflict.

From the narrative, we already know how it ends. And we know, too, that in the heat of the moment the trooper had no time to reflect on our three resolution principles. But we do. How, if we had been there, might we have advised him to act? That depends, in large part, on which of the principles seemed most compelling.

If we look at these circumstances from the ends-based, utilitarian point of view, we'll ask what's the greatest good for the greatest number. On first blush, there don't seem to be many numbers here: It's just the trooper and the driver on an isolated stretch of highway. So the "greatest number" may strike us as one—the driver alone. After all, the ends-based thinker will ask, what are his prospects for survival? The cab is on fire and could blow up any moment. And even if the trooper had the tools to extricate the driver, to try to do so would endanger his own life as well—raising the probability that the "greatest number" could suddenly become two, not one. If, then, the greatest number is indeed two, what is the greatest benefit? To save one is better than losing both. And to reduce the misery of the one who is probably going to be lost in any case is better than to prolong his agony. Utilitarianism, then, may well argue for shooting him—although the case could be made that the "greatest number" here is society at large, which will benefit in the long run by a "rule utilitarianism" that upholds the "never kill" dictum even though somebody (namely, the driver) has to suffer mightily for it.

To all of which the Kantian thinker strongly objects—on the grounds that the above arguments are pure consequentialism. Predicated on speculation, they assume as fact what can only be guessed—that the cab will indeed blow up, and that the driver must inevitably be killed. Since the trooper can never be certain of that (or any other) outcome, the rule-based thinker insists that he stick by the largest and safest precept he can—the one he would want every trooper, from now to eternity, to follow in such a situation. That precept may well be "Don't kill."

Such a position probably seems absurdly rigid and theoretical to the ends-based thinker, who feels so deeply the suffering of the driver. He understands that real situations have real results. "You want the trooper just to stand there," queries the utilitarian, "and watch the guy suffer the consequences?"

"Consequences!" retorts the Kantian. "Let me tell you about consequences. You've told the trooper to shoot him, and he's done so. And now, with the smoke still lingering in the gun-barrel and the sound of the shot still reverberating in the trees, he hears another sound: a siren. Within half a minute a fire truck has pulled up beside the wreck—how it got there he has no idea. In another half minute the fire is out. And there lies the driver dead, because the trooper shot him. So much for your silly little efforts of trying to foresee all possible consequences!"

These two guidelines, then, may well give us different answers. What guidance do we get from the Golden Rule? Here, the "other" is clearly the driver. If you were caught in the cab, what would you want a trooper to do to you? If you were pleading for him to shoot you, wouldn't that be pretty powerful evidence of what you want? Shouldn't the trooper respect your wishes?

Well, yes and no. Usually, such a request is fair evidence of one's deepest wishes. But this is clearly an extreme circumstance. Is the driver capable of thinking clearly? His plea, after all, has a strong streak of consequentialism about it: He cries out for this particular solution because, in his fear, he can see only one horrible outcome ahead. But should his plea be honored? Lifeguards understand that drowning swimmers will often strike out and attack their rescuers. Should lifeguards, therefore, interpret that behavior as a clear signal whose meaning is "Please leave me alone: I prefer to drown"? Hardly. They're taught to knock such persons out, if necessary, and drag them ashore against what seems to be their will. Should the trooper here assume that "Shoot me!" means what it says? And is that the interpretation he would most want another to put on his words if the situation were reversed?

Several points emerge from this discussion. First, the recorded outcome followed a course of action that defied the initial conception of the situation. It seemed to be a *di*-lemma, permitting only two outcomes: Either you reduce suffering by killing, or you refuse to kill.

The trooper here found a third way—a kind of middle ground through the extremes that reduced suffering without killing. How did he find it? Not, clearly, by a conscious process of rational discourse like the one we've just been through. But it may be significant that he took the time to agonize over the decision (as indicated by his withdrawing his gun and then returning it to his holster twice) before he acted. In that moment, it would seem, the alternative occurred. Out of the dilemma came (in a metaphor given currency by Ambassador Harlan Cleveland) a *trilemma*—a third way forward, a middle ground between two seemingly implacable alternatives.

Dilemmas don't always resolve themselves in this way. They often leave us with no option but to choose one or the other side. But sometimes a noble compromise emerges. That's especially true, I find, if we're willing to step back long enough from the issue to analyze the paradigms and apply the resolution principles. As we do so, we're more apt to uncover a way forward that we hadn't seen. The role of the resolution process, then, is not always to determine which of two courses to take. It is sometimes to let the mind work long enough to uncover a third.

The second point about the trooper's dilemma concerns his role as a law enforcement officer. The law of the land is clear: You don't kill. In a legal sense, then, the trooper has no option. He probably must refuse to kill under any circumstances, or risk jeopardizing his standing as an officer and, possibly, his career. But that's only in the legal sense. Ethics, as we noted earlier, goes well beyond the law and into "obedience to the unenforceable." Like all of us, the trooper has feelings. Like any of us, he may encounter circumstances where moral courage calls on him to take an ethical stand that is higher than the law allows. If the law is well crafted, these situations should be few and far between. But to suggest that the trooper in this case faced no ethical dilemma, but only a moral temptation to do the "wrong" thing, is to try to collapse all of ethics into the narrow confines of the law. It is to assume, in other words, that ethics and law are identical. To be sure, had the trooper killed the driver, he might well have been subject to strict *legal* proceedings. But would that make his action wrong? Or would we credit him with a moral heroism and praise him for acting up to his highest sense of conscience?

2. The Social Service Counselor

As a counselor on sexually transmitted diseases, May worked at a social service agency for women. One day she discovered that she herself had two such diseases.

Knowing she had no sexual relationships with anyone but her longtime companion, she reasoned that the diseases could only have come from him. Confronting him with her concerns, she accused him of transmitting the diseases to her—in effect charging him with promiscuity, since he could have contracted the diseases only through sexual relations with other women. He denied it adamantly, refusing even to submit to medical testing. She subsequently ended their relationship.

Some months later, a young woman May did not know came in for counseling after having contracted a sexually transmitted disease. In their discussion, the client revealed the name of her boyfriend. To May's astonishment, it turned out to be her own former boyfriend—a fact apparently unknown to the young woman.

May's dilemma: Does she maintain her professional demeanor and give no hint that she knows anything about the man? Or does she warn the young woman of what she knows?

(Chapter Five, pp. 125–126)

May's loyalty to her profession and its standards of objective counsel would argue against her revealing to the young woman her past relationship. But the truth of the matter, in her eyes, is that her former boyfriend is a potentially serious health threat to the young woman. For that reason, she should warn her. She most clearly faces a truth-versus-loyalty dilemma. In fact, other paradigms may apply as well. The self-versus-other paradigm makes it plain that May is balancing the needs of community safety against the etiquette of her profession: To tell the girl might protect the community against the further spread of disease, but to keep quiet would honor her own professionalism, thereby helping promote her career and certainly reducing her entanglements with what could become a sticky case. There's also a short-term-versus-long-term component: To tell the girl is to forestall an immediate threat of yet another case of disease, though it may undercut the agency's long-term credibility as an objective provider of counseling services.

The utilitarian, called upon to advise May, thinks about consequences. What will happen if she doesn't tell? The woman may well contract the remaining disease, which she may then spread to others in the community. Furthermore, if May's diseases should become public knowledge and could be traced back to her boyfriend—and if it were to become public that May knew of the boyfriend's relations with the young woman—it might look as though she had deliberately withheld information from the young woman as a form of revenge against her old boyfriend's new lover. Yet what will happen if she does tell? The young woman may think May is deliberately trying to scare her away from the boyfriend. If the client then blows the whistle, May's boss may well accuse her of an unwarranted personal intrusion into what should have been a thoroughly professional relationship. Given these consequences, the greatest good for the greatest number—if that number is the community at large—may be to tell the young woman. To be sure, that may cause damage, both to the emotions of the young woman and to May's career. But if one or two have to suffer for the good of the whole, so be it. That's where the "greater good" is served.

To the rule-based thinker, the above is a tissue of speculation. What's more, it's not particularly useful speculation: Predicting consequences, you can take either side with nearly equal force. Better far, then, to determine the rule you most want to see followed for all time by counselors in May's position. That rule is probably some version of "Save life." But what exactly does that mean in this case? Does it mean "Save the life of this young woman sitting in front of my desk right now"? If so, then May must tell. Or does it mean "Protect the ability of the social-service agency to save lives in the future"? That might cause you to put the credibility and long-term viability of the agency above the needs of any single individual.

In this case, the Golden Rule offers perhaps the clearest guidance. Putting herself in the young woman's shoes, May would no doubt want to be told the truth—especially if she could be assured that what she was hearing would indeed be motivated by the demands of integrity rather than the desire for revenge. And since May already knows herself to be truthful, she would want to be told the truth by someone in her position. The Golden Rule, then, will probably tell her that, regulations aside, she should care enough about the young woman to tell her what she should know.

Should it bother us that in several cases these guidelines produce no firm conclusions? Yes; but it's probably inevitable. Ethics is complex. It calls upon us to weigh judgments and exercise discretion. That may mean, in the end, that we have to choose between two different ways of making a choice. We may have to decide, in other words, which version of the ends-based or the rule-based thinking is the most acceptable.

As we do so, we naturally begin to investigate some third alternatives. In this case, for instance, an obvious one comes to mind: Let May excuse herself from this case and turn it over to another counselor. That would surely preserve the professionalism of the social service agency's relationship to the young woman. But would it help warn her of what she needs to know? Even here, there may be no way around it: May faces a tough choice, which can be resolved only in accordance with her highest moral decision-making.

3. The Loyal Employee

As head of a small liberal-arts college, Bill faced a dilemma of the self-versus-community variety.

> *Among the small staff of administrators with whom he worked closely was Maud, a single woman in the comptroller's office whose loyalty to the school knew no bounds. In twenty years of service, she had held a number of different positions. Yet she never quite proved suited to any of them. Big-hearted with her fellows and careful in her tasks, she was nevertheless a slow, deliberate worker unable to grasp the newer technologies and easily flustered by changes in routine. Bill had several conversations with her about her work, each ending in tears on her part. He knew that, six years away from retirement, she had little accumulated savings and no family. Her life seemed completely wrapped up in the school.*
>
> *Bill was also aware, however, that with increasing costs and a leveling of enrollments, he had to make adjustments to his staff. It was clear to all involved that Maud's work could be nearly eliminated by new computer equipment. It was also clear that there was no obvious position into which she could be moved, and that her salary was a significant drain on the budget. The requirements of the community made it plain that she should be released. The needs of the individual, however, urged Bill to keep her in place for another six years.*
>
> *(Chapter Six, p. 133)*

The good utilitarian, advising Bill, has little difficulty with this one. After all, the self-versus-community paradigm seems ready-made for an ends-based calculus focusing on lesser versus greater numbers. The good of the whole community, apparently, will be advanced by removing Maud's drain on resources. Yes, she is fiercely loyal. Yes, she should have been let go years earlier. Yes, it will be a hardship for her. But you cannot let the progress of the entire school be held hostage to the needs of a single individual. By its very nature, the greatest good for the greatest number implies that there are times when a few have to suffer.

To the good Kantian, that sounds a bit crass. "There you go again, thinking only of consequences," says this rule-based thinker. "How do you know that you won't find just the right niche for her where she'll shine? How do you know that the very quality she best expresses, loyalty, might not be just what you need in some position you have yet to establish—in alumni relations, for instance, or as a highly confidential administrator for the board of trustees? How do you know, in fact, that her rich uncle isn't just on the point of honoring your school with a massive gift in recognition of your years of caring for his favorite niece? Since you can't know consequences, don't try to guess at them. Stick to the rule."

But what rule? The answer, here, might be something as simple as one that Kant developed as his second formulation of the categorical imperative: "Act in such a way that you always treat humanity, whether in your own person or in the person of any other, never simply as a means, but always at the same time as an end." In other words, don't use people. Don't treat them merely as instruments toward some goal, but as the goal itself, with full attention to their dignity and humanity. If everyone always treated everyone else as ends, the Kantians ask, would that not produce the world we would most like to inhabit? To treat Maud as a means would be to measure her value only in terms of her ability to make a strong contribution to the school. As that contribution declined, so would her worth. And as the executive charged with maximizing worth, Bill would logically conclude that he should terminate her. But to treat her as an end—deserving love and respect, sympathy and nurture for no better reason than that she is human—Bill might conclude that he and the school had an obligation to her going well beyond any legal relationship. He might wish his predecessor had been honest with her about her future, given her a fixed term in which to adjust or depart, and helped set her up in a benefits plan that would ease her transition. But that didn't happen. So he now must treat her less as an employee and more as a member of the family.

Yet the rule-based thinker might also look on this from another perspective. Bill's job is to help the school prosper, in order that it may best serve its students and the world. The most applicable rule, then, may be "Always do what strengthens the team." But what is that? That may mean "Fire her, so that others can do better work." But it may mean "Keep her, thereby sending a signal to the entire community that this is the sort of school that cares deeply about its people."

Which, of course, is the argument that the care-based thinker will want Bill to make. Here, however, the identity of "the other" is problematic. Is Maud the one with whom Bill, as the actor in this dilemma, should imagine exchanging roles? Or is it someone else on his staff? If it's Maud, the answer is clear: Keep her on staff. But if it's someone else, isn't that person looking to Bill to provide leadership, strong management, and a courageous sense of direction? Doesn't the staff expect him to make the tough decisions that, however painful in the short term, will help them prosper in the long term? Will they accuse him of wimping out if he fails to let her go?

In several ways, this dilemma is different from the other two above. Hardly anyone comes across burning wrecks—especially with gun in hand. Relatively few have sexually transmitted diseases. But nearly everyone has encountered a situation where the person and the position simply don't fit. The resolution in such cases depends less on the terms of the immediate situation—is the truck burning? is this disease dangerous?—than on the long-term assessment of the character of the individuals involved. To resolve this dilemma properly you must know Maud—intimately, over many years, and with a rich depth of understanding of her attitudes, responses, strengths, and weaknesses. You must know her as you could never know her from a few paragraphs in the kind of case study provided here. The best we can do in a book of this sort is to sketch the outer limits of character. Real resolutions, by contrast, are built upon a rich inwardness of understanding—which is why, in our seminars, we ask participants to share with us dilemmas drawn from the full color of their own experience.

4. The Girls' Basketball Team

When his small public high school chalked up a winning season in girls' basketball, Allen was delighted. Now, ten months later, things looked even better to the principal: Four of last year's starters were back again as seniors this year.

> *But one November day, several weeks before the team was officially allowed to form and begin practices, these four girls left school at nine o'clock in the morning, walked downtown to a bar, got smashingly drunk, and returned to school in time to catch the buses home at 2:30. There was no hiding their condition. No sooner had they set foot in the building than the entire school erupted in controversy. Within minutes Allen's office was packed with faculty and staff in a frenzy of argument. One side insisted that the girls be suspended immediately, given significant detention when they returned, and kicked off the team—or, since there was no official team as yet, at least be prevented from playing on it once it convened. Justice, they said, must be done: These girls must be made clear examples to the student body.*
>
> *The other side called attention to the circumstances of the case, noting that to get drunk and* then to return to school *was a transparent cry for help. Wasn't Allen aware, they asked, of the miserable domestic conditions of these children, several of whom came from abusive homes where alcoholism was prominent? These kids did not need suspension and detention: They needed detox clinics and professional counseling. Mercy, they said, must take precedence here; if the school was to set an example, let it be an example of caring.*
>
> *Justice and mercy: Allen had to make the call, and he could not apparently satisfy both sides at once.*
>
> *(Chapter Six, p. 142)*

Suppose Allen is a scrupulous utilitarian. What will he do? The most relevant "greatest number," for him, is probably the school community—the students, faculty, staff, parents, and townspeople who follow basketball and love to feel good about their team. The greatest good for that community may well be to smooth over the infraction, find a way to let the girls play, and look toward an even better season than last year's. Might there be some adverse consequences? Yes, indeed. If the girls prove unrepentant and continue to be obstreperous, they might send a signal to younger students that such behavior is not a serious problem. They might also prove to be so full of themselves that, unlike last year, they don't coalesce into a team, refuse to take orders, and act like prima donnas. But those are uncertain consequences, to be weighed against the apparently unavoidable certainty that, without these four girls, the team will plummet to the basement of the standings. *If* the adverse consequences seem manageable, and *if* the girls are sufficiently repentant, and *if* the coach agrees, and *if* and *if* and *if* . . . then Allen may well let them play.

The Kantian may see it another way. Disentangling the argument from its consequentialist threads, she will point out that whatever Allen does must be what he wants every principal to do in similar circumstances from now on. Does he want rules to be followed or broken, she asks? The highest rule here, in fact, may be "Enforce the rules." If every principal took a tough-minded stand as a disciplinarian—tempered with mercy, of course, but nevertheless sending a clear signal that athletics and alcohol don't mix—the long-term health of interscholastic athletics would be greatly improved. What's more, if every principal put the educational and emotional needs of the students ahead of the entertainment needs of the sports-loving public, the entire culture of education would be benefited. Lose a season? Sure, if by doing so you save some students from a life of delinquency, alcoholism, and misery.

The Golden Rule, as usual, raises the question of the identity of "the others." The easiest role-reversal to imagine is with the students: If Allen were one of them, what would he want to have happen? On the surface, of course, all of us long to escape punishment. So part of the answer would have to be to mitigate the penalties for their actions. But at a deeper level, all of us long to live in a world where authority speaks firmly, protects the lives of the weaker, and cares enough to exercise a kind of tough-minded love. If those who saw this behavior as a transparent cry for help were right, the cry should be answered. The highest sense of the Golden Rule calls for Allen to do something that reforms and rehabilitates—though at the same time it may have to punish and restrict.

The Language of Ethics

There's a telling turn of phrase that shows up regularly in the above discussions. It centers on words like "perhaps," "probably," "possibly," "might," and "may." It creeps in just when the heart longs for a clear, definitive answer. And it always seems to float to the surface right when the moral principles are being translated into particular positions. Just as we're about to hear what resolution the utilitarians would advise, for instance, along comes the conditional: They might argue this way, or they could argue that way. If the greatest number is this group over here, then they should do *A*—although, if the greatest number is really that group over there, then *B* is the obvious course of action.

Is this really a process of resolution? Or is this just a fancy way of talking? Are we simply soaking our dilemmas in a verbal marinade—adding a new touch of flavor to the same old tough cut of meat? Or are we actually using language to penetrate the haze, spot the disjointed landmarks, identify the moral signposts, and bring the light of principled decision-making to bear on the question?

There is no question that language is capable of the latter. Nor is there any question that language, applied properly to ethical dilemmas, can guide toward morally consistent decision-making. But language itself is poised between two opposite demands: the need for precision, and the desire for expansiveness. And that in itself poses a dilemma. On the one hand, we want our words to be sharp, crisp markers, bearing one-for-one correspondences to the things of the world. We want such clarity of expression that no ambiguities remain, all shadows are banished or accounted for, and all meaning is fixed. On the other hand, we want our words to sing, to open avenues of uncharted thought in a world new-made for every inhabitant. We want words that don't so much *define*—which means "to limit" or "to set boundaries around"—as *narrate*, words rich with the storyteller's art, capturing the infinite nuances and fine-tunings of individual lives. We want a language through which meaning is not simply conveyed but created, in which characters stand up and take charge of their history and destiny, and relationships are as fluid and evocative as they are in everyday life.

What we need, then, are two sorts of language. The language we use to narrate our ethical dilemmas—the way we tell ourselves and others what's going on in the world—is not necessarily the language we use to analyze and resolve those dilemmas. The former tends to be flexible, subjective, artistic. The latter tends to be firm, objective, even scientific. Yet since what's under the microscope of this scientific language is itself a narrative—because we're trying to analyze the stories we tell each other—the resulting analysis tends to run to one of two extremes. At times, it can seem so fuzzy, amorphous, and slippery as to contribute little to our understanding. At other times, it can seem so rigid and buttoned-down that the understanding it conveys, while accurate, is hardly worth having.

In this, as in many of our ethical dilemmas, the most satisfactory way forward is along the ridge of middle ground between these peaks. There will be times when the analysis will seem unsatisfactory—when, say, a desire to adhere to the rule-based principle will throw up two opposing rules that could readily be universalized. There will be other times when the most reasonable avenue will seem puerile, stark, and indefensible—as when ends-based thinking leads us to conclude that we must kill *these* babies so that *those* can live. At those times we may be tempted to blame the decision-maker and find fault with ourselves—or to criticize the decision-making system for failing to hand us a clear-cut resolution. In fact, the problem lies in language itself. Ethics is, at bottom, a verbal activity. And words are not always as clear as we would like.

Yet it's only fair to note that, somewhere along this pathway of narration and analysis, resolutions begin to take shape. The more we work with these principles, the more they help us understand the world around us and come to terms with it. The metaphor is apt: We *come to terms* by finding the terminology, the discourse, that helps give meaning to our lives. What that meaning is, and how the terms illumine it, differs for each of us.

Little wonder, then, that there can be no formula for resolving dilemmas, no mechanical contraption of the intellect that churns out *the* answer.

Yet little wonder, too, that in the act of coming to terms with the tough choices, we find answers that not only clarify the issues and satisfy our need for meaning but strike us as satisfactory resolutions.

And little wonder, finally, that as we practice resolving dilemmas we find ethics to be less a goal than a pathway, less a destination than a trip, less an inoculation than a process.

Chapter Eight

"There's Only 'Ethics' . . ."

In 1958, in the infancy of the U.S. space program, a twenty-eight-year-old aerospace engineer named Ted Gordon was called into the office of his superior, J. L. (Jack) Bromberg. As chief project engineer for the Douglas Aircraft Company's Thor program, Bromberg was responsible for overseeing the flight tests for the air force's new sixty-two-foot-tall intermediate-range ballistic missile.

Bromberg had in mind no idle conversation. On October 4, 1957, the Soviets had launched *Sputnik I,* the first earth satellite. They followed in less than a month with *Sputnik II,* this time with a live dog in the payload. With those launches, the Soviet Union had leapfrogged into apparent technological supremacy in the race into space—and shamed the American research and educational establishment into a wholesale reexamination of its goals and outcomes. More important, however, the Soviets had sent tremors throughout the U.S. military and political establishments. Soviet premier Nikita Khrushchev's threat that the grandchildren of Americans would live under communism was taken with frigid sincerity. The Soviets were known to have an atomic bomb, making them a major threat both to the Western nations and to the newly created third-world countries that had recently spun loose from decades of European colonialism. The Soviet alliance with China, cemented eight years earlier, meant that communism now stretched from the Adriatic to the Bering Straits and down to the China Sea. The Korean War, which cost the lives of thirty-four thousand American military personnel, had already demonstrated the expansionist intentions of the Communists. Now they seemed intent on expanding into space as well. In that turbulent hour, Western military power was inextricably linked to U.S. economic supremacy, which in turn depended on technological success. And the showpiece of U.S. technology was the budding space program.

By 1958, the nation was supporting two parallel space efforts. One, headed by Dr. Wernher von Braun, focused on the Redstone missile developed by the army's Ballistic Missile Agency—the group that, on January 31, 1958, put the first U.S. satellite into orbit from Cape Canaveral, Florida. The other, centered on the Thor, was an air force enterprise. It was here that Bromberg and his young protégé found themselves in stiff competition not only with the Soviets but with the army. So far, the record was not good. Bromberg, whom Gordon once described as "a hard-driving taskmaster who accepts no alibis, no excuses, no reasons why a task is not completed on time," was nicknamed "Thorhead" by his team. As head of the program, he had overseen the first three launches of the Thor Intermediate Range Ballistic Missile (ICBM). To his dismay, every one of them failed for technical reasons, some crashing on the launchpad. In a mixture of desperation and hope, he turned to young Gordon with an unprecedented opportunity: to write the countdown for the upcoming launches, and to become test conductor for the Thor program at Cape Canaveral.

Writing the countdown, as Gordon recounts it, was no simple task. Each launch of a Thor required that some three hundred thousand parts all function perfectly at the proper time. Thousands of parameters needed to be taken into account, involving hundreds of precisely calibrated actions by scores of engineers and mechanics. Each had to be done exactly right, and in just the proper sequence. Missiles, as Gordon recalled in his book *First into Outer Space*, are "vastly complex, and this complexity is occasionally their undoing. Each system must work, each component part must function when commanded. A missile flight seldom fails because of a basic inadequacy in design; usually a two-bit part fails, a seemingly insignificant link in a basically strong chain."

So all the two-bit parts are tested and retested—right up to the final ignition. Among the last tests to be performed, with less than a half-hour to go, was one involving a switch located on the back end of the missile as it sat upright on its pad. The switch, set to operate the moment the missile lifted off, locked open all the valves that allowed fuel to reach the engines. It was secured by a pin preventing it from opening prematurely, a pin that was to be removed by hand in the final minutes of the countdown. But before the pin was removed, the switch was to be checked electrically to make sure it was not faulty.

Gordon, who is now the retired chairman of the Futures Group and one of the world's leading futurists, recalls that day vividly. A multistage Thor was on the launchpad. He was in the cramped concrete blockhouse when, to his horror, he saw the control panel light up, signaling that the first-stage main oxygen and fuel valves had suddenly opened. That meant that kerosene and liquid oxygen were being fed into the rocket's combustion chamber, where they formed a volatile and extremely explosive mixture. The mixture, having nowhere else to go, gushed out of the chamber and dropped to the steel exhaust-deflector plate on the launchpad many feet below. The mechanics and engineers working on the pad scattered in every direction. They knew what could happen: They had already seen rockets on the launchpad engulfed in orange balls of fire and melting down into white-hot wreckage. They were literally running for their lives, fleeing the holocaust that an accidental spark or electrical shock could ignite.

The spark never came. The oxygen warmed up and evaporated, and the potential inferno reduced itself to an oily but essentially harmless mess. Later, Gordon and his colleagues pieced together what had happened. The mechanic in charge of testing the fuel switch, it seems, had simply reversed the procedure specified in the countdown. He pulled the pin first, and then tried to do the test. That test tripped the switch, sending up the message that the rocket had left the pad, opening wide the valves for the launch and showering the pad with tens of thousands of pounds of fuel and oxygen.

What to do now? The launch was scrubbed, but the rocket could be refueled and the launch rescheduled without great difficulty. No lives had been lost; no one had even been injured. Yet the potential for disaster had been enormous. Had there been a spark, the explosion would have been catastrophic—not only in lives lost, but in damage done to the morale, public approval, and congressional support for the budding space program. Had there been a spark, there might very possibly have been no more Thor or Jupiter launches, no continued enthusiasm for the National Aeronautics and Space Administration (NASA), and no landing of U.S. astronaut Neil Armstrong on the moon in 1969. In the absence of that spark, one question remained: What to do about the mechanic in whose hands the whole future of the nation's space program might have been placed?

As the launch team sat around the blockhouse, Gordon recalls, smoking their ever-present cigars and waiting a half-hour for the liquid oxygen to boil off the pad, opinions flew thick and fast. Fire him immediately, someone said. Suspend him with stiff penalties, said someone else. Transfer him to something less dangerous, said another. Above all, they agreed, just get him out of here. There was apparently no dilemma involved. He had done wrong. The only question was how, not whether, to punish him.

To all of which Gordon listened, until the time came for him to deliver his opinion—an opinion that created a dilemma where none had seemed to exist.

"There's one thing we know about him for sure," Gordon recalls saying. "He'll never, ever, as long as he lives, do anything like that again. Maybe he'll become our most reliable mechanic. Maybe we shouldn't fire him. Maybe we should *promote* him!"

In the end, Gordon recalls, that's what happened. The Thor tests went forward as planned, the U.S. space program flourished, and it was not a Soviet but an American crew that reached the moon. And never again did that mechanic blow a countdown.

Nine Checkpoints for Ethical Decision-Making

The American poet E. E. Cummings, writing about the sculptor Gaston Lachaise in the 1920s, coined a phrase that in many ways describes not only aesthetic but ethical processes. Lachaise, he wrote, exhibited "intelligence functioning at intuitional velocity."

It's an apt characterization for ethical decision-making. As Gordon's dilemma suggests, ethical issues can arise in the least suspecting moments. Just when everything seems to be progressing with utmost order, something can come along and deliver potentially deadly blows before we've even begun to grasp their significance. To grapple with them requires rational acts of the mind. But the mind is often called upon to operate without a full understanding of causation, with only

The Prisoner's Dilemma

Why be moral? One of the most common answers comes from the rationalist perspective. It argues that reason, assessing arguments for and against morality, will inevitably conclude that immorality is irrational.

But morality is a complex topic—nowhere more so than in tough conundrums concerning one's own future. One such conundrum, rooted in a 1950 lecture on game theory given by distinguished Princeton mathematician Albert W. Tucker, seeks to show that reason and morality may not coincide.

The hypothetical case, widely cited in decision-making literature, centers on two prisoners accused of conspiring against the state. They are hauled before a judge, who points out that each has two alternatives: to confess, or not to confess. The judge, in a plea-bargaining arrangement, lays out the deal:

- If one confesses and the other does not, the confessor will be released and the nonconfessor will be imprisoned for ten years.
- If both confess, both go to prison for five years.
- If neither confesses, both go to prison for a year.

Suppose they agree not to confess. They are sentenced to one year each. But why, then, would not one of them confess at that point—setting himself free, though plunging the other into ten years' incarceration? Since that temptation is strong on both sides, however, why wouldn't the other also confess—thereby reducing his ten-year sentence to five? In other words, would it not be in the interests of each to confess if he had the slightest suspicion that the other was going to do so?

But suppose they could confess in secret. They may have made a solemn pact with one another never to confess. But isn't it still to the rational advantage of each to confess? And if so, must not each prisoner strongly suspect that the other will do so?

The dilemma? On one hand, it is right to keep one's word. On the other, it is right to maximize one's freedom from imprisonment.

Furthermore, it is only by adhering to the promises made in their don't-confess agreement that each can be sure of serving less than five years.

Yet if rationality is the only basis for ethical choice—and that's a very large "if"—neither will adhere to those promises. By behaving unethically and breaking promises, they enter a crapshoot that might set them free but might make things worse. Yet to behave ethically and keep their word guarantees that there will be some minimal punishment all around.

Tough choice? Indeed—if rationality is the only standard. It is on this question of sacrificing self-interest—even enduring some "irrational" hardship for the sake of the general good—that so much of ethics turns.

a hint of possible consequences, and with little room for reflection. If sound decisions are to be made, the intelligence truly must function at "intuitional velocity."

That does not mean, however, that there is no logical and sequential process for ethical decision-making. True, we may not be aware that a pattern exists. That does not mean there is no pattern. We're surrounded, in fact, by evidence of highly patterned processes that happen at intuitional speed. The jazz pianist improvising in an up-tempo riff is not mentally saying, "Now I must move to a D-seventh chord, since I've just come from an A-minor-seventh." But that's exactly where she's moving. Neither does the pitcher, whirling to fire to first base and stop a would-be steal, consciously calculate angle, distance, speed, and torque before hurling the ball. Yet all those parameters have been factored into his throw. Developing real skill at jazz or baseball—or ethics—requires that intelligence fuse with intuition, that the processes be internalized, and that decisions be made quickly, authoritatively, and naturally. For musician, athlete, and moral thinker, making good decisions usually requires a patient investment in process—and plenty of practice.

So far, this book has provided opportunities for such practice by laying out a number of examples, along with a good deal of commentary on ethical thinking. It's time now to wrap these threads together into a coherent process—not necessarily as a checklist to be applied in the heat of the moment, but as a guide to the underlying structure of ethical decision-making. The following nine steps, or checkpoints, suggest an orderly sequence for dealing with the admittedly disorderly and sometimes downright confusing domain of ethical issues.

1. Recognize that there *is* a moral issue. This step is vitally important for two reasons. First, it requires us to identify issues needing attention, rather than to brush past them without another look. Second, it requires us to sift genuinely moral questions from those that merely involve manners and social conventions—or that take us into realms of conflicting values that are not so much moral as economic, technological, or aesthetic. This recognition is not always easy. Nor is it without danger. Too much diligence here can turn us into self-righteous hypermoralists sensing sin at every turn. Yet too little can lead us into an apathy or a cynicism that breezily dismisses even the most compelling ethical challenge.

2. Determine the actor. If this is a moral issue, whose is it? Is it mine? The operative distinction here is not whether or not I am *involved.* In matters of ethics, we're all involved. Why? Because we all live within a context of community, and communities depend on ethical interrelations. Reminding us that "no man is an island, entire of itself," John Donne instructed us never to "send to know for whom the bell tolls; it tolls for thee." So the question is not whether I am *involved* but whether I am *responsible*—whether I am morally obligated and empowered to do anything in the face of the moral issues raised. Warning: In some formulations of ethical decision-making, this determination of actors includes a determination of stakeholders. The problem with stakeholder analysis, however, is that the very assumption that there are "stakes" in a dilemma implies an outcome-oriented mode of thinking. Those who venture into such analysis are typically so predisposed to an ends-based utilitarianism that they overlook other ethical principles. That severely limits their options. Rule-based thinkers, after all, couldn't care less about "stakes," since what's at issue is obedience to a fundamental principle so universal that it operates equally for everyone. Both Kantians and utilitarians, however, need to know the actor.

3. Gather the relevant facts. Good decision-making requires good reporting. That is especially true in making ethical decisions.

Not to know the way events have unfolded, what finally happened, what else might have happened, who said what to whom, who may have suppressed information, or who was culpably ignorant or innocently unaware—not to know these things leaves crucial voids in the understanding. Why? Because ethics does not happen in a theoretical vacuum but in the push and pull of real experience, where details determine motives and character is reflected in context. Also important to fact-gathering is an assessment of future potential: Robert Frost, in his famous decision-making poem about the two roads that "diverged in a yellow wood," notes that before deciding which way to go he "looked down one as far as I could" until it disappeared "in the undergrowth." Part of fact-gathering involves just that kind of peering as far as possible into the future.

4. Test for right-versus-wrong issues. Does the case at hand involve wrongdoing? Here various tests apply. The *legal test* asks whether lawbreaking is involved. If the answer is an obvious "yes," the issue is one of obedience to the enforceable laws of the land, as opposed to the unenforceable canons of a moral code. The choice, in that case, is not between two right actions but between right and wrong—a legal rather than moral matter.

If the answer to the legal test is less obviously "yes," three other tests are useful:

• The *stench test*, relying on moral intuition, is a gut-level determination. Does this course of action have about it an indefinable odor of corruption that makes you (and perhaps others) recoil and look askance? The stench test really asks whether this action goes against the grain of your moral principles—even though you can't quite put your finger on the problem. For many people, it's a common and surprisingly reliable indicator of right-versus-wrong issues.

• The *front-page test* asks, "How would you feel if what you are about to do showed up tomorrow morning on the front pages of the nation's newspapers?" What would be your response, in other words, if what you took to be a private matter were suddenly to become entirely public? If such a consequence makes you uncomfortable, you had best not do it.

• The *Mom test* asks, "If I were my mother, would I do this?" The focus here is not only on your mother, of course, but on any moral exemplar who cares deeply about you and means a lot to you.

If putting yourself in that person's shoes makes you uneasy, think again about what you're on the verge of doing: It could well be wrong.

It may be worth noting here that the latter three tests align themselves with our three decision-making principles. The stench test is at bottom a form of rule-based reasoning, asking not about consequences but about visceral principles. The front-page test, by contrast, is a form of ends-based reasoning that looks to outcomes: Only if people know what I'm doing (it seems to assume) will there be any consequences, and consequences are what matter. The Mom test, requiring care-based reasoning, is a form of the Golden Rule that asks you to put yourself in the shoes of another—in this case, a person of high moral stature—to determine the rightness or wrongness of an action.

If an issue fails these tests, there's no point going on to the following steps. Since you're dealing with a right-versus-wrong issue, any further elaboration of the process will probably amount to little more than an effort to justify an unconscionable act.

5. Test for right-versus-right paradigms. If the issue at hand passes the right-wrong tests, the next question is, What sort of dilemma is this? Try analyzing it in terms of the four dilemma paradigms: truth versus loyalty, self versus community, short-term versus long-term, and justice versus mercy. The point of identifying the paradigm, remember, is not simply to classify the issue but to bring sharply into focus the fact that it is indeed a genuine dilemma, in that it pits two deeply held core values against each other.

6. Apply the resolution principles. Once the choice between the two sides is clearly articulated, the three resolution principles can be brought to bear: the ends-based or utilitarian principle; the rule-based or Kantian principle; and the care-based principle based on the Golden Rule. The goal, remember, is not to arrive at a resolution based on a three-to-nothing or two-against-one vote. Instead, it is to locate the line of reasoning that seems most relevant and persuasive to the issue at hand.

7. Investigate the "trilemma" options. This step, listed here for convenience, can kick into action at any point throughout this process. Is there, it asks, a third way through this dilemma? Sometimes that middle ground will be the result of a compromise between the two rights, partaking of each side's expansiveness and surrendering a little of each side's rigidity. Sometimes, however, it will be an unforeseen and highly creative course of action that comes to light in the heat of the struggle for resolution.

8. Make the decision. This step, surprisingly, is sometimes overlooked. Perhaps that's because the intellectual wrestling required in the previous steps can seem exhaustive, leaving little energy for the final decision. Or perhaps it's that a quasi-academic mind-set comes into play, confusing analysis with action and failing to move from the theoretical to the practical. Whatever the reason, one thing is clear: At this point in the process, there's little to do but decide. That requires moral courage—an attribute essential to leadership and one that, along with reason, distinguishes humanity most sharply from the animal world. Little wonder, then, that the exercise of ethical decision-making is often seen as the highest fulfillment of the human condition.

9. Revisit and reflect on the decision. When the tumult and shouting have died and the case is more or less closed, go back over the decision-making process and seek its lessons. This sort of feedback loop builds expertise, helps adjust the moral compass, and provides new examples for moral discourse and discussion.

When we test Ted Gordon's dilemma against these nine checkpoints, what do we find?

First, Gordon knew there was a moral issue here. Indeed, his colleagues were shouting it out to him from all sides: Something terribly wrong had been done (however innocently) and restitution had to be made. There was no way, apparently, that he could walk away from the decision-making process.

Second, it was apparent that Gordon was the actor: He was in charge, and the issue truly was his.

Third, the facts were apparent by the time Gordon gathered his team to discuss the fate of the mechanic. Notice, however, how vital those facts were to the decision. Suppose the mechanic had blown the countdown because his foot had slipped just as he was pulling the pin—the result of a blob of grease left behind by another careless team member. Suppose the countdown itself had been wrongly written or inaccurately typed. Suppose the fuel had started to gush *before* he had pulled the pin—evidence of a failure elsewhere in the system. Any such mitigating factor would have significantly altered the discussion in the blockhouse. And, of course, suppose there had been a spark. Suppose lives had been lost, the rocket destroyed, the nation's space program aborted. Could Gordon have argued as easily that the mechanic should be retained?

Fourth, there was plenty of wrong done here. But Gordon himself was not facing a right-versus-wrong choice. There was no *legal* requirement that the mechanic be disciplined. Nor was there any notable stench, any fear of publicity, or any concern about Mom. This was, for Gordon, a right-versus-right issue.

Fifth, the paradigm that most seems to fit here is justice versus mercy. The voices surrounding Gordon were howling for justice—and in many ways they were right. He chose mercy—also right.

Sixth, from what we know of the reasoning at the time, Gordon seems to have placed strongest emphasis on the ends-based resolution rule. What mattered to him were the consequences. How would this employee behave in the future? Gordon thought he could tell and based his decision on that assessment, which in the end proved right. He did not, apparently, reason that he would not want to be fired if he had made such a mistake (a care-based approach), nor that the potential danger was so great that discipline should be enforced regardless of the fact that no explosion occurred (a rule-based approach).

Seventh, this outcome reflects a decision based on one side of the dilemma—clearly in support of mercy—rather than a "trilemma" compromise down the middle. It could have been the latter, of course: Gordon might well have agreed to keep the employee on, but to penalize him severely while doing so.

Eighth, a decision was actually taken. The discussion in the blockhouse was no idle chatter. It led to action.

Ninth, through the years the decision has given grounds for reflection—so much so that, thirty-five years later, it surfaced in one of our seminars as a key experience in Gordon's own personal history. We don't know, from the narrative given here, the extent to which it stood out in the lives of the others involved at Cape Canaveral or found itself woven into the culture of space-program lore as a point of commentary. It is probably fair to say, however, that it has been the subject of some revisiting by at least one person other than Gordon: the mechanic who, the next day, still had his job on the launch team.

Public and Private Ethics: Distinctions Without Differences

The nine steps listed here, then, clearly apply to dilemmas raised in aerospace engineering. But are they relevant elsewhere? Indeed they are. They apply to:

- the doctor trying to help a family decide whether or not to use heroic procedures to save an aging parent;
- the teacher pressured by worried parents to divulge something their son has told her more or less in confidence;
- the editor deciding whether to print a story written by a journalist who gathered information by posing as a prostitute;
- the laboratory chemist who realizes that her line of research, if carried to its logical conclusion and widely publicized, could cost millions of dollars in lost sales for some sector of the nation's farming and food-processing operations;
- the public official weighing the merits of a policy that benefits the entire nation but costs jobs in his district;
- the student whose best friend confesses he is on drugs but swears her to secrecy.

The list of possible actors and potential dilemmas, in fact, is as endless as human inventiveness and as relevant as tomorrow's headlines. Yet in each case the dilemmas lend themselves to the same process of discussion and analysis. Why? Because at bottom there is no such thing as "aerospace engineering ethics" that can be distinguished in any significant way from "medical ethics," "education ethics," "journalism ethics," or ethics in any other field.

This point may not be as obvious as it should be. A great deal has been made of the different flavors of professional ethics. We're tempted to think that each discipline, profession, and avocation has its own set of moral principles, its own unique ways of thinking about ethical dilemmas, its own patented resolutions. True, each specialty has issues unique to its field. There's as little reason for real estate agents to think hard about the ethics of cloning, for example, as there is for genetic researchers to be concerned about making up-market homes available to minorities. But when you strip away the specifics and penetrate to the core values underlying these dilemmas, the resulting ethical structures lend themselves to just the sort of analysis and resolution developed here.

That fact is important for two reasons. First, it helps deflate a subtle form of ethical relativism that insists that all ethics flows out of, and is bounded by, the situational specifics of a particular case. Such a view starts by saying, "Different professions, different ethics." Carried to its extreme, it insists that you and I have divergent ethical standards simply because we are individuals—"Different *people*, different ethics." Such a thesis, refusing to acknowledge any common ground of shared values, guts the potential for building consensus on any basis but fear, ignorance, or malice. Second, the fact that there's only ethics removes a divide. It helps dispel the notion that *public* ethics is fundamentally different from *private* ethics, and that the way an individual behaves and makes decisions in one of those arenas has no real relevance to what he or she does in the other.

This public/private discussion has a long history. Socrates insisted that the two realms were essentially separate. For him, only the individual who remains in private life can remain fully principled, since public life demands compromises that make true morality impossible. Following a similar line, the American writer Henry David Thoreau argued that since one's private conscience could be the only reputable guide to behavior, any involvement with public life would inevitably erode the moral sense. "The only obligation which I have a right to assume is to do at any time what I think right," he wrote—a view that naturally led him to scorn any public or political "obligation" that would compel him to act against his conscience. Even the English philosopher Thomas Hobbes, taking an opposing road, arrived at much the same destination. He argued that individuals in public positions who allowed private morality to influence their decision-making were in fact doing a disservice to the political sphere. Such an individual, Hobbes felt, had agreed to be subject to a public morality; to pursue the interests of a private set of values would be to violate that agreement. For Socrates, Thoreau, and Hobbes, the old distinction between public and private morality was a very real one.

Recently, however, this distinction has frayed. Some of the shredding comes from feminist philosophers, who point out that this view compounds the problem of abuse against women, especially rape and violence occurring in the home. Until quite recently, such abuse has often been written off as a private matter of no real relevance to the public world—a view that, of course, depends on the recognition that public and private are distinct. In the world of business, too, the public/private split can seem artificial. "There's only 'ethics,' " says James K. Baker, chairman of Arvin Industries, a Fortune 500 manufacturer located in Columbus, Indiana, and former president of the U.S. Chamber of Commerce. "What you do over here is no different from what you do over there. Let's not think that you've got to adhere to one standard at home and another standard at work. There's only one thing."

The distinction also comes to grief on the shoals of common sense. Few people, these days, are under the illusion that an employee who is unethical in personal financial matters is likely to be thoroughly principled at work, or that a corporate executive can be a cad in family matters and a paragon of virtue in the office. This very issue, in fact, was tested in 1987 during the presidential campaign in the United States when candidate Gary Hart, a married man, asserted that his dalliances with Miami model Donna Rice were irrelevant to his public life and should be of no concern to the public. The public and the press—particularly *The Miami Herald*, which broke the story—thought otherwise. That attitude marked a clear shift from the 1960s, when the widely observed extramarital affairs of President John F. Kennedy were scrupulously suppressed by news editors. These days, few candidates find cover behind the public-private distinction. Ethics is increasingly seen to be woven into a seamless whole, as the public grows more insistent that one's public and private lives must fuse into a morally consistent entity.

Moral consistency, in fact, is an effective test for ethical action—a point illustrated in our seminars by Bill, a recently retired former senior executive for a major manufacturing corporation in the United States. During the peak years of the Vietnam War, he found himself working for a company that, among its many products, supplied matériel for the armed forces. Because it was a good job in an area of work he very much enjoyed, he did not spend much time dwelling on the military aspects of the corporation.

But in the 1968 presidential campaign, he found himself attracted to Democratic candidate Eugene McCarthy, the senator from Minnesota who staked out a strong antiwar position. When a friend asked Bill if he would volunteer an evening's time at the local campaign headquarters, he agreed. One thing led to another, however, and before long he found himself cast as the leading spokesman for the campaign in his community, quoted in the newspapers and clearly identified with McCarthy's positions.

One day, a few months before the Democratic convention in Chicago, his boss called Bill into his office. The topic for discussion: Bill's political activities. The corporation, with a staunchly conservative bent and a long tradition of support for the nation's military, was uncomfortable. It was awkward, Bill's boss said, having one of its senior people take such an outspoken role against what appeared to be the interests of the corporation and, in its view, of the nation. Might Bill want to consider scaling back the level of his political activities?

Sobered, Bill talked it over with his wife. The dilemma was clear: Should he stick with his political activities or with his job? In fairness, he realized, the corporation had not made the dilemma quite so explicit: There was no threat to fire or demote him. There was just an expression of discomfort—although, Bill felt, the possible consequences could be read between the lines. In discussing the situation at home, the usual issues arose: the children's schooling, the mortgage on the house, the difficulty in finding a comparable job. One side argued strongly for the freedom of political expression—the right, guaranteed by all that the nation stood for, to express dissent openly and honestly without fear of reprisal. The other side argued strongly for corporate allegiance—the need, felt by any organization, for a sense of unity and common purpose around an agreed-upon set of objectives. Furthermore, one side argued for the unfettered individual conscience, while the other argued for the compromises that produced a salary and helped make family life pleasant and affordable.

Given the nine steps set forth above, it's clear that Bill was aware of the moral issue (step 1). It's also clear that he was the actor (step 2). Did he know enough (step 3) to make the decision? He thought he did, especially since he felt he could see through the conversation with his boss to a deeper but unspoken threat. Nor was he placed in a right-wrong issue (step 4), since there was nothing inherently bad about his political activities. The most appropriate dilemma paradigms (step 5), as he explained them during our seminar, were truth versus loyalty (his need to stand up for what he thought was "true" about the nation's role in the war versus his allegiance to his corporation) and self versus community (his own need to retain his job and support his family versus the corporation's need for unity and commitment).

The resolution (step 6) involved some deep thinking—which, even though Bill was not then using the exact terms we've used here, probably followed similar lines of reasoning. Ends-based, utilitarian thinking might well have argued that the "greatest number" here was not himself and his own political conscience but his family—in which case he would have abandoned the campaign. Or it could have argued that the corporation was the greatest number—also leading him to give up McCarthy's quest. But it also might have argued that the nation as a whole superseded either his family or the corporation, leading him to stay with his campaign. The rule-based approach, by contrast, would have looked for overarching maxims, which could have ranged all the way from "Don't bite the hand that feeds you" (urging him to align himself with the corporation) to "Follow your conscience" (demanding that he stay with the campaign). Under the care-based reasoning of the Golden Rule, Bill might have leaned toward the views of his boss by putting himself in the corporation's shoes. But he could also have asked, "What kind of 'others' do I wish to live with in this society? Do I most want others to get involved in the activities of a civil society? Or do I most want them to mind their own business and leave public affairs to others?" Under that logic, he would probably have chosen the campaign over the corporation.

Was there (step 7) a trilemma option here? Bill didn't see one. So his decision (step 8) was simply to persist in his political work—knowing that, as the convention approached, he would be even more visible than before.

In the end, Bill chose to continue working with the campaign. As he revisited his decision (step 9) several decades later, he told us he felt it had been the right one. He heard nothing further from the boss. McCarthy lost the election. And Bill remained happily employed by that corporation until he moved to another firm eight years later.

Bill's dilemma may not strike some readers as a genuine moral problem. It may seem right from the outset that the only ethical resolution would be to do what he ultimately did—phrased as "taking a stand for principle" or "following the dictates of conscience" or "doing what you've got to do." After all, if this had been a novel or a film, it would probably have been cast as the morally courageous lead character, Bill, standing up to the big, bad, faceless corporation. We're so accustomed to seeing that stereotype, in fact, that we tend to overlook some of the important step-three pieces of information. Bill liked his job. He liked his colleagues. He approved of most of what the corporation did. He believed in paying his bills, providing security for his family, and contributing to his community as a prosperous, taxpaying citizen. Only as we cut through the stereotype and let these facts speak do we see this as a real dilemma.

Yet the very fact that we cheer on Bill in his quest for individual expression suggests an important point. All of us place a high value on this thing called moral consistency. We expect that the "right" resolution, here, will be one that aligns Bill's life as a public citizen with his life as an employee and a family man. We expect his values to be the same in each sphere. Had he chosen not to pursue the campaign, we would have been tempted to say he "buckled under pressure." Had he done that, the word *hypocrisy* might have come to mind to describe Bill's willingness to hold one set of personal views (against the war) while working for a firm that publicly (as a military supplier) espoused another. What we applaud in Bill's choice is moral consistency—a clear congruence between the actions and the values.

Nowhere, apparently, do we applaud that congruence more loudly than when the consistency bridges the apparent gap between public and private ethics. The truly consistent individual, the one who generally wins our highest praise as an exemplar of virtue, is the one whose actions in public and in private are morally identical. In theory, we may appreciate the distinction between public and private ethics. In practice, we not only merge the two but tend to hold in some suspicion those who don't. That's not to say that those around us—or even we ourselves—always act up to this level of moral consistency. It's simply to say that we intuitively seem to recognize that, when public and private ethics diverge, something is morally amiss.

Condoms, Communists, and Conservation: Three Public Issues

So far, we've considered dilemmas that have arisen largely in the private realm. Can this process help us make sense of dilemmas that lie squarely in the public sphere—those that affect the entire nation or the entire world, but in which we may be "actors" only by virtue of being citizens? Yes. To see how, consider three contemporary issues that are rooted in today's news but have ramifications well into the twenty-first century: the condoms-in-the-schools controversy, the post-Communist world order, and the environment-versus-development tension.

Ethics, AIDS, and safe sex

When U.S. basketball superstar Magic Johnson announced on November 7, 1991, that he was HIV positive, he recharged the debate over "safe sex." Earlier that year, when New York City adopted a plan to distribute condoms to students to help prevent the spread of AIDS, the ensuing political surf swept away the city's schools chancellor, Joseph A. Fernandez, who was voted out of office by the city's board of education. So when in 1993 the New Haven, Connecticut, public schools voted to distribute condoms to fifth-graders, the debate intensified. With AIDS in that city a leading cause of death among men and women aged twenty-five to forty-four, some school board members felt they had to act. Not surprisingly, they couched their actions in moral terms. "If there is anything that you can do to prevent [such deaths], then it is your moral obligation to do so," school board chair Patricia McCann-Vissepo told *The New York Times* after the vote. The opposition, too, took a moral stand. Board member Arthur J. Bosley, Jr., who voted against the policy, worried that condom distribution "can and will send a message [to students] that we are sanctioning their [sexual] activities."

Like all significant ethical debates, this one features two core values in opposition. On one side stands respect for life, emphasizing that you don't kill and that you help prevent others from being killed. Those who hold to this value seek to protect even those who, ignorantly or willfully, pay no heed to the deadly danger of AIDS.

On the other side stands respect for sexual continence, emphasizing that you don't indulge promiscuity and that you encourage others not to do so. Those who cleave to this position argue that continence is vital to society, since it is a cornerstone of the marriages that build stable families and communities.

The first value argues that, since AIDS is so often fatal, the highest good is to prevent death at all costs. If that requires supplying teenagers with condoms, so be it. In this view, the right to avoid death takes precedence over all other rights: Even if it could be shown that supplying condoms destroys family values and wrecks the social fabric, the right to live would still have priority. Here three arguments suggest themselves:

• **Finality.** Death is, of course, terminal. Once surrender the right to life, and all other rights are meaningless, since the individual will not live to see them put into practice. What does it matter that we arrive at a good society if so many must be killed to create it?

• **Centrality.** Respect for life is one of the most widely discussed of human values. It underlies such powerful issues as abortion and euthanasia. Extended to other species, it lies at the center of debates over the environment and some forms of vegetarianism. Taken to its extreme, it informs some brands of pacifism. And, of course, it surfaces in discussions of crime, violence, and capital punishment. Surely (so the argument goes) a value so close to the heart of what it means to be human should take precedence over other values.

• **Compassion.** The highest form of compassion resides in affirming another's right to exist. That may require that we help protect others—especially the young—from the subtle influences of self-deceit, sensuality, and self-denigration that cause them to indulge in promiscuous sexuality without realizing its implications. At least (so the argument goes) keep them alive until they are mature enough to take responsibility for their own actions.

On the other side stand those who argue that, to prevent the growth of a sex-on-impulse society, teenagers ought to be discouraged from premarital sex. If a society can be kept alive only by indulging its wanton sensual impulses, what sort of life is that? Surely self-discipline is also at the core of what it means to be human—since self-restraint naturally leads one away from killing, while merely refusing to let others kill themselves does not necessarily teach self-restraint. Here, too, three arguments arise:

• **Chastity.** Often assumed to mean simply *sexual abstinence*, its primary and more useful dictionary definition is "freedom from unlawful sexual activity." Though popularly seen as outmoded, the concept is central to any serious consideration of sexuality. Why? Because if chastity were irrelevant, the assumption would have to be that sexual activity is an unqualified good and should be practiced without restraint. Were such license given rein, it would destroy commitment, affection, and trust—qualities that characterize the most intimate human relationships.

• **Childrearing.** With the advent of birth-control devices, sexual relations are increasingly separated from their natural consequences—pregnancy and childbearing. But love, sex, and the perpetuation of humankind are tightly bound together. To pretend otherwise is to fragment an immensely powerful social compact. It is also to subject those raised under the free-condom regime to one of two things after marriage: a jarring adjustment to a new and unfamiliar life of fidelity, childrearing, and the greater good of the community; or the perpetuation of early habits of promiscuous sexual activity, with its well-documented damage to marriage, family, and society.

• **The broader community.** When sexuality focuses on immediate personal gratification—as it often does among teenagers—the larger context gets lost. The community depends on the transmission to the young of stable, long-term values. Doing "whatever turns you on" is the attitude that promotes drug addiction, alcoholism, and greed—hardly an adequate ethical standard for sustainable communities. Distributing condoms fuels the conviction that it's okay to follow your instincts, and that there will be no adverse consequences of doing so.

There are powerful arguments, then, behind both the don't-kill and the don't-permit-adultery principles. For some, saving lives is worth any possible offense against sexual mores. For others, satisfying the desires of some teenagers is hardly worth the long-term debasement of family and community.

The paradigm? Long-term versus short-term fits well. If the issue is the short-term saving of lives, preventing AIDS is essential; if it's the far-reaching good of society, chastity is vastly superior to condoms. Also relevant here are the claims of the self against the needs of the community, where *self* argues for lifesaving condoms in the schools and *community* for family-saving efforts to inhibit the increase of sexual license.

How might an ends-based attitude judge this one? Here, the greatest number might well seem to be the teenagers who are at risk of dying—in which case, hand out the condoms. One could argue, on the other hand, that society as a whole is the greater number. In this view, taking measures that reduce AIDS without promoting sexual activity will be far better for far more people in the future: What does it matter if we save a few teenagers and destroy society in the process? The problem with this view, in part, lies in public perception. Today's teenagers have names and faces. Unlike the anonymous multitudes of future generations, these people can be counted, and the benefit of a condom policy can be measured in real numbers. Utilitarianism, then, builds a strong case for the condom policy.

By contrast, a rule-based approach asks, "What rule would I like to see universalized in the behavior of everyone else from now on?" Does the distribution of condoms set up a rule—"Sexual indulgence is okay at any age"—that creates a sustainable society? Most of us, handed a choice between an impulsive, sex-on-demand world and a community of liberty hedged with self-restraint, would choose the latter. Is such a community worth dying for—or, more precisely, letting the young die for? In the past, some have thought so: Patriotism has always taken its energy from those for whom some values (like freedom, independence, and self-government) took precedence over their own right to live. The rule-based thinker, here, may come down on the side of a rule that says, "Don't commit adultery"—despite consequences that include the death of some unwary teenagers. In practice, such thinkers may feel strongly that such a rule is especially appropriate for fifth-graders—more so, perhaps, than for older teenagers.

Care-based thinkers, facing these issues, will extend themselves into the consciences of the teenage population. Yes, they may say, if I were a teenager I would want to be shown the virtues of abstinence, the power of true affection, and the joy of sexuality in the context of deep and constant love. But I would also want to be protected against the raging tides of my own libido and the consequences of uncontrolled passion. Keep me alive, and I may become good; let me die, and I'll never get to goodness. Thus the Golden Rule may come down on the side of condom distribution.

Here, as in so many public issues, society is longing for a trilemma resolution. Is there a way to quench teenage sexuality so that it never needs to get to the free-condom level? Or is there a way to remove the danger of AIDS so that teenagers, however much they lack responsibility, will survive? To date, modern medicine is shuffling toward the latter without much success. More hopeful, many feel, are programs now being developed in the schools that instill the virtues of abstinence and self-discipline. For the time being, however, debate continues over this genuine dilemma.

The Post-Communist World Order

Much ink has been shed dissecting the military, political, and economic consequences of the collapse of communism. That's fitting: It's the major international development of our time. When the Berlin Wall was breached in November of 1989, it signaled the end of a Cold War between the superpowers that had been the single most powerful political determinant in the world since the 1950s. By at least three measures of greatness, that change has left the United States as the only great power in the world. One of those measures is the ability to project military force across the globe, in which the United States stands head and shoulders above any other single nation. Another is in the development of breakthrough technologies, where America still takes the lead.

The third measure, less widely understood, has to do with the ethical ideals that undergird the civil society. The United States remains the only nation founded not on border tiffs or ethnic rivalries but on a set of ideals about freedom, equal rights, and the individual's relation to the state. True, these ideals sometimes seem badly tattered in a society that permits escalating levels of homelessness, poverty, violence, and addiction. Yet they still exert a powerful field of moral magnetism around the world. Every country whose citizens long for the tremendously infectious idea of democracy calibrate that yearning against the American standard. Some, seeing only the America of *Dallas* and Madonna, turn away in revulsion. But many more, seeing the

America of *The Federalist Papers* and Horatio Alger, strive for emulation. The fact remains that the values of civil society are nowhere more understandable, appealing, and exportable than in the United States.

That fact, and the nation's newfound position as the lone world-class power, has profound ethical implications for America's future. Why? Three trends seem relevant here.

The first concerns security and military power. In the Cold War era, defense efforts by the member nations of the North Atlantic Treaty Organization (NATO) had essentially one goal: to prevent the spread of communism. Western governments, having made the moral choice in favor of democracy, knew which side to take when regional conflicts erupted: They looked to see where the Communists were, and chose the other party. To be sure, that stand produced as strange a gaggle of authoritarian bedfellows as democracy ever had, including the Shah of Iran, Philippine strongman Ferdinand Marcos, and Nicaraguan dictator Anastasio Somoza Debayle. But the presence of the overarching moral imperative—to keep communism at bay—relegated any qualms about abusive dictators, rightly or wrongly, to the ethical backseat.

Exit communism, and the ethics leaps to the front. Without the Cold War's rigid categories, the West must now sort out the morality of regional conflicts on a case-by-case basis. Is it right to send back the Haitian boat-people? Should we try to stop the killing in Nagorno-Karabakh? Should we pay for a United Nations peacekeeping force in Cambodia? Should we intervene in Bosnia? Should we send soldiers to Somalia? Needed: a framework for ethical analysis to replace instinctual anticommunism.

The second trend concerns the ethical vacuum surrounding the citizens of formerly Communist nations. If ethics is obedience to the unenforceable, and if law is obedience to the enforceable, the past seventy years of communism have seen a deliberate, concerted effort to replace ethics by law. In a state where everything is regulated, nothing of consequence need be left to individual discretion—at least in theory. Conceptually, then, there is little need for ethics. In practice, of course, many citizens in the formerly Communist countries survived with their ethics intact. Sadly lacking, however, is the public tradition of ethical behavior—the habit of right actions taken not out of fear of punishment or promise of reward but simply because it's the right thing to do. That ethical vacuum mightily complicates the efforts of Western businesses and governments to build trading relations in many of these countries. Reports of corruption, personal greed, and every-man-for-himself-ism, brought back by Western visitors, continue to defy imagination. Question: Can the really important export—democracy—take root without an ethical base?

The third trend arising from the collapse of communism is a reconsideration of American individualism. Since the days of Emersonian self-reliance and the frontier mentality, Americans have tilted toward the rights of the individual over those of the group—despite de Tocqueville's warning that excessive individualism would finally destroy the "public virtues" of the nation. In the face of communism, that tilt became a profound list—not only from fear of being called "pinko" or "fellow traveler," but out of concern that the forces of Big Brother were poised to crush out all individuality. These days, Westerners have less to fear from a Communitarian balancing of the rights of the self with the needs of the community.

These three trends raise a profound dilemma for the West. On one hand, it is right to extend a helping hand to the post-Soviet world, however much it may be mired in the leftover amorality of communism. It is right for several reasons. Our self-interest dictates that we expand trade, to benefit ourselves while we help others. Our commitment to democracy urges us to spread its values widely in an effort to make the world a safer, fairer, and more peaceable place for its citizens. And our compassion requires that these citizens, as fellow sojourners on a shrinking globe, be provided with a full complement of human rights. Nor is such a helping hand unprecedented. The Marshall Plan, through which American money rebuilt Europe after World War II, helped create the global prosperity we enjoy today.

On the other hand, it is right to prevent ourselves from falling into foreign relationships that sap our vitality and confine our own ability to grow. The nation's founders rejoiced that an ocean lay between them and the European courts—for the simple reason that, imagining that they were self-sufficient, they thought they had no need for artfully crafted treaties and the entanglements of alliances. Isolationism has a long and noble history in the United States. If, as author Paul Kennedy argues so persuasively in *The Rise and Fall of the Great Powers,* a nation's security is intimately tied to its economic strength, the United States may need a period of internal housecleaning after seventy years of what Professor Kennedy calls "imperial overstretch." Having fallen from the role of the world's largest creditor in the 1970s to the world's largest debtor at present, it needs to get its own economy back on track before taking on further altruistic obligations.

These two views are both right—and apparently exclusive of each other. On two points, however, there is no disagreement. First, this is a moral (rather than merely legal) question. Second, the United States, as the sole remaining superpower, is unavoidably the actor. The paradigm? Self versus community, where "self" is a single nation and "community" is the world. Also relevant here is justice versus mercy, where the latter calls for helping others while the former reminds us to be fair to our own citizenry first.

What do the resolution principles tell us? So far, most of the discussion surrounding approaches to the post-Communist world has been ends-based. Consequences loom large: The literature is filled with forecasts, future scenarios, and a bevy of speculative "what-ifs." What is right is often deduced as a kind of back-formation: Determine where you want to come out, decide how to get there, and declare that to be the "right" thing to do.

A rule-based approach, setting aside such consequentialism, insists on following fundamental maxims. The most applicable global "rules," perhaps, are those contained in the United Nations' Universal Declaration of Human Rights (1948) and the Helsinki Final Act (1975). These agreements combine a number of political rights pertaining to the security of the person with a number of economic and social rights designed to meet basic human needs. Those who cleave to these precepts make adherence to human rights a litmus test for governments: In 1977, President Jimmy Carter spoke for this view when he declared in a speech to the UN General Assembly that "no member of the United Nations can claim that mistreatment of its own citizens is solely its own business." Though often scorned by pragmatists, this rule-based approach has had results. In the restructuring of the world order in the late 1980s, writes Harlan Cleveland, these rights played a key role. "No government," says Cleveland, "not even the totalitarian Soviets or military dictators or even the long dug-in South African authorities, seemed able to ignore entirely the ultimate enforcer that the U.S. Declaration of Independence calls 'the general opinion of mankind.' "

Our third resolution principle, using the care-based approach, asks us to extend ourselves into the minds and hearts of the post-Soviet citizenry. So we try to answer such questions as "If we were the Russians, what would we want to have done to us?" To do so, we must first grasp the concept of *otherness* and learn to feel what it is like to be "the Russians." Here the dimension of cultural understanding comes into play. We often find we understand this otherness better through art than diplomacy, literature than politics, feature writing than news reporting, movies than statistics, music than lectures. The care-based approach begins with empathy, with feeling the life of another from the inside out, and with understanding the currents and desires of that life in its own context. As global communications improves, the potential for care-based resolutions increases: As more and more Westerners see Russian films, and as they travel in the post-Soviet world, the human face comes more sharply into focus. Result: The care-based approach may well argue for significant economic aid to Russia—although, if the otherness we identify is that of America's homeless and unemployed, we might well oppose such aid.

The bottom line? The new world order seems to be bringing a new moral order. As a result, the domination of utilitarian pragmatism may naturally begin to break. Moving closer to center stage may be a set of rule-based convictions—fired by the success of such human-rights campaigns as those of Amnesty International, Freedom House, and the Helsinki Watch organizations—and the care-based principles that naturally flourish whenever humans get close enough to one another's cultures to feel compassion.

Conservation Versus Consumption

One of the major ethical issues of the global future pits environmentalists against developers. That's nothing new. Eight years before the official closing of the American frontier in 1890, Norwegian playwright Henrik Ibsen wrote *An Enemy of the People,* a polemic exploring the ethical issues surrounding a financially profitable but contaminated and unhealthy swimming-bath in a small Norwegian town. The dilemma facing Dr. Stockmann and his fellow townspeople was stark: shut the baths to control disease, or keep them open to maintain the town's lifestyle. Within another few years, America would be plunged into its first major preservation-versus-exploitation debate in the controversy over the Hetch Hetchy dam in Yosemite

National Park. In 1930, the American poet Hart Crane captured the essence of such issues in a telling image:

> The last bear, shot drinking in the Dakotas
> Loped under wires that span the mountain stream. . . .

Since then, environmental issues have rolled forward in a kaleidoscope of events: Rachel Carson's *Silent Spring* in 1962, the Endangered Species Act in 1973, the two hundred million people in 140 countries turning out for Earth Day in 1990, the ongoing spotted owls–versus-loggers debate in the American Northwest. At the heart of each lies the same core dilemma: how to protect the natural environment while permitting human development.

If that issue is serious today, it will be crucial tomorrow. The reason: global population growth. While often seen as a problem in and of itself, population growth would in fact be irrelevant were it not for its impact on the environment. If the biosphere were infinitely expandable—if, as in the past, new populations could simply move onward into uninhabited lands so vast that a human presence made hardly a dent—population growth would hardly matter. The problem is quite otherwise. Rapidly rising populations are confronting a finite and oddly fragile environment. As George D. Moffett points out in *Critical Masses: The Global Population Challenge,* the impact can be spelled out in a litany of familiar statistics:

• Population growth now adds some eleven thousand people to the globe every hour—the equivalent of a new Dallas or Detroit in two days, a new Germany every eight months, a new Africa and Latin America combined every ten years.

• More than 90 percent of this growth will take place in the one hundred or so nations of the developing world that are least able to provide for these new individuals.

• Most of it will occur in urban areas. Many cities in third-world countries are doubling in size every twelve to fifteen years.

• This growth is unprecedented. It took us hundreds of thousands of years to reach, by the early 1880s, our first billion people. Now, at 5.5 billion, we add a new billion each decade, heading toward a total of between 9 billion and 20 billion in the next century.

Yet the very pressure that gives such cogency to environmental concerns also fires the need for development. Are we willing to let all these new people starve and freeze in the dark? Will we deny them access to the same resources that have sustained us? Will we promulgate regulations and ideals that enshrine nature's rights at the expense of human rights? Of course we must control future population growth—but what do we do in the here and now with all those who have already been born?

Even if you live in the relative comfort of North America, with its low population density and immense tracts of preserved land, these issues shape your future. Sometimes they cause us real anguish, as in the case of the beluga or white whales—the species celebrated by Herman Melville in *Moby Dick.* An endangered species in the Gulf of St. Lawrence, belugas eat so much fish in those toxic-laden waters that their bodies are considered to be "hazardous waste" when beached along the shore. Sometimes, however, such issues simply provoke sighs over man's inanity—as when a paper mill in rural Maine, clearing the grating on its water-intake pipe of rocks lodged there during raging spring torrents, was solemnly ordered by state officials not to return the perfectly clean rocks to the riverbed but to truck them thirty miles to a soon-to-be-overloaded landfill.

Whatever the case, these issues feature two opposing core values. On one hand stands the value of preserving nature from the onslaughts of man. Humans are broadly adaptable, able to live on arctic ice floes and equatorial deserts, in dense cities or deserted mountains. Most other species are not so flexible: Wipe out their habitat, and they disappear. Some of the most vigorous and scrappy animals are acutely sensitive to habitat changes. Burrowing owls, for example, can endure all kinds of predators and still come out on top. But they depend on abandoned prairie dog holes for their nests. Wipe out prairie dogs, as western ranchers have been doing, and even the hardiest of burrowing owls can't survive.

To save habitats, then, is to save species. Why does saving species matter? One reason is their beauty and the lessons they teach. Another has to do with effective management of natural lands: Most species have an important niche in the habitat as food for something or consumer of something else. Still another is for science: We're only now learning, for example, how to take genes from a certain kind of wild Mexican maize and merge them into commercial corn to produce vigorous and disease-resistant strains. Finally, of course, is the sheer right of a species to exist—or, to put it another way, the unconscionable human pride that thinks it has the right to destroy forever another form of life.

Such preservation, at bottom, is one of the deepest symbols of our humanity. No other species is gifted with such capacity for rational foresight and long-range planning. To defer immediate gratification for the sake of offspring we will never see is an intensely human act: To plant oaks beside your house on the frontier, knowing that a century later they will shade your great-grandchildren, is to show conscious respect for an environmental future in ways no other species can. Conservation, then, is not simply a luxury that we can overlook if we choose. It is part and parcel of our very humanity.

On the other hand stands an equally valid core value concerning human development. Among the most fundamental duties that humans have to one another are those that guarantee safety, warmth, food, shelter, and the right to propagate. The faces of the world's children, peering through our television screens from refugee camps or third-world slums, cry out for policies that could put even a few scraps of food into their mouths. Such help could conceivably come in the short term, of course, through a straightforward redistribution of current wealth: If rich countries simply taxed themselves to death, some of these children would be fed. But the best long-term help comes through the development of economic opportunities.

Such development depends on education, religious approval, willingness to work, family structures that recognize the needs and rights of women, and many other intangibles. But it also depends on creating something of value that someone else needs and wants to buy. That usually requires raw materials and energy—the very things nature has always provided. To be sure, there are environmentally "clean" service-oriented jobs in banking, insurance, advertising, tourism, communications, and other areas. But even those depend upon the prosperity generated somewhere in the world through a manufacturing base, which almost always involves some exploitation of natural resources. To refuse that exploitation, then, is to condemn the world's poor to continued poverty—a condemnation that seems all the more inequitable when promoted by those in the developed world who already enjoy significant prosperity.

These two sides, clashing together, produce the environment-versus-development dilemma. It seems to fit three paradigms:

- It is right to honor the *short-term* demands for survival by developing economic paths out of poverty. Yet it is right to respect the *long-term* demands for survival by assuring a sustainable environment.

• The rights of the *individual* require us to supply food, clothing, and shelter despite the hardship on the environment. The rights of the *community* require that our common environmental heritage be protected despite the hardship on the individual. (This paradigm, however, can be put the other way: It is right for me as an individual to have access to unblemished wilderness tracts, though it may be right that, in order for my community to survive, everyone has access to the resources on that tract.)

• The greatest *justice* will be served by saving the environment out of fairness to those yet to be born, while the greatest *mercy* will be to provide for those who are suffering today.

How do our resolution principles help us? Ends-based thinkers, brooding upon consequences, lay out sober prophecies of future doom and gloom—on both sides of the issue. Estimates of global warming vie for our attention with prognostications of job losses and welfare increases. To the ends-based thinker, a close study of such figures, and the methodologies behind them, is essential: How else will we know what "the greatest good" will be? Not surprisingly, then, the policy-makers' well-known penchant for utilitarianism plunges modern society into endless rounds of expert testimony, scientific debate, and statistical saber-rattling—the assumption being that whoever gets it intellectually right will also have captured the moral high ground.

Rule-based thinkers look on all this with wry detachment. The moral sense, to them, has little to do with such arcane debates. What rule, they ask instead, should be universalized? If it is to save species at all costs, then that must be done regardless of consequences. If, on the other hand, it is to honor every individual's basic human dignity by supplying food and shelter, that must take precedence no matter what happens. What gives these thinkers the shudders is the spectacle of moral inconsistency, a waffling set of policies that change every few years depending on scientific fashion or public whim. Get the rule right, they argue, and carry it out in full trust that it will produce the highest sense of goodness.

The care-based thinker may well dismiss both these views—the first for its cold disregard of suffering, the second for its rigid demand for consistency. What, they ask, would I want to have done to me? Living in a Manila slum, I would want a meal, an education, a job, a sense of hope—not a lecture on saving the whales. Living in a Los Angeles suburb, however, I would want a set of policies that would compel my entire community—myself included—to support alternatives to the gasoline-powered cars whose exhausts engulf me in smog. Placing my highest emphasis on caring for others—and observing that there are more slum-dwellers than suburbanites—I might finally come down more in favor of supporting the former than the latter.

This dilemma also gives us a clear look at another part of the resolution process: locating the trilemma options. Among the most encouraging signs of progress in the last decade has been the growth of coalitions that involve both environmentalists and developers. From a past filled with the strident animosities of stark opposition, we seem to be moving toward a greater recognition of the fact that, like all true dilemmas, this one has a lot of right on both sides. The trilemma goal—saving the environment while at the same time providing economic development—is being met in some areas. Already, electric companies are supplying more efficient bulbs rather than building new plants. Some kinds of seafood are being farmed rather than drift-netted out of the open ocean. Unleaded fuels, more efficient cars, and smokestack scrubbers are helping clean the air. Debt-for-nature swaps are helping turn third-world tracts into parks and preserves. Ecotourism is on the rise, helping travelers visit unspoiled areas without damaging them. In these and other ways, a resolution process as old as Aristotle's Golden Mean is on the twenty-first century's agenda.

More Public Issues

The discussion of these three public issues—involving AIDS, the new world order, and the environment—is meant to help us bring the lens of ethics to bear on problems of a national and international scope. These are not, by any means, the only problems needing ethical analysis and resolution. Dozens of other global issues cry out for attention, including:

- Immigration across international borders: Do we keep them out or let them in?
- The human genome project: What are the ethical ramifications of designer babies and cloned humans?

- The computer-communications revolution: Who pays, who benefits, who gets excluded, and why?
- Free trade: A boon for all, or a boondoggle for a few?
- Big science: Should the world's taxpayers fund a few supercolliders and space stations, or thousands of smaller research projects?
- Censorship: If violence on television produces violence in the street, is there an ethical way to control either?
- Military forces: Should gays serve?
- Character education: Can ethics be taught in the schools without trampling on religious freedom?
- Medicine: Which patients should benefit from big-ticket, heroic surgical procedures—and who decides?
- Homelessness: Is having a home a right or a privilege?
- Child care: As women become more educated and contribute more to the working world, who raises the next generation?
- Global business: Can ethical standards survive in countries where bribery is endemic?

If ethics is as valid in a public as in a private arena, these issues ought to be amenable to thoughtful analysis from an ethical perspective. That's not to say they won't also benefit from more familiar forms of analysis through economic, technological, historical, or political lenses. They will. Subjected to ethical scrutiny, however, they yield up a different kind of understanding. Through that scrutiny, we come closer to answering the question that, more than any other, seems to be commanding public attention as we move into the twenty-first century: Of all the things we *could* do, what's the *right* thing to do?

Chapter Nine

Epilogue: Ethics in the Twenty-first Century

Some years ago, in my high-school chemistry class, the teacher set us working on acid-alkali reactions. As we mixed the two components, the solution seethed and the test tubes got warmer and warmer. Then the reaction fizzled out. The acid and alkali had neutralized each other, leaving behind nothing but salt and water.

Our teacher then began his own experiment. Starting a similar reaction in a large flask, he dropped in a few flakes of platinum foil, small shiny squares like bits of metal confetti. The reaction nearly exploded. It bubbled madly, casting off a furious discharge of vapor and heating the flask until it was too hot to touch. Within seconds it was over, the reagents consumed in far less time than in our test tubes.

When he emptied the flask, we expected to see only liquid. To our surprise, out came the platinum bits. They were the same size they had been when they went in. Nothing had eaten into them. Nothing had dissolved them. Nothing had even dulled their finish. They were untouched.

Through that simple experiment we came to understand the meaning of the word *catalyst*. As a catalyst, the platinum never enters into the reaction. It simply provides a surface on which the reaction takes place. But something in its structure speeds the reaction immensely. When it's all over, everything in the surrounding environment is different. The once-powerful reagents, transformed by the interaction of their opposite natures, are irreversibly altered. The catalyst comes out unchanged.

Explaining this phenomenon, our teacher added one more comment. The catalyst, he said, comes out unchanged only if it goes in pure. Put in an impure catalyst, he said, and it will be eaten up by the intensity of the reaction.

In that simple morning's work, we grasped not only an important scientific concept but a powerful metaphor for the human condition. Wherever humanity comes to a decision point, it seems, we're surrounded by reactions. Some bubble along slowly. Others churn and froth. Some produce good results, while others create noxious poisons. Some are hardly noticeable. Others shake the rafters and spew out sparks.

That is nowhere more true than in ethical decision-making. Core values are like moral reagents: They sometimes clash together with plenty of energy and fervor. There are no conflicts as challenging, long-lasting, or intractable as those that grow out of moral issues. Yet there are no more important issues to resolve than those on the ethical landscape.

There are times, of course, when the prudent teacher douses the experiment—rinses out the flask before things get out of hand. And there are times when moral reactions, as they threaten to turn into white-hot arguments that melt the walls of their containers, need to be stifled. But that's not usually the case. Most of the time the tough choices we face could use a little catalysis. Most of the time, when the end result is desirable, the process deserves a good nudge.

Ethical thinkers are catalysts. The moral viewpoint, however gently added to a situation, has an uncanny way of stimulating the process. Positions that were uncertain take on a new sharpness. Attitudes that were grudgingly congruent can suddenly diverge. People who once whispered can begin to shout. That can be unnerving. As the ethical battle rages, all sorts of stench can erupt—and all sorts of sludge can precipitate to the bottom. But it can also be exhilarating. There is nothing more satisfying than to see apathy overcome, stagnation broken, and decisions made that absolutely transform their surroundings for the better. And there is nothing more comforting than to feel some assurance that such decisions, when arrived at through ethical processes, constitute the highest level of right we can reach.

Ethical fitness makes ethical thinkers. If you've come this far in this book, you've invested a fair amount of energy and time in your own ethical fitness. Don't be surprised, then, if the result is sometimes volatile. Like it or not, you're becoming a better catalyst. The ideas you cast into the discussion—sometimes without even opening your mouth—form the surface upon which things happen. You'll speed things along, and you'll come out unchanged—if, that is, you go into it with your purity intact.

What is purity? These days it's a puzzling word, confounded with overtones of goody-goody moralists and self-righteous busybodies. At bottom, however, it describes a condition we all long for. Clean air, fresh water, sharp focus, unadulterated friendships, honest motives, straightforward answers, untainted candidates—we crave purity at every turn. In the chemical metaphor of the catalyst, *pure* simply means unalloyed, uncorrupted, unmixed. In ethics, it means adhering to core values, exhibiting moral consistency, being true to one's ethical compass—and avoiding hypocrisy at every turn.

In my experience, nothing chews up would-be ethical thinkers faster than hypocrisy. Why? Because, lacking that central purity, they can't avoid becoming part of every reaction they enter. Perhaps they only mean to provide the surface for the catalysis. But bit by bit they erode, lose luster, get used up.

How do you protect purity? I once bought an old French horn, which I greatly enjoyed but never learned to play very well. I wanted it to shine. If it was polished and then lacquered, I was told, it would keep its shine without any effort—though the lacquer would soon yellow with age. Or I could leave it unlacquered and keep it polished myself. In that case it would take lots of work. But it would always shine more brightly than its lacquered neighbors.

Some people seek to protect purity with a veneer of protective film. That's fine for looks, but it destroys the catalytic properties: Varnish the platinum, and you might as well drop a plastic bag into the test tube. The only way to protect purity, I suspect, is to work at it. Ethics, as I said earlier, is not an inoculation. It's a process. I've never met anyone who has good judgment simply because they *once had* good judgment. They have it because they keep exercising it. That's what ethics is all about: practice, exercise, and doing right at every turn.

Future Ethics: New Challenge, New Urgency

To an age waffling in relativism and awash with political correctness, the demand for ethical exercise may seem a tall order. Why bother? If ethics takes all that effort, why not just settle for compromise? Why does it matter that we're ethical?

The answer has a lot to do with the age we're entering. Successful moral leadership for the twenty-first century will be grounded in centuries-old concepts of ethics that may never change. Yet it will also be flexible, adaptable, and inventive. Why? Because the moral landscape of the next century will be shaped by three conditions our ancestors could not have imagined.

First, we will face *entirely new ethical issues.*

Second, we will live in an age of *increasing moral intensity.*

Third, we will experience unprecedented pressures to drop out of society and make a *separate peace*—to carve out moral enclaves disconnected from the ethical issues of the world.

Let's examine these one by one.

New Issues

On the evening of November 2, 1988, a twenty-three-year-old graduate student, Robert Tappan Morris, sat down at his computer terminal at Cornell University and committed what some pundits have called the crime of the century. Finding a security flaw in the computer programs of the Advanced Research Projects Agency (ARPA) network—an international grid of telephone lines and satellite hookups created by the Department of Defense in 1969 to link governments, corporations, and universities—he launched a "worm" into a computer hundreds of miles away at the Massachusetts Institute of Technology. The program began sending itself through the network, growing like a tapeworm through the sixty thousand computers of the system until it soaked up so much of their memory that they began to crash. In the end, Morris did something no one else had yet done: He broke into and paralyzed a major computer network.

Morris had no criminal record, no motive for revenge, no scheme for economic gain—and no discernible moral restraints. "It was a mistake, and I am sorry for it," he told the court. His father, one of the nation's leading computer-security experts, called it "the work of a bored graduate student." *Time* called it "one of the most sophisticated and infectious computer viruses the world has yet seen." U.S. District Court Judge Howard Munson, in the nation's first prosecution under the federal Computer Fraud and Abuse Act of 1986, handed Morris a light sentence that included community service and a $10,000 fine.

Was Morris an oddity, a unique exception, a whacko in an otherwise normal world of computer enthusiasts? Probably not. The frontier of technology, like all frontiers, has among its citizens a distinct breed of intellectual gamblers, gunslingers, and grubstakers. For them, the moral issues pale to insignificance before the lure of discovery. In the computer world they're known as *hackers*. The fact that something can be done is, for many of them, reason enough to try it. Yet the fact that no one has ever done it before—nor thought hard about the ethical consequences involved—places a peculiar responsibility upon these discoverers. Some pause to assess the moral landscape before proceeding. Others simply gallop ahead.

A society that develops ideas at only moderate rates can perhaps afford to let its ethics catch up with its inventions. But in the twentieth century, as futurist Alvin Toffler explains, the pace of change has accelerated exponentially. Noting that the history of humankind has spanned eight hundred "lifetimes" of sixty-two years each, Toffler writes that "only during the last six lifetimes did masses of men ever see a printed word. Only during the last four has it been possible to measure time with any precision. Only in the last two has anyone anywhere used an electric motor. And the overwhelming majority of all the material goods we use in daily life today have been developed within the present, the eight-hundredth, lifetime." These words, accurate when he wrote them in 1971, are even more true today.

Result: The sheer growth of inventiveness has created ethical questions that simply did not arise in the past. Already, entirely new dilemmas face us at every turn:

• Should unmarried teenage girls use the pill? The question never surfaced until the 1960s, when oral contraceptives came on the market.

• How should software be protected from unlicensed copying? Only a computer age would want to know.

• Should dashboard radar detectors, whose sole purpose is to help people disobey traffic laws, be banned? The issue didn't arise until high-speed interstate highways and low-cost transistor technology joined hands in the 1980s.

• Should the much-diminished sea urchin population along America's Atlantic coast be protected? No one would have thought so before there were regular overnight flights to Japan, where live urchin is an expensive delicacy.

• Should New England ship its nuclear waste to Texas? Had you asked Harry Truman, who authorized the dropping of the atomic bombs that devastated Hiroshima and Nagasaki in World War II, you would have been dismissed as a science-fiction freak: No one had ever thought of the problem.

• Should fifth-graders get free condoms? Before AIDS, the question would have seemed prurient and scandalous.

• Should you and I clone ourselves? The question has yet to come up—but it will.

What will this pace of change mean for the twenty-first century? Go back to our earlier example: computers. Predictions are that everything about them—their size, speed, weight, and cost—will improve by a factor of ten thousand over the next two decades. When computers are as ubiquitous as the electric motors that run our hair-dryers, clocks, and toys—and about as cheap and easy to replace—they will have a profound impact on the way we live. But if Robert Morris's worm is any indication, they will also open vistas of ethical complexity we can't even imagine.

Moral Intensity

When Michigan pathologist Jack Kevorkian helped Janet Adkins end her life in 1990 by using his "suicide machine," he was doing nothing new. Socrates himself was assisted in his suicide by those who gave him hemlock to drink. What makes Kevorkian's work different is the demographics of aging. The fastest-growing cohort of the American population is the over-eighty-five crowd. Similar increases in longevity are occurring worldwide. While many of these people are in excellent shape, increasing numbers are alive without their health. Facing the prospect of life maintained only by biological interventions, sometimes in great pain and often feeling hopeless and alone, more and more of them may express a wish to die.

The ethical issues surrounding euthanasia—"an easy death," as my dictionary defines it—have been well explored by others. The point here is simply to note that the invention and use of *illegal machinery* for euthanasia—and the publicity surrounding it—crank up the intensity of this issue in ways that the physicians of our grandparents' generation never had to face. Now and then, perhaps, they encountered an elderly patient who asked them about suicide. These days, with a drumbeat of news stories about a growing list of customers for Kevorkian's grim machinery, new questions arise about old laws governing euthanasia. Maybe, the public is asking, such machinery is not only *relevant*. Maybe it should be *legal*.

As once-esoteric concerns over euthanasia are lifted from their academic context and plopped down on coffee tables around the world, they join scores of other ethical issues pressing in upon us for attention. Reason: the extended reach of the global news media. There is nothing new in the subjects the media cover: There have always been wars, famines, plagues, and disasters, and they have always had grisly effects on populations. But only now can we see them played out in our living rooms every night. Problems that once did not trouble us—since we didn't know about them—now wring us with moral anguish and outrage. Fifty years ago we would not have cared about civil war and starvation in Somalia—because we would have been ignorant of it. Now, having seen it, we cannot live with ourselves if we *don't* take action. Multiply that single case by dozens of others, factor in all the direct-mail appeals for help from worthy causes, add up all the genuinely new ethical issues now facing us, and it's little wonder we live in such an age of moral intensity.

In the donor community, where foundations and charitable organizations fund nongovernmental organizations and volunteer groups, a term has recently surfaced for this intensity. It's called *compassion fatigue.* Faced with so many requests from so many worthy organizations engaged in such profoundly moral battles, our ability to care risks being numbed. Rather than be overwhelmed, we tune out. Earlier ages may have had an easier time of it: They merely had to support good causes. Our task, as president Peter Goldmark of the Rockefeller Foundation likes to observe, is harder. It's no longer enough, he says, to fund causes that are merely worthwhile. Our job is to back causes that are essential.

Separate Peace

The danger, of course, is that unless we find mental and emotional structures for addressing these causes, we may well become ethical tortoises, retreating into our shells rather than facing a world of such moral intensity. Or we may simply try to respond to ethical overload by longing for its opposite: a simpler, easier world where moral issues exist in an ordered framework. That longing should come as no surprise. In humanity's social progress, strong movements often launch trends toward their opposites. In recent times, the lunge into a high-tech world has produced what author John Naisbitt has called "high touch"—the explosion of interest in handmade crafts, one-of-a-kind objects made in age-old methodologies and materials. Hard rock, blanketing the airwaves with often-incomprehensible lyrics and jarring rhythms, has provoked new enthusiasm for country music with its storytelling diction and mellifluous harmonies. Hiking—one of the slowest ways to get anywhere—has never been more popular than in an age of high-speed travel. Despite the convenience and thrift of plastic containers, consumers now pay a premium for milk in glass bottles.

These opposites all have in common a return to more traditional ways, as well as a desire to come out and be separate from the unfulfilling materialism of modern life. Put those two powerful impulses together with a charismatic leader, and the results can be ghastly. That was the story when, on April 19, 1993, David Koresh and his followers touched off their fatal conflagration at his compound in Waco, Texas.

Koresh, whose tangled and mystical biblicalism caused his followers to hoard large caches of arms on their isolated farmland retreat, had triumphed over a bungled raid on February 28, in which several federal officers were killed. Then came the long standoff. Finally, impatient with stasis and concerned for the welfare of Koresh's several hundred followers—especially the children—the feds moved in. As they did so, a wind-whipped fire apparently set by Koresh's Branch Davidians erupted into truly Texan proportions. Within minutes, Koresh and his legions perished.

Separatism doesn't always end that way. But the incident at Waco points up three ethical issues that will increasingly tear at the fabric of civil society as the twenty-first century unfolds:

• **Religion.** David Koresh clearly established a cult. His followers seemed absolutely dependent upon his personality and unwilling to think for themselves. But the pejorative term *cult* probably got in the feds' way, allowing them to brand him a kook and misapprehend his weird but formidable notions. The feds, for instance, say they never suspected Koresh would torch himself. They should have. Koresh showed repeated fascination with fire imagery in the Scriptures. He also knew well the Old Testament story of Shadrach and his Hebrew friends who, tossed into a "burning fiery furnace," escaped unsinged because of their faith. His biblicalism, however strange, was serious. A clear grasp of twenty-first century values will require us to dispense with stereotypes and seek to understand diversity from the inside out—no matter how bizarre, antisocial, or flatly illegal it may be. Insofar as the future is a place of increasing separatism, the need for this understanding will commensurably increase.

• **Terrorism.** Why did the feds miss the fire imagery? Perhaps because they wrongly identified the Branch Davidians as terrorists. That's not surprising: On February 26, two days before the shootout with the feds, international terrorists blew up the garage at the World Trade Center in New York. Like terrorists, these people in Waco seemed to be anarchists taking the law into their own hands, demanding publicity and willing to use violence. But terrorists commit suicide only as a last extremity. Besides, their hostages want freedom. Religious separatists, by contrast, often seek out martyrdom—and their "hostages" are actually followers who choose to die with them. Never mind that expert psychologists employed by the feds declared Koresh unlikely to commit suicide. "Suicide," like "cult," was not a helpful concept: Psychological tests would not have found Shadrach "suicidal," either, yet he willingly faced death for his beliefs. The point: Under the separatist thrust, terrorism and religious fanaticism may fuse and blur. Needed: a moral construct willing to care enough about motives to analyze them carefully and take appropriate action.

• **The role of the civil society.** Ultimately, however, the role of community goes far beyond law enforcement. Given the arms stashed in Waco, the evidence of child abuse, and the killings of federal agents in the February raid, the feds had to act. But the real purpose of the community is to make itself so fair, caring, and tolerant that a Koresh can attract few followers. The frightened and uneasy, longing for a higher vision, must be able to find meaning in their lives without falling prey to a quasi-religious mesmerism. As the next century progresses, the pressures on those less stable may well intensify. Yearning for a separate peace, they may be especially prime targets for cultish behavior. Legislation can help by making weaponry less accessible and violence less permissible. In the end, however, only a well-balanced civil society can promote a healthy vision of a moral universe. Only a society of ethical thinkers will create a community where the lonely and unsure need not be tempted by an enclave mentality. Only a truly moral community can counter separatism wherever it shows up—whether as ethnic cleansing and hatred of refugees on the international front, or as special-interest pleading and a whining me-firstism on the domestic scene.

Resolving the Dilemmas: A New Morality of Mindfulness

These three trends—toward new inventions, higher intensity, and greater separatism—are already shaping the ethical landscape. Neither fuzzy relativism nor dogged absolutism has proved capable of addressing them. Nor, for that matter, has any compromise between those two poles. Perhaps the American poet E. E. Cummings said it best when he noted that "joy is a mystery at right angles equally to pain & pleasure, as truth is to fact & fiction." The ethics that will shape our future is not to be found on some sliding scale where fact shades into fiction or pleasure into pain—or, Cummings might have said, where relativism shades into absolutism. Like joy and truth, the most practical ethics for the twenty-first century will be found in a dimension perpendicular to the political tugs-of-war and academic tiffs over absolutism, liberalism, family values, outcomes-based education, and the dozens of other hot-button words surrounding the ethics debate. That does not mean ethics is a mystery. It means only that it's not simply a set of politically correct views on specific issues, or a particular moralistic stand, or a bully flag planted in the sand. It's a way of looking at the world. It's a process that helps us come to terms with our toughest dilemmas. It's not a compromise; it's a lens.

In the end, our ethics defines the way we participate in the community around us. Yet it's also a deeply personal construct, developing powerful standards and practices in each of us. It calls upon us to be impartial. Yet it demands that we be engaged—that we have, in other words, a point of view.

Lest this book appear to hint at the values-neutral relativism so corrosive to ethical endeavors, let me share in closing my own point of view concerning the four dilemma paradigms. These four are, of course, statements of right versus right. So there is no invariably "right" side to each one. But imagine a level playing field, on which both sides have equal weight and nothing in the situation drives you

Values Clarification

A popular but controversial approach to moral education, values clarification seeks to help students identify their own beliefs. It is rooted in the work of Louis Raths, who with coauthors Merrill Harmin and Sidney Simon explained the process in their highly influential book, *Values and Teaching,* published in 1966. Raths, as Simon later wrote, was "not concerned with the *content* of people's values, but the *process of valuing.*" He set forth seven steps for helping students become aware of their own values, grouped under three headings: *prizing* one's own beliefs and behaviors, *choosing* freely which ones to follow, and *acting* consistently upon those choices.

Simon, with whose name values clarification is now usually associated, developed and promoted the methodology. He set it forth as "a process for selecting the best and rejecting the worst elements contained in the various value systems which others have been urging [students] to follow." Often working in groups, and guided by a teacher who listens carefully, the students work through a number of strategies or games intended to help them clarify their values.

It is here that the controversy arises. Values clarification has been strongly attacked for promulgating an "anything goes" atmosphere, where the teacher remains neutral, uncommitted, and accepting of all expressions of values regardless of their moral implications. (In fairness, Simon points out that the teacher *should* share his or her own values with the class at the appropriate moment—always with the proviso, however, that "the particular content of his values holds no more weight than would anyone else's.") It is also condemned for some of its classroom exercises—like "The Fallout Shelter Problem," in which students must decide which of ten people is to be saved from a nuclear attack by taking refuge in a shelter that holds only six, or the "Cave-in Simulation," in which students must determine which of their own group, facing an imaginary collapse of an underground cave, should be allowed to survive based on each one's reasons for wishing to remain alive. These exercises, while generating lively discussion, are sometimes criticized for suggesting to students that ethics is a highly competitive game of winners and losers, taking place in an imaginary world unrelated to their own.

Used widely in classrooms over the last twenty-five years, values clarification—along with the moral discussion approach promoted by Lawrence Kohlberg—has been the subject of intensive evaluations of its effectiveness in changing values-based behavior. Analyzing that body of research, James S. Leming concludes that "the moral discussion approach works, and the values clarification approach does not."

more toward one of these sides than toward the other. All things being equal, here is where I tend to come down as I encounter these four paradigms:

• Compelled to choose between *truth* and *loyalty*, I would (all things being equal) come down on the side of truth. One reason: The history of this century suggests that those who put loyalty above truth (loyalty to Hitler, Mao, Stalin, Saddam Hussein, and even Richard Nixon) are capable of doing terrible damage to the world. It's hard to imagine that kind of damage arising when truth is put above loyalty. Having to choose, I feel safer and more comfortable honoring what is true than following human allegiances.

• Compelled to choose between *the individual* and *the community*, I would (all things being equal) lean toward the community. One reason: Individualism and its emphasis on *rights* has run to such extremes in this century that it has done serious damage to community and its emphasis on *responsibilities.* Were I a citizen of a post-Soviet country, I might feel otherwise: Seventy years of oppressive communism might have driven me to support the individual at any cost. But I'm not: My history, and that of my culture, has been different.

Another reason: Community includes self, but self does not always embrace community.

• Compelled to choose between *short term* and *long term*, I would (all things being equal) favor the long term. One reason: The long term always includes the short term, whereas short-term thinking (as the history of greed in the American 1980s demonstrates) does not always provide for the long term.

• Compelled to choose between *justice* and *mercy*, I would (all things being equal) stick with mercy, which to me speaks of love and compassion. One reason: I can imagine a world so full of love that justice, as we now know it, would no longer be necessary. But I cannot imagine a world so full of justice that there would no longer be any need for love. Given only one choice, I would take love.

The world, of course, hardly ever presents a truly level playing field. All things are rarely equal. An action that is right in the abstract may, in the push and pull of human interchange, be less right than some other. That's where the tough choices arise.

By themselves, these four paradigms won't make those choices for us. It's hard to imagine a leader who succeeds simply by staking out one side of a paradigm and doggedly adhering to it no matter what happens. That's not to say people don't try: In a society schooled on quick fixes and educated by sitcoms that solve everything in half an hour, there is an undeniable temptation to find a formula and live by it. Too often, however, these Johnny-one-notes of the values chorus miss the point. Clinging to one value to the exclusion of others, and failing to assess the complexity of the issues surrounding them, they substitute thoughtless moralizing for moral thinking.

And for that there is no longer any room. More than ever before, our age is making short shrift of those who preach without acts, indulge selfrighteousness without humility, and chastise others' wrongs without understanding their own. A morality of repetition—mouthing unexamined values inherited from a ghostly past—is rapidly giving way to something new.

What's coming? That will depend in large part on our responses to the world around us. What's coming, unfortunately, may be a resurgent morality of relativism, in which core values fall into cynical disrepute and cold-blooded self-will finally drives out all vestiges of honesty, love, fairness, and respect.

On the other hand, what's coming may be a new morality of

mindfulness, in which the light of ethical reason and intuition dispels shadows, builds firm conclusions, and leads to goodness, worth, and dignity.

We will not survive the morality of repetition: The twenty-first century's choices are simply too tough. Nor will we survive the morality of relativism: There is too much leverage these days behind even a single unpunished act of evil. We'll survive by a morality of mindfulness. We'll survive where reason moderates the clash of values and intuition schools our decision-making. There's no better way for good people to make tough choices.

Notes

Chapter One Overview: The Ethics of Right Versus Right

24 Immanuel Kant's "categorical imperative": Immanuel Kant, *The Moral Law: Kant's Groundwork of the Metaphysic of Morals,* trans. H. J. Paton (London: Hutchinson and Co., 1961), p. 88.
24 "Worth of character": Kant, *The Moral Law,* p. 66.

Chapter Two Right Versus Wrong: Why Ethics Matters

31 The story of a moral meltdown: For accounts of the incident at Chernobyl, see Zhores A. Medvedev, *The Legacy of Chernobyl* (New York: W. W. Norton & Co., 1990); and Grigori Medvedev, *The Truth About Chernobyl* (New York: Basic Books, 1991).
40 "Character education . . . with clear community support": James S. Leming, *Character Education: Lessons from the Past, Models for the Future* (Camden, Me.: The Institute for Global Ethics, 1993) p. 30.
44 "Pam, a Minnesota college student": Douglas Wallace, *Career World* (Highland Park, Ill.: Curriculum Innovations Group, March 1993), pp. 7–8.

44 "You manufacture keys, and you are accused" case scenario: Wallace, *Career World,* p. 9.
44 "You are an interviewing supervisor" case scenario: Ethics questionnaire, Walker Research, Inc. (Indianapolis: August 24–25, 1993).
45 *New York Times* stories under "ethics": Deni Elliott, "In Tomorrow's News . . . Ethics will be a frequent story subject," *Fineline,* Vol. 1, No. 12 (Mar. 1990), p. 6.
46 College student who found $6,100 in cash: Christopher Heredia, "Good Samaritan Did Right Thing—Twice," *The Arizona Republic/ Phoenix Gazette* (July 17, 1991), p. B1.
46 Survey on teenagers who do volunteer work: *Volunteering and Giving Among Teenagers 12 to 17 Years of Age,* Independent Sector (Washington, D.C.: 1992).
47 Poll finds "personal ethics" at top of the list: Board of Directors, Korn/Ferry International, Sixteenth Annual Study (Los Angeles: 1989).
47 Gallup Organization polls find a "strict moral code" is "very important": Gallup Organization survey 187–6 (Princeton: Dec. 11–Dec. 14, 1981); and Gallup Organization survey A1–877 (Princeton: Jan. 1–Jan. 26, 1989).
47 Josephson Institute survey on U.S. high school students and cheating: Michael Josephson, "The Hole in the Moral Ozone: Ethical Values, Attitudes, and Behaviors in American Schools," *Ethics: Easier Said than Done,* Nos. 19 and 20 (1992), pp. 35–45.
47 Center for Business Ethics surveyed *Fortune 1000:* Judith B. Kamm, "Ethics Officers Gaining Acceptance at Many Firms, Survey Reveals," *Ethikos,* Vol. 7, No. 4 (Jan./Feb. 1993), pp. 7–10.
47 McFeely Wackerle Jett surveyed four thousand upper-level executives: Clarence E. McFeely, Frederick W. Wackerle, and Charles C. Jett, *The McFeely-Wackerle-Jett Survey on Ethics* (Chicago: 1987).
48 "Americans believe the United States is in decline as a nation": Gallup Organization survey of Americans' attitudes conducted for Knight-Ridder Newspapers (Ohio) and Cable News Network, cited in R. Boyd, "The American Nightmare," *Akron Beacon Journal* (Sept. 13, 1992), pp. A1, A6.
48 Survey indicated dissatisfaction with ethical standards: McFeely, Wackerle, and Jett, *Survey on Ethics.*
48 Respondents to a Shearson Lehman survey thought that the United States was "pretty seriously on the wrong track": "Life in America Survey Series," No. 1 (New York: Shearson Lehman Brothers, Inc., 1992).
48 Harris Poll ranked groups with good moral and ethical standards:

Harris Poll, cited in "Snapshots," *USA Today* (Sept. 3, 1992), p. 1.
48 J. Walter Thompson researchers ranked the ten sleaziest ways to make a living: James Patterson and Peter Kim, *The Day America Told the Truth: What People Really Believe About Everything That Really Matters* (Englewood Cliffs, N.J.: Prentice-Hall, 1991), p. 144.
49 Louis Harris survey showed level of cheating in high school students: Robert Coles and James Hunter, *Girl Scouts Survey on the Beliefs and Moral Values of America's Children*, Girl Scouts of the United States of America (New York: 1990), p. xvii.
49 Pinnacle Group survey examined level of lying in business students: Pinnacle Group, Inc., *Business Ethics Survey* (Minneapolis: 1989).
49 Rutgers professor surveyed college students for cheating: Donald L. McCabe, "The Influence of Situational Ethics on Cheating Among College Students," *Journal of Sociological Inquiry*, Vol. 63, No. 3 (1992) pp. 365–74.
51 An informal poll found potential cheaters in business students: Marvin Cetron, in conversation with the author, Aug. 13, 1993.
52 When these people finally enter the workforce: Shearson Lehman Brothers, Inc., "Life in America."
52 Roper Survey examined eighteen- to twenty-nine-year-old responses: Roper Organization Survey for Insurance Research Council, cited in *Bangor Daily News* (Nov. 9, 1991), p. 33.
52 J. Walter Thompson researchers found that nine in ten citizens regularly lie: Patterson and Kim, *The Day America Told the Truth*, p. 45.
52 *USA Weekend* survey examined honesty of thirteen- and seventeen-year-olds: *USA Weekend* survey, cited in *USA Today* (Aug. 21–23, 1992), p. 5.
52 Girl Scouts survey showed ethics declines as age increases: Coles and Hunter, *Girl Scouts Survey*, p. 55.
53 College athletes score lower in moral reasoning than nonathletes: For a brief survey of research suggesting that "the longer an individual participates in sports, the less moral his actions become," see Jennifer M. Beller and Sharon Kay Stoll, "A Moral Reasoning Intervention Program for Student-Athletes," *The Academic Athletic Journal* (Spring 1992), pp. 43–57. The quotation is found on p. 52.
53 Josephson Institute surveyed older Americans about their cheating habits in high school: Josephson, "The Hole in the Moral Ozone," p. 40.
53 "Most people will cheat or lie when it is necessary to get what they want": Josephson, "The Hole in the Moral Ozone," p. 36.
53 Georgia professor examined high school views on honesty: Fred Schab, cited in Josephson, "The Hole in the Moral Ozone," p. 40.

53 Upper-level executives viewed Americans as less ethical than twenty years ago: McFeely, Wackerle, and Jett, *Survey on Ethics.*
54 McCabe findings showed wealthier students more likely to cheat: McCabe, "Cheating Among College Students," pp. 365–74.
54 *USA Weekend* survey found that people believe schools should teach values: *USA Weekend* survey, cited in *USA Today* (Aug. 21–23, 1992), p. 7.
54 Nation's business executives feel that companies should teach values: McFeely, Wackerle, and Jett, *Survey on Ethics.*
55 The future of both our youth and society are in danger: James S. Leming, "Should Character Education Be Taught in Schools?" *Insights on Global Ethics,* Vol. 3, No. 4 (Camden, Me.: The Institute for Global Ethics, Apr. 1993), p. 8.

Chapter Three Ethical Fitness

64 "All that a philosophic theory can do": Michael K. Hooker, *How to Think About Ethics* (Camden, Me.: The Institute for Global Ethics, 1992), p. 21.
66 "Law and Manners" piece on the three great domains of human action: Lord Moulton of Bank, "Law and Manners," *The Atlantic Monthly*, Vol. 134, No. 1 (July 1924), pp. 1–5.
68 A study of character education: James S. Leming, "Should Character Education Be Taught in Schools?" *Insights on Global Ethics,* Vol. 3, No. 4 (Camden, Me.: The Institute for Global Ethics, Apr. 1993), p. 6.
72 The concept of restraint in the novel's character Kurtz: Joseph Conrad, *Heart of Darkness* (New York: W. W. Norton & Company, 1963), pp. 58–59.
74 Retired French musical instruments salesman interested in tracing his Jewish ancestry: Alan Riding, "A Mother's ID Card Exposes French World War II Secrets," *The New York Times* (Apr. 7, 1993), pp. A1, A6.

Chapter Four Core Values

77 The elements of a powerful moral dilemma: William Stafford, *Traveling Through the Dark* (New York: Harper & Row, 1962), p. 11.
82 "Every man who looks at a woman": Matthew 5:28, in J. B. Phil-

lips, *The New Testament in Modern English* (New York: Macmillan Publishing Company, 1958).

83 Quality of life in the world in which we live: "Always Take the High Road: The McDonnell-Douglas Code of Ethics," pamphlet prepared by McDonnell-Douglas (St. Louis: 1983).

83 Sanford McDonnell code of ethics: From an interview with McDonnell by Sukie Bernard, "Sanford N. McDonnell: Boy Scout Extraordinaire," in Rushworth M. Kidder, ed., *Heartland Ethics: Voices from the American Midwest* (St. Louis: The Principia, 1992), p. 10.

84 Corporate ethics codes: Ronald E. Berenbeim, "Corporate Ethics Practices," The Conference Board Report No. 986 (New York: 1992).

87 A case that put ethics ahead of marketing: Laura L. Nash, *Good Intentions Aside: A Manager's Guide to Resolving Ethical Problems* (Boston: Harvard Business School Press, 1990), p. 39.

88 "Tylenol was the tangible proof of what top management had said": Nash, *Good Intentions Aside,* p. 40.

89 Professor Brandt's findings on universal ethics: Richard P. Brandt, *Ethical Theory: The Problems of Normative and Critical Ethics* (Englewood Cliffs, N.J.: Prentice-Hall, Inc., 1959), p. 95.

89 "Anthropologists have come to find much more common ground": Brandt, *Ethical Theory,* p. 286.

89 "Every culture has a concept of murder": Clyde Kluckhohn, "Ethical Relativity: Sic et Non," *Journal of Philosophy,* Vol. LII (Jan.–Dec. 1955), p. 672.

90 Philosopher Alan Gewirth on "common morality": "Common Morality and the Community of Rights," in Gene Outka and John P. Reeder, Jr., eds., *Prospects for a Common Morality* (Princeton, N.J.: Princeton University Press, 1993), p. 29.

90 Philosopher Bernard Gert's ten rules of moral values: Bernard Gert, *The Moral Rules: A New Foundation for Morality* (New York: Harper & Row, 1970), p. ii.

91 German theologian Hans Küng's "five basic commands to human beings": *Global Responsibility: In Search of a New World Ethic* (New York: The Crossroad Publishing Company, 1991), p. 57.

91 If you could formulate a global code of ethics: Rushworth M. Kidder, *Shared Values for a Troubled World: Conversations with Men and Women of Conscience* (San Francisco: Jossey-Bass Publishers, 1994).

93 Professor Gardner on objective truth: John W. Gardner, in conversation with the author, Jan. 1994.

93 Professor Ronald Howard on "universality of agreement" in different cultures: From an interview with Howard by Rushworth M.

Kidder, "He Calls Ethics Crucial to Survival," in *The Christian Science Monitor* (June 19, 1989), p. 14.
94 Quote on quantum mechanics: Rushworth M. Kidder, "Making the Quantum Leap: A Five-Part *Monitor* Series" (reprint), *The Christian Science Monitor* (June 13, 1988), p. 1.
95 The concept of probability using a baseball example: Kidder, "Making the Quantum Leap," p. 19.
95 Physicist David Gross on the principle of nonnegligible probability: Kidder, "Making the Quantum Leap," p. 19.
95 Physicist Edward W. Kolb on leading an ordinary life despite quantum probabilities: Kidder, "Making the Quantum Leap," p. 20.
96 "If men come to really believe that one moral standard is as good as another": Walter T. Stace, *The Concept of Morals* (New York: Macmillan Publishing Company, 1937), pp. 58–59.
97 Situation ethics: Quotations are from Joseph Fletcher, *Situation Ethics: The New Morality* (Philadelphia: The Westminster Press, 1966), pp. 27–28, 36, 50, 87, 119, 120, 121, 124.
104 The "conceptually undecidable" moment when life begins: Michael Hooker, *How to Think About Ethics* (Camden, Me.: The Institute for Global Ethics, 1992), p. 5.
104 "It cannot be made real when you reduce it to the level of molecular biology": Hooker, *How to Think About Ethics,* p. 6.
107 Poem, "Musée des Beaux Arts": W. H. Auden, *Collected Shorter Poems 1927–1957 (New York: Random House, 1967), p. 123.*

Chapter Five Right Versus Right: The Nature of Dilemma Paradigms

111 Do Men and Women Have Different Moralities?: Quotations are from Carol Gilligan, *In a Different Voice: Psychological Theory and Women's Development* (Cambridge, Mass.: Harvard University Press, 1982), pp. 3, 19, 66, 105, 174.
113 The difficulties of communicating as shown by T. S. Eliot's character: "Sweeney Agonistes," *The Complete Poems and Plays: 1909–1950* (New York: Harcourt, Brace & World, 1952), p. 83.
119 "What does truth mean?": John 18: 37–38, in James Moffatt, *A New Translation of the Bible* (New York: Harper & Brothers, 1922).
119 "The opinion which is fated": Walter Lippman, *A Preface to Morals* (New York: The Macmillan Company, 1929), p. 129.
120 Lying as defined by Sissela Bok: Sissela Bok, *Lying: Moral Choice in Public and Private Life* (New York: Pantheon Books, 1978), p. 13.

121 The effect of truth-telling . . . is to promote trust: Bok, *Lying,* p. 33.
121 Loyalty—the perceptions of allegiance: Josiah Royce, *The Philosophy of Loyalty* (New York: Macmillan, 1908), p. 105.
121 "Some of the strongest moral epithets in the English language": George P. Fletcher, *Loyalty: An Essay on the Morality of Relationships* (New York: Oxford University Press, 1993), p. 8.
122 Survey for *Industry Week* on loyalty: "Purview," supplement to *pr reporter,* Vol. 8, No. 30 (Apr. 5, 1993), p. 13.
122 Survey done by the Lewis Harris Organization on loyalty: Robert Coles and James Hunter, *Girl Scouts Survey on the Beliefs and Moral Values of America's Children,* Girl Scouts of the United States of America (New York: 1990).
123 Poem by Emily Dickinson: Poem 1129, in Thomas H. Johnson, ed., *The Complete Poems of Emily Dickinson* (Boston: Little, Brown and Company, 1960), p. 506.

Chapter Six Three More Dilemma Paradigms

128 "Individualism is a calm and considered feeling": Robert N. Bellah, Richard Madsen, William M. Sullivan, Ann Swidler, and Steven M. Tipton, *Habits of the Heart: Individualism and Commitment in American Life* (Berkeley: University of California Press, 1985), p. 37.
128 "We are all animated with the spirit of an industry": Bellah et al., *Habits of the Heart,* p. 36.
128 "It is not from the benevolence of the butcher, brewer, or baker": Adam Smith, *The Wealth of Nations* (Oxford and New York: Oxford University Press, 1993), p. 22.
128 "There would be those who would argue": Bellah et al., *Habits of the Heart,* p. 33.
128 "Society everywhere is in conspiracy": Ralph Waldo Emerson, "Self-Reliance," *Essays and Lectures* (New York: Library of America, 1983), p. 261.
130 Leadership and community: John W. Gardner, *On Leadership* (New York: The Free Press, 1990), pp. 116–18.
130 Community and "the reinforcement of our moral inclinations": Amitai Etzioni, *The Spirit of Community: Rights, Responsibilities, and the Communitarian Agenda* (New York: Crown Publishers, 1993), p. 31.
135 Values of productiveness versus values that promote consumption: Andrew Bard Schmookler, *The Illusion of Choice: How the Market*

Economy Shapes Our Destiny (Albany, N.Y.: State University of New York Press, 1993), p. 148.

135 The shift from self-control to self-realization: Daniel Horowitz, *The Morality of Spending: Attitudes Towards Consumer Society in America, 1875–1940* (Baltimore: Johns Hopkins University Press, 1985), p. xxvii; cited in Schmookler, *The Illusion of Choice,* p. 149.

135 "By the 1950s American culture had become primarily hedonistic": Daniel Bell, *The Cultural Contradictions of Capitalism* (New York: Basic Books, 1976), p. 70; cited in Schmookler, *The Illusion of Choice,* p. 149.

135 Sociologist David Riesman's term, "transaction mentality": William H. Donaldson, "Capitalism and the Challenges of the 1990s," address delivered Nov. 30, 1992, for the annual Baird Lecture Series of the University of Wisconsin–Milwaukee School of Business Administration, pp. 2, 5, 7.

136 Global population expansion adds roughly a million people every four days: See George D. Moffett, *Critical Masses: The Global Population Challenge* (New York: Viking Penguin, 1994).

136 "The problem . . . is the management of human behavior": Harlan Cleveland, *Birth of a New World: An Open Moment for International Leadership* (San Francisco: Jossey-Bass Publishers, 1993), p. 197.

136 "If you do not think about the future, you cannot have one": John Galsworthy, *Swan Song* (1928), Part II, Chapter 6.

136 "There is no finer investment for any community than putting milk into babies": Winston Churchill, "Post-War Planning," radio broadcast, Mar. 21, 1943, in Robert Rhodes James, ed., *Winston S. Churchill: His Complete Speeches 1897–1963,* (New York: Chelsea House Publishers, 1974), Vol. VII, p. 6761.

140 The original meaning of justice "lies in the realm of personal passions": Robert C. Solomon, *A Passion for Justice: Emotions and the Origins of the Social Contract* (Reading, Mass.: Addison-Wesley Publishing Company, 1990), p. 9.

141 How laws must be abolished if they are unjust: John Rawls, *A Theory of Justice* (Cambridge: Harvard University Press, 1971), p. 3.

141 "The liberties of equal citizenship are taken as settled": Rawls, *A Theory of Justice,* p. 4.

141 "The difficulty is that the love of several persons is thrown into confusion": Rawls, *A Theory of Justice,* p. 190.

141 "The relationship between love and justice": D. B. Robertson, ed., *Love and Justice: Selections from the Shorter Writings of Reinhold Niebuhr* (Louisville, Ky.: Westminster/John Knox Press, 1957), p. 9.

141 "Love is the final or highest possibility in man's relationship to man": Robertson, *Love and Justice,* p. 11.
141 "[An ethic] must give guidance": Robertson, *Love and Justice,* p. 9.
141 "Forgiving love" must take precedence over "tolerable harmonies" of justice: Robertson, *Love and Justice,* p. 13.
146 The Potter Box: See Ralph B. Potter, "The Structure of Certain American Christian Responses to the Nuclear Dilemma," Ph.D. dissertation, Harvard University, 1965, and his article "The Logic of Moral Argument" in ed., Paul Deats *Toward a Discipline of Social Ethics* (Boston: Boston University Press, 1972), pp. 93–114. See also Clifford G. Christians, Kim B. Rotzoll, and Mark Fackler, *Media Ethics: Cases and Moral Reasoning* (New York: Longman, 1983), pp. 2–8.
148 "No ideas but in things": "A Sort of a Song," *Selected Poems of William Carlos Williams* (New York: New Directions, 1949), p. 108.
148 "Not Ideas About the Thing but the Thing Itself": *The Collected Poems of Wallace Stevens* (New York: Alfred A. Knopf, 1954, rpt. 1965), p. 534.

Chapter Seven Resolution Principles

151 "Were it left to me to decide whether we should have a government without newspapers": Thomas Jefferson, letter to Col. Edward Carrington, Jan. 16, 1787, in Julian P. Boyd, ed., *The Papers of Thomas Jefferson,* (Princeton, N.J.: Princeton University Press, 1955), Vol. II, p. 49.
152 Anecdote about the ethical dilemmas of journalism: Kay Fanning, "A rock and a hard place," in Frank McCulloch, ed., *Drawing the Line: How 31 Editors Solved Their Toughest Ethical Dilemmas* (Washington, D.C.: American Society of Newspaper Editors, 1984), pp. 37–39. Reprinted by permission of the *ASNE Bulletin.*
155 Mill on utilitarianism: John Stuart Mill, "Utilitarianism," in F. E. L. Priestley, ed., *Collected Works of John Stuart Mill,* Vol. X (Toronto: University of Toronto Press, 1969), pp. 211, 218.
157 "An action done from duty": Immanuel Kant, *The Moral Law: Kant's Groundwork of the Metaphysic of Morals,* trans. H. J. Paton (London: Hutchinson and Co., 1961), pp. 67–68.
157 "What is essentially good": Kant, *The Moral Law,* p. 84.
157 The measure of rightness or wrongness: Kant, *The Moral Law,* pp. 68, 69, 70.
158 "I ought never to act except in such a way": Kant, *The Moral Law,* p. 70.

159 "The invasive do-gooding . . . Kantian theory": Barbara Herman, *The Practice of Moral Judgment* (Cambridge: Harvard University Press, 1993), p. 23.
159 Similar formulations appear at the center of Hinduism: W. A. Spooner, "The Golden Rule," in James Hastings, ed., *Encyclopedia of Religion and Ethics,* Vol. 6 (New York: Charles Scribner's Sons, 1914), pp. 310–12.
159 The Golden Rule as "a principle of great antiquity": Marcus G. Singer, "Golden Rule," in Lawrence C. Becker and Charlotte B. Becker, eds., *Encyclopedia of Ethics* (New York: Garland Publishing, 1992), p. 405.
159 Imagine yourself as the *object* rather than the *agent* of that action: Gene Outka, "Augustinianism and Common Morality," in Gene Outka and John P. Reeder, Jr., eds., *Prospects for a Common Morality* (Princeton, N.J.: Princeton University Press, 1993), p. 121.
160 "Attempt to put oneself in another's shoes": Outka, "Augustinianism and Common Morality," p. 119.
160 "Merely derivative of our principle": Kant, *The Moral Law,* p. 97.
160 "It was never intended as a guide": Sissela Bok, "The Golden Rule", in *Oxford Companion to Philosophy* (Oxford and New York: Oxford University Press, forthcoming).
160 The veil of ignorance: John Rawls, *A Theory of Justice* (Cambridge, Mass.: Harvard University Press, 1971) pp. 136–42.
171 "Act in such a way that you always treat humanity": Kant, *The Moral Law,* p. 96.

Chapter Eight "There's Only 'Ethics' . . . "

178 Bromberg as "a hard-driving taskmaster": Theodore J. Gordon and Julian Scheer, *First into Outer Space* (New York: St. Martin's Press, 1959), p. 48.
178 "A missile flight seldom fails because of a basic inadequacy in design": Gordon and Scheer, *First into Outer Space,* p. 43.
180 Lachaise . . . exhibited "intelligence functioning at intuitional velocity": E. E. Cummings, "Gaston Lachaise," in George J. Firmage, ed., *E. E. Cummings: A Miscellany Revised* (New York: October House, 1965), p. 17.
181 The Prisoner's Dilemma: William Poundstone, *The Prisoner's Dilemma* (New York: Doubleday, 1992).

183 On man and community: John Donne, *Devotions* (1624), Vol. XVII.
184 Robert Frost's famous decision-making poem: Robert Frost, "The Road Not Taken," *Complete Poems of Robert Frost* (New York: Holt, Rinehart and Winston, 1949), p. 131.
189 The only obligation is to oneself: Henry David Thoreau, "Civil Disobedience," cited in Larry May, "Public and Private Morality," in Lawrence C. Becker and Charlotte B. Becker, eds., *Encyclopedia of Ethics,* Vol. 1 (New York: Garland Publishing, Inc., 1992), pp. 1043–47.
190 "There's only 'ethics' ": Rushworth M. Kidder, *Shared Values for a Troubled World: Conversations with Men and Women of Conscience* (San Francisco: Jossey-Bass Publishers, 1994), p. 169.
194 School board member opposed to distribution of condoms: Clifford J. Levy, "Fifth Graders Get Condoms In New Haven," *The New York Times* (July 28, 1993), p. B1.
201 Prof. Paul Kennedy and "imperial overstretch": Paul Kennedy, *The Rise and Fall of the Great Powers: Economic Change and Military Conflict from 1500 to 2000* (New York: Random House, 1987), p. 515.
201 Jimmy Carter's human rights speech: Harlan Cleveland, *Birth of a New World: An Open Moment for International Leadership* (San Francisco: Jossey-Bass Publishers, 1993), p. 123.
203 Poem on the issue of environment versus development: Hart Crane, "The River," *The Bridge* (New York: Liveright, 1933), p. 17.

Chapter Nine Epilogue: Ethics in the Twenty-first Century

212 Graduate student paralyzes major computer network: Jonathon Littman, "The Shockwave Rider," *PC Computing,* Vol. 3, No. 6 (June 1990), p. 142.
213 "One of the most sophisticated and infectious computer viruses": *Time,* cited in *Washington Monthly* (Jan. 1989), p. 21.
213 Futurist writes that mankind has spanned eight hundred "lifetimes": Alvin Toffler, *Future Shock* (New York: Bantam Books, 1971), p. 9.
214 Prediction about the future of computers: Author's conversation with futurist Ted Gordon, Camden, Me., Aug. 1992.
215 The ethical issues surrounding euthanasia: See, for instance, Peter Singer, *Practical Ethics,* 2d ed. (Cambridge, England: Cambridge University Press, 1993), pp. 175–217.

216 The concept of "high touch"—going back to handmade items: John Naisbitt, *Megatrends* (New York: Warner Books, 1982), p. 1.
218 "Joy is a mystery at right angles": E. E. Cummings, *Adventures in Value,* Vol. 3 (New York: Harcourt Brace Jovanovich, 1962), p. 1.
219 Values clarification: Quotations from Simon are from Sidney B. Simon, Leland W. Howe, and Howard Kirschenbaum, *Values Clarification: A Handbook of Practical Strategies for Teachers and Students* (New York: Hart Publishing Company, 1972), pp. 16, 19, 27, 281, and 287. The quotation from Leming is from *Character Education: Lessons from the Past, Models for the Future* (Camden, Me.: The Institute for Global Ethics, 1993), p. 8.

Index

Institute for Global Ethics
Founded by Rushworth M. Kidder in 1990

Many of the real-life dilemmas used in *How Good People Make Tough Choices* were originally shared by participants in seminars presented by the Institute for Global Ethics, a non-profit membership organization. The Institute offers ethics training, programs, and management consulting for corporations, schools, government agencies, and non-profits, and provides publications about ethics and current affairs for its members around the world. For more information please contact the Institute:

Institute for Global Ethics
P.O. Box 563
Camden, Maine 04843
(207) 236-6658

World Wide Web: http://www.sourcemaine.com/ethics